The

# NEW
# NEW

Thing

Also by Michael Lewis

*Liar's Poker*
*The Money Culture*
*Pacific Rift*
*Trail Fever*

W. W. Norton & Company • New York   London

The

# NEW
# NEW

Thing

**A Silicon Valley Story**

## Michael Lewis

For information about permission to reproduce selections from this book,
write to Permissions, W. W. Norton & Company, Inc., 500 Fifth Avenue,
New York, NY 10110

The text of this book is composed in Weiss, with the display set in Meta.
Composition by Julia Druskin.
Manufacturing by The Haddon Craftsmen Inc.
Book design by Chris Welch.

Library of Congress Cataloging-in-Publication Data

Lewis, Michael (Michael M.)
The new new thing : a Silicon Valley story / Michael Lewis.
p.   cm.
**ISBN 0-393-04813-6**
1. Clark, Jim, 1944–    . 2. Businessmen—United States Biography.
3. Computer software industry—United States—History.   I. Title.
HD9696.63.U62C585    1999
338.4'70053'092—dc21
[B]                                                      99-43412
CIP

W. W. Norton & Company, Inc., 500 Fifth Avenue, New York, N.Y. 10110
www.wwnorton.com

W. W. Norton & Company Ltd., 10 Coptic Street, London WC1A 1PU

1 2 3 4 5 6 7 8 9 0

For Tabitha

The age demanded an image
of its accelerated grimace

—*Ezra Pound*

# Contents

This book is about a search that occurs on the frontiers of economic life. Maybe the best way to introduce it is to explain why I bothered to write it.

In the second part of the 1990s Silicon Valley had the same center-of-the-universe feel to it as Wall Street had in the mid-1980s. There was a reason for this: it was the source of a great deal of change. Up until April 4, 1994, Silicon Valley was known as the source of a few high-tech industries, and mainly the computer industry. On April 4, 1994, Netscape was incorporated. Suddenly—as fast as that—Silicon Valley was the source of changes taking place across the society. The Internet was a Trojan horse in which technogeeks entered all sorts of markets previously inhospitable to technogeeks. Wall Street, to take just one example, was turned on its head by new companies and new technologies and new social types created just south of San Francisco. The financial success of the people at the heart of this matter was unprecedented. It made 1980s Wall Street seem like the low-stakes poker table. As yet, there is no final reckoning of the wealth the Valley has created. Hundreds of billions of dollars, certainly; perhaps even trillions. In any case, "the greatest legal creation of wealth in the history of the planet," as one local capitalist puts it.

The money was only part of what I found interesting. I really do think, and not just because I happen to be writing a book about it, that the business of creating and foisting new technology upon others that goes on in Silicon Valley is near the core of the American experience. The United States obviously occupies a strange place in the world. It is the capital of innovation, of material prosperity, of a certain kind of energy, of certain kinds of freedom, and of transience. Silicon Valley is to the United States what the United States is to the rest of the world. It is one of those places, unlike the Metropolitan Museum of Art, but like Las Vegas, that are unimaginable anywhere but in the United States. It is distinctively us.

Within this unusual place some people were clearly more unusual than others. Many of those who sought and found fortune in Silicon Valley in the 1990s could just as easily have found it on Wall Street in the 1980s or in London in the 1860s. But a certain type of person who has recently made it big in Silicon Valley could have made it big at no other time in history. He made it big because he was uniquely suited to this particular historical moment. He was built to work on the frontier of economic life when the frontier was once again up for grabs. He was designed for rapid social and technological change. He was the starter of new things.

Oddly enough, this character at the center of one of history's great economic booms, who, in effect, sits with the detonator between his legs, could not describe what he did for a living. When a person sets out to find the new idea or the new technology that will (a) make him rich and (b) throw entire industries into turmoil and (c) cause ordinary people to sit up and say, "My God, something just changed," he isn't doing science. He isn't engaged in what any serious thinker would call thought. Unless he makes a lot of money, he isn't even treated as a businessman, at least not by serious businessmen. He might call himself an "entrepreneur," but that word has been debased by overuse. Really, there's no good word for what he does. I first noticed this problem when I watched one of these people—a man who had made himself a billion dollars—try to fill in a simple questionnaire. On the line that asked him to state his occupation, he did not know what to write.

There was no name for what he did. Searcher? He couldn't very well put down that.

For that matter, there is no name for what he's looking for, which, typically, is a technology, or an idea, on the cusp of commercial viability. The new new thing. It's easier to say what the new new thing is not than to say what it is. It is not necessarily a new invention. It is not even necessarily a new idea—most everything has been considered by someone, at some point. The new new thing is a notion that is poised to be taken seriously in the marketplace. It's the idea that is a tiny push away from general acceptance and, when it gets that push, will change the world.

The searcher for the new new thing conforms to no well-established idea of what people should do for a living. He gropes. Finding the new new thing is as much a matter of timing as of technical or financial aptitude, though both of those qualities help. The sensation that defines the search is the sweet, painful feeling that you get when you can't think of a word that feels as if it's right on the tip of your tongue. For most people the relief they experience upon finding it is almost physical. They sink back in their chairs and try not to stumble upon any more difficult words. The person who makes his living searching for the new new thing is not like most people, however. He does not seriously want to sink back into any chair. He needs to keep on groping. He chooses to live perpetually with that sweet tingling discomfort of not quite knowing what it is he wants to say. It's one of the little ironies of economic progress that, while it often results in greater levels of comfort, it depends on people who prefer not to get too comfortable.

From the start of my investigation of Silicon Valley, I knew I was trying to describe a process: how this fantastic wealth got created. It just so happened that the process was best illustrated by this character. After all, the greatest legal creation of wealth in the history of the planet came directly from the new new thing. When you asked, "How is it that an entire economy made this little leap?" you were really asking, "How is it that some person gave an entire economy a little push?" Believe it or not, there are people, inside and outside of Silicon Valley, who consider it almost their duty to find the new new thing. That person may not be entirely typical of our age. (Is anyone?) But he is, in this case, representative: a disruptive force. A catalyst for change and regeneration. He is to Silicon Valley what Silicon Valley is to America. And he has left his fingerprints all over the backside of modern life.

What I've tried to write, in a roundabout way, which is the only way I could think to write it, is a character study of a man with the gift for giving a little push to Silicon Valley, and to the whole economy. To do this I had to follow him on his search. I hope the reader will, too. At any rate, I hope he or she gets a sense of what it feels like to be so oddly, and messily, engaged. Progress does not march forward like an army on parade; it crawls on its belly like a guerrilla. The important events in capitalism no longer occur mainly in oak-paneled offices, if indeed they ever did. They can happen in the least likely of places. On a boat in the middle of the Atlantic Ocean, for instance.

As it turned out, the main character of this story had a structure to his life. He might not care to acknowledge it, but it was there all the same. It was the structure of an old-fashioned adventure story. His mere presence on a scene inspired the question that propels every adventure story forward: What will happen next? I had no idea. And neither, really, did he.

The

# NEW
# NEW

Thing

## 1

## The Boat That Built Netscape

he original plan, which Lord knows didn't mean very much when that plan had been made by Jim Clark, was that we would test the boat quickly in the North Sea and then sail it across the Atlantic Ocean. If nothing went too badly wrong, it would take us six days to sail down to the Canary Islands and another ten to the Caribbean. I had seen Clark in so many different situations that I felt sure I knew him, and the range of behavior he was capable of. But there is nothing like sixteen days on the high seas with a small group of people who have a lot of doubts about each other to test one's assumptions about human character. On the Atlantic crossing *Hyperion* would carry only the captain and his seven crew members, one or two computer programmers, Clark and me.

Why Jim Clark was so worthy of study was another matter, and I'll come to that soon enough. For now I'll just say that the quirks in the man's character sent the most fantastic ripples through the world around him. Often starting with the best intentions, or no intentions at all, he turned people's lives upside down and subjected them to the most vicious force a human being can be subjected to, change. Oddly enough, he was forever claiming that what he really wanted to do was put up his feet and relax. He could not do this for more than a minute. Once he'd put up his feet, his mind would spin and his face would redden and he'd be disturbed all over again. He'd thought of something or someone in the world that needed to be changed. His new boat was a case in point.

For all I knew, Clark would be remembered chiefly as the guy who created Netscape and triggered the Internet boom, which in turn triggered one of the most astonishing grabfests in the history of capitalism. Maybe somewhere in a footnote it would be mentioned that he came from nothing, grew up poor, dropped out of high school, and made himself three or four billion dollars. It might even be said that he had a nose for the new new thing. But to my way of thinking these were only surface details, the least interesting things about him. After all, a lot of people these days have a billion dollars. Four hundred and sixty-five, according to the July 1999 issue of *Forbes* magazine. And most of them are no more interesting than you or me. You have to trust me on this.

Along the stretch of canal outside of Amsterdam where the water is deepest, the swollen tankers and stout tugs come to rest. Neither the driver nor I had the slightest idea where in this stand of massive industrial ships one might park a pleasure boat. It was not a place anyone would normally come for fun. The driver finally turned around and asked me exactly what I was looking for, and I told him I was looking for the sailboat that would take me out to sea. He laughed, but in the way people do who want to prove they get the joke. The Dutch do this a lot. They appear to live in terror of being mistaken for Germans, and to compensate by finding a funny side to life where none exists. Tell a Dutchman that your dog just died, and he will pretend that you have just made some impossibly witty remark. This is what the driver did when I told him I was about to go sailing in the North Sea. It was early December, the winds were up around thirty-five miles an hour, and the North Sea—well, the North Sea in winter is not the place to be in any kind of sailboat. The driver roared in the most un-Germanly fashion. "Yachting!" he said, and burst out laughing again, far too loudly, as if he had seen me my one joke and raised me another. "Yes," I said, which only brought forth more peals.

The great mast rescued us. One moment we were lost; the next we turned a corner and spotted on the horizon the tall, rigid white rod. Its brightly colored pennants flew in relief against the gray sky, and its five spreaders reached up into the clouds like a chain of receding crucifixes. They beckoned everyone within five miles to drop his jaw in wonder. It was then that the driver finally stopped laughing. "Yacht," after all, is a Dutch word.

Three minutes later we drove onto the dock up near the low white sailboat, next to the name painted in blue cursive on the side: *Hyperion*. You could tell the driver knew at least a bit about sailboats because he immediately called the boat a "sloop." A sloop is a sailboat with one mast, to distinguish it from a sailboat with two masts, called a "ketch." "How long is this sloop?" he asked me. "One hundred and fifty-five and a half feet," I said. "That is the biggest sloop I have ever heard of," he said. I said that that was because it was the biggest sloop ever built. His eyes moved from the hull to the mast, and from the mast to the boom, and from the boom to the sails, which, unfurled, would cover a football field. "How many men are needed to handle the sails?" he asked. "None," I said, "at least in theory."

The Dutchman laughed again, but nervously, as if deciding whether it was better to be mistaken for a German or a fool. It wasn't until I told him that the boat did not exactly require a crew, that it could be completely controlled by a computer, that conviction returned to his laughter. The whole thing, after all, had been some foreigner's idea of a joke.

When I arrived that morning of the first North Sea trial, Wolter Huisman was standing on the deck beneath the mast. Wolter owned the boatyard that had built *Hyperion*. Wet snow dribbled from his rain gear, and his woolen cap drooped around his ears. His chin sunk glumly into his dark tattered parka, and his old Dutch shoulders sagged like a commuter's at the end of a long day. He seemed to be melting. Coming up from behind, I caught him muttering to himself. Later I learned that Wolter hadn't slept. He'd stared at the ceiling all night, worrying.

"What's the worst weather you ever tested a sailboat in?" I asked him.

"Dis wedder," he replied. Then he sighed and said, at once apropos of nothing and everything, "When Yim wants something, Yim gets it."

In his pessimism Wolter had found a strategy for getting through this life and onto a new and better one: so long as he insisted to himself that tomorrow would be worse than today, it did not matter as much if it was. He still had the Dutch habit of laughing at whatever you told him, just in case it happened to be a joke. But his laugh was harsh and unhappy. Wolter was pushing seventy, and his heart was old and weak, but this gloom of his was young and vital. Who could blame him? His fate was now intertwined with *Hyperion's*. And *Hyperion* was at this very moment the most spectacular maritime disaster waiting to happen since the launching of the *Titanic*.

Of course, every new yacht that left the Huisman Shipyard was, so far as Wolter was concerned, an accident waiting to happen. It had taken Wolter, and his father before him, and his father's father before him, decades to build their reputation as perhaps the world's finest makers of yachts. Each time Wolter launched a new yacht, that reputation went up for grabs. But this was different. This was new.

"Where is he?" I asked.

"Behind duh computer," said Wolter. Pause. "When Yim sits behind duh computer, he is not any more in dis world."

That was true. He was creating a new one.

On that bitterly cold December morning *Hyperion* left its moorings so silently that the programmers didn't notice. The programmers were three young men Jim Clark had flown over from Silicon Valley to the North Sea to help him turn his new yacht into a giant floating computer. Technogeeks. Each was in his early thirties, each possessed a wardrobe that appeared to consist of nothing but T-shirts and blue jeans, and each was a former employee of Clark's first technology startup, Silicon Graphics. They clambered up on deck from below, where they had been typing away on their keyboards, to see what they'd wrought. It was as if they hadn't quite believed that *Hyperion* would float.

The bridge was a technogeek fantasy. Where an experienced sailor would expect to find a familiar row of gadgets—radar, sonar, radio, GPS, and so on—were four large flat-panel computer display screens. The three young men took seats in front of these and started pressing buttons. Soon enough they were making small quivering sounds that suggested all was not right with the computers. On one of the screens was a map of Holland. The map focused on the area immediately around us, perhaps twenty square miles. A miniature *Hyperion* inched stealthily across it, like a boat in a video game. But according to the computer map we were chugging on top of a farmer's field, and heading toward an airfield. The slender canal we were actually on lay three miles to the east. Any captain using the computer to run the boat would think he was heading full tilt into an aircraft watchtower.

I walked out onto the deck to find that the same map occupied the computer screen in front of Allan Prior, the man Clark had hired to captain *Hyperion*. Allan was from the old school. He'd won the Whitbread around-the-world race in a sailboat so stripped down that it looked vandalized. Allan himself looked vandalized; the wind and the sun had ravaged his complexion. Allan did not believe that sailboats should be run by computers. Now he was staring straight ahead, attempting to avoid a large ferry that was making a dash across the canal. "Don't bother me with that," he said when I asked him why his boat was in the middle of a wheat field. "That's a computer problem." Clearly, he was in no mood to consider the undeniable fact that his entire boat was a computer problem.

I returned to the programmers on the bridge. After a couple of minutes of furious typing, they had the boat back on the water. Yet the head programmer, a fellow named Steve Hague, retained a certain dubiousness. His eyes darted back and forth between the edge of the canal and the map on which *Hyperion* chugged along. All of the computer's gauges seemed to be either inadequate or inaccurate. A captain steering off them—which Allan Prior at that moment declined to do—would not only think that he was sailing through a wheat field. He'd think he was sailing through a wheat field *in the wrong direction*. For no apparent reason a red light flashed on one of the screens. It said, DANGER, DANGER, DANGER.

Steve punched some buttons. According to the computer we'd been grounded. "It is truly unfortunate that we find ourselves in this situation," he said, at length.

Yes it was. Just a few hours earlier the weatherman had predicted Force 4 sailing conditions. Force 4 implied pleasant winds of twenty knots and seas of perhaps six feet. Even before we left the canal and passed through the locks into the North Sea, the report lost its credibility. The gauges on the boat that measured the speed of the wind had frozen at fifty knots—the computer had not been programmed to register winds any higher.

As we passed through the lock and into a harbor, we could finally see why Wolter Huisman muttered to himself. Fifteen-foot waves crashed against the seawall and flicked their white foam thirty feet in the air, where it mingled with falling snow. Gusts of wind blew at seventy miles an hour. The boat suddenly began to rock too violently for anyone to stare very long into his computer. The programmers scrambled out from the bridge and onto the deck, where Allan and Wolter stood together in the snow with pretty much everyone else: twelve boatyard workers, seven crew members, two Dutch friends of Clark's, a photographer, and a German television crew present to document the launching of the world's first computerized sailboat. The only person missing was Clark himself, but, then, people who knew Clark knew better than to expect him to be where he was meant to be. Sooner or later he'd turn up, usually when he was not wanted.

"It's too goddamn windy out there," Wolter Huisman shouted, to no one in particular. "It is wedder to test people, not boats." He shot Allan a meaningful look, who shot it right back to him. They both knew that the weather was the least of their problems.

When *Hyperion* left the seawall behind, it put itself at the mercy of a furious North Sea. Instantly, the boat was seized by forces far greater than itself; its magnificence was trivialized. A furious partial corkscrewing motion pulled us up to the right and then down to the left. We'd dip into a trough, experience a brief, false moment of calm, and then be picked up and twisted again. The German television soundman dropped to his knees, crawled over the side of the boat, and vomited. There was no question of his suppressing the urge; it was as if someone had pushed a button on the computer that instructed the man to be sick. There, prone and puking on the violent deck, he lifted his microphone into the air to capture the ambient noise. Room tone. A young Dutch friend of Clark's along for the ride chuckled and said, "The Germans. They will always do the job they are given no matter *what*."

But the German soundman was a trend setter. It took about a minute and a half before the first Dutch boatyard worker leaned over the safety ropes and vomited the Saint Nick's cake he'd been served an hour before. A minute later he was joined by two poor colleagues who had been down below monitoring the engines. A few minutes after that the three fellows working on the foredeck came back to join the party. Then came the rest of the German television crew. *Hyperion* rose and twisted and plunged and settled, then rose and twisted and plunged and settled all over again. Within twenty minutes eight men had gone as lifeless as if they had been unplugged from their sockets. Those who weren't sick pretended to be amused. They clustered around the captain and clung to the rails and smiled crazily at each other.

Eventually, Allan reduced the engine speed and hoisted the sail. He did this by pushing a button, which told the computer to hoist the sail, which the computer, for once, did. The mast was hatched with cross-bars, called spreaders. The sail rose with a great flapping sound past them one by one until at length it reached the second-to-last spreader. Just when you thought there could be no more sail, more sail appeared. The mainsail alone was 5,600 square feet, a bit more than a quarter of a football field. The world's largest sail, as it happened. It was expected to handle up to eleven tons of wind. That is, the force on its ropes was the equivalent of dangling from their ends an eleven ton steel block. Already the ropes were being tested. "The wind is too strong to let it all out," Allan shouted to Wolter. Wolter nodded solemnly.

Not until you have hoisted a sail and turned off the engine can you fully appreciate the euphoria that accompanied the invention of the steam engine. The boat, now engineless, was subjected to a grosser, more primal force. The waves crashed and the spray came in sheets and the partial corkscrewing motion became a full corkscrewing motion. The eight men in Puker's Alley retched all over again. This time it wasn't so funny to the others. A wave washed over the deck and knocked two of the Dutch shipyard workers on the bow off their feet; they were saved from the sea by their safety ropes, which they alone wore. The three technogeeks clung to the rails and tried not to remember that they didn't belong here. They knew without being told that anyone who went overboard was as good as gone. A person tossed into the North Sea in December would last only a few minutes before freezing to death; and in these conditions it might take an hour to pick up a man overboard, if you could find him. Maybe for this reason no one bothered to don a life jacket.

It was then I noticed Wolter, his arm wrapped tightly around a rail, trying not to look at everything at once. It was Wolter whose ass was really on the line out here. If a Huisman mast snapped, or a Huisman hull leaked, and a Huisman yacht sank, a long and glorious family tradition bubbled to the bottom of the North Sea floor. That is why Wolter and his three hundred stout and sturdy craftsmen back in their tiny village in the north of Holland resisted change. They did not cling to the past mindlessly. But they were as immune as people can be to the allure of a new way of doing things. Traditional, in a word.

Wolter had spent the past three years wrestling with a great force that had neither the time nor the taste for tradition. The struggle had turned Wolter into an old man. Before Jim Clark had come to the boat-yard at the end of 1995, Wolter had never heard of Silicon Valley, or of the Internet, or, for that matter, of Jim Clark. Yim, as Wolter called him, had sat down amid the exquisite models of ships built centuries before, and the old black-and-white photographs of Wolter and his ancestors at work building them. He had seen a yacht Wolter had just finished building, he said, and wanted one like it. Only bigger. And faster. And newer. He wanted his mast to be the biggest mast ever built. And he wanted to control the whole boat with his computers. Specifically, he wanted to be able to dial into his boat over the Internet from his desk in Silicon Valley and sail it across the San Francisco Bay. It was as if someone had distilled manic late twentieth-century American capitalism into a vial of liquid and poured it down Wolter's throat.

Only a small part of the discomfort experienced on that wintry, gray December afternoon on the North Sea was physical. Most of it occurred inside of people's minds. Clark pushed people into places they never would have gone willingly. Often the people who'd been pushed assumed, for one reason or another, that Jim Clark, the rich man from Silicon Valley who seemed to know what was about to happen before anyone else, would make sure that it didn't happen to them. The prob-lem with their assumption was that it wasn't true: all Jim Clark ever guar-anteed anyone was the chance to adapt. His penchant for disrupting his environment was at the bottom of every new company he created; now he'd used it to transform a sailboat. The many strange deep sen-sations on board—Wolter's dread, Allan's frustration, the computer geeks' unlikely feelings of responsibility—all were the doing of Clark and his new technology. It was a single great, messy experiment, which, in retrospect, was bound not to end well. And it didn't.

At the moment when the seas were most fierce, the boat's tiny pop-ulation huddled together on the stern. *Hyperion* pitched and rolled; its passengers clung to the rails and to each other. Even Allan, who had sailed around the world three times in boats the size of Clark's bathtubs back in California, was numb as a mummy. "It's not sailing," he hollered to Wolter. "It's more like throwing something into a washing machine to see what breaks."

It would have occurred to no sane person at this point to crawl along the side and have a look around. But that is what Clark did. He emerged from his cabin, where he'd been fiddling with his computer, and made his way up the safety ropes along the side. Since *Hyperion* was 157 feet long, and he was six foot three, this took some doing. I should say that he did not look as he was expected to look; his appearance was just another element of surprise in a surprising universe. He was tall and broad in a way computer nerds are not supposed to be. His blond hair was neatly combed. His features were small and delicate: one could easily imagine that he resembled his mother. He was handsome. Unlike most men who make billions of dollars for themselves, he had an expansive, easy manner. At any rate, that's the first impression he made. If you looked closely, you could see that each of the slow and easy gestures was countered by another that was small, tense, almost involuntary. His body language was engaged in a debate with itself. It was as if he had an itch that he was refusing to scratch.

When he reached the bow, he climbed up toward the world's tallest sailboat mast, which rose to a point 189 feet over the deck. He put his hand on it, to steady himself. There he stood for some long while, a large yellow lump of Gore-Tex, directly beneath the tall, rigid white rod of his ambition. He was looking, it appeared, straight up at the sky. What he was looking for, no one could say. Probably he was thinking about something he might like to change. Possibly he was not thinking at all but groping. That is how his mind worked—the logic always came after the initial, inexplicable, primal impulse. But whatever he was doing he didn't do it for long. Once he'd found his footing, his mast began to sway. At first its movements were barely perceptible; then they became more pronounced; at last they were violent.

Later someone who had been on the bridge said he had heard a loud crack. The rubber at the base of the world's tallest mast had shattered. The foot-wide seal that kept Clark's 189 feet of carbon fiber standing straight had frozen into a crystal, and then broken to bits. The mast came loose in its socket. Its three and a half tons rocked wildly back and forth, like a broomstick rattling around inside a garbage can. As quickly as he could press a button, Allan Prior lowered the sail, before the mast itself broke and fell over into the sea.

"Yesus," Wolter Huisman muttered, and looked away.

## 2

It couldn't have been more than a few hours after the last guest stumbled out his front gate that Clark called and made his suggestion. "I'm going up in the helicopter," he said. "Want to come?" His voice was deep and thick and unsteady. Apparently, he hadn't slept. It was just before eight in the morning on the fifth of July. He'd spent the past three hours writing computer code, and the seven hours before that drinking with seventy of his favorite engineers who worked for the companies he'd created and then, more or less, abandoned.

By then I knew that the only way to spend time with Jim Clark was to leap onto one of his machines. You didn't interact with him so much as hitch a ride on the back of his life. Once you proved to him that you wouldn't complain, or weep, or vomit into the gearbox, he was not unwilling to pick you up. He offered you a choice of vehicles: helicopter, stunt plane, motorbike, various exotic sports cars of the type that no one but really rich people ever even know exist, and, of course, the computerized sailboat. His array of possessions was hardly original. He could be made to seem like yet another newly rich guy trying to demonstrate to the world just how rich he'd become. Either that or one of those people who try to prove how interesting they are by risking their lives in various moronic adventures. This was not his motive, however. He didn't need to show how much money he had; the number was in the newspaper every day. It was public knowledge that Jim Clark owned 16 million shares in Netscape and that Netscape, on July 5, 1998, was trading at $25 a share. Twenty-five times 16 million equaled $400 million. That was $650 million less than Clark had been worth two years ago and, for that matter, $3 billion less than he would be worth nine months from now. The number was always changing.

In any case, it never would have occurred to Clark that anyone of his machines was a mere display of wealth, or some kind of thrill ride. No matter how reckless his mode of travel might appear, he never considered himself anything less than the soul of caution. No, for him all the joy came from mechanical intimacy. Machines! He loved to know about them, to operate them, to master them, to fix them when they were broken. More than anything he liked to upgrade and improve them. I came to believe they were the creatures in the world to whom he felt closest. They were certainly the only ones he really trusted.

If anything, Clark used his machines not to impress other people but to avoid them. They were his getaway vehicles. Once it became clear that a person would not permit himself to be gotten away from, Clark would load that person into the back of his stunt plane, launch him five thousand feet straight up in the air, and switch off the engine. The maneuver was known as the reverse hammer. The plane would plummet back toward earth, tail first, spinning like a top. The passenger rarely returned for a second trip.

Unsettling as these rides often were, they were never dull. Something always happened on them that wasn't supposed to happen.

An hour after Clark phoned, he picked me up in one of his designer sports cars. He wore dark sunglasses and the pained expression of a man enduring the aftershocks of two bottles of fine Burgundy. I lobbed into the haze a series of conversation starters before he took a swing at one of them: a book I had first mentioned a few weeks before, Thorstein Veblen's *The Engineers and the Price System*. Veblen was a quixotic social theorist with an unfortunate taste for the wives of his colleagues in the Stanford economics department. Between trysts he coined many poignant phrases, among them "leisure class" and "conspicuous consumption." Back in 1921 Veblen had predicted that engineers would one day rule the U.S. economy. He argued that since the economy was premised on technology and the engineers were the only ones who actually understood how the technology worked, they would inevitably use their superior knowledge to seize power from the financiers and captains of industry who wound up on top at the end of the first round of the Industrial Revolution. After all, the engineers only needed to refuse to fix anything, and modern industry would grind to a halt. Veblen rejoiced at this prospect. He didn't much care for financiers and captains. He thought they were parasites.

When I told Clark about Veblen, he did a good imitation of a man who was bored out of his skull. When he didn't want to seem too interested, he pretended he wasn't paying attention. Now, his head splitting, he was particularly keen on the idea of the engineer grabbing power from the financier. "That's happening right now," he said. "Right here. In the Valley. The power is shifting to the engineers who create the companies."

That, Clark thought, was only as it should be. Engineers created the wealth. And during the 1990s Silicon Valley had created a fantastic amount of new wealth. The venture capitalist John Doerr, Clark's friend and Valley co-conspirator, liked to describe the Valley as "the greatest legal creation of wealth in the history of the planet." He may have been right about that. But such a great new event in economic history raised great new questions. For example, why had it happened? What caused this explosion? Why had it happened *here*? The old economic theories of wealth creation—that wealth comes from savings or investment or personal rectitude or the planet earth or the proper level of government spending—failed to capture what was happening out here in the engineering division of the American economy.

The people who make a living trying to explain where wealth comes from were just starting to get their minds around the phenomenon. In the mid-1980s a young economist named Paul Romer had written a couple of papers that put across a theory, which he called New Growth Theory. Soon after Romer published his papers, Robert Lucas, the Nobel Prize–winning economist from Chicago, delivered a series of lectures at Cambridge University on the subject; inside of ten years New Growth Theory had become something like the conventional wisdom in the economics profession and the business world. New Growth Theory argued, in abstruse mathematics, that wealth came from the human imagination. Wealth wasn't chiefly having more of old things; it was having entirely new things. "Growth is just another word for change," said Romer, when he paused for breath between equations. The metaphor that Romer used to describe the economy to noneconomists was of a well-stocked kitchen waiting for a brilliant chef to exploit it. Everyone in the kitchen starts with more or less the same ingredients, the metaphor ran, but not everyone produces good food. And only a very few people who wander into the kitchen find entirely new ways to combine old ingredients into delightfully tasty recipes. These people were the wealth creators. Their recipes *were* wealth. Electricity. The transistor. The microprocessor. The personal computer. The Internet.

It followed from the theory that any society that wanted to become richer would encourage the traits, however bizarre, that led people to create new recipes. "A certain tolerance for nonconformism is really critical to the process," as Romer put it. Qualities that in eleventh-century France, or even 1950s America, might have been viewed as antisocial, or even criminal, would be rewarded, honored, and emulated, simply because they led to more . . . recipes. In short, the new theory conferred a stunning new status upon innovation, and the people responsible for it. The Prime Mover of Wealth was no longer a great industrialist who rode herd on thousands of corporate slaves, or the great politician who rode herd on a nation's finances, or the great Wall Street tycoon who bankrolled new enterprise. He was the geek holed up in his basement all weekend discovering new things to do with his computer. He was Jim Clark.

Clark drove far too fast—in the car pool lane—through the lower half of the Valley to the San Jose Jet Center. The Jet Center is the place where they keep the growing number of private planes in Silicon Valley. Waiting for us, beside Clark's new McDonnell Douglas helicopter, was a very large San Jose police officer. Clark had hired a local cop to teach him how to operate his latest acquisition. The cop had flown helicopters in the Vietnam War. He had been in combat. He hadn't crashed or been shot down. It was a start.

The first half hour Clark spent sluggishly running down a safety checklist. He wore a pale blue open-necked shirt, khaki slacks, and a pair of tattered and soiled sneakers with a tag poking off them that read MEPHISTO. Even when he headed out to start a new company, he looked as if he were dressed for a day of bait fishing. The cop barked out a list of parts, and Clark located each of them and ensured it was in the right place.

"Anti-torque pedals checked?"

"Checked."

"Anti-torque pins in?"

"In."

The exercise could not have been more tedious; Clark could not have enjoyed himself more thoroughly. It was his own peculiar cure for a hangover. At one point he looked up and said it was such a beautiful machine that he thought he might buy the company that made it. He was perfectly serious. He'd already looked into it. He'd talked it over with his friend Craig McCaw, who had made his fortune in cell phones and had now moved on to putting enough satellites into geosynchronous orbit that a person could log onto the Internet by satellite modem anywhere on the planet. Clark and McCaw were thinking of submitting a private bid for the helicopter company—as a kind of hobby.

Anyway, as he bounced around his new machine, pushing and pulling levers and buttons and blades, Clark was completely absorbed. His headache waned; he entered into a silent spiritual discussion with the shiny metal objects. The cop, perhaps sensing he was being ignored, offered a bone-chilling lecture on the perils of helicopter flight. The history of helicopters, he argued, is a story of mechanical failure. Not long ago the two finest helicopter pilots on the local police department lost the main rotor blade in flight. The whole mechanism for remaining aloft just flew right off the top. "When we got to the crash site," said the cop, "there was nothing. There was nothing left of the helicopter. Just dust."

Clark yanked out the new back seat he'd just installed, and complained it was the wrong color.

Once all the parts were checked, Clark and the cop climbed into the front seats equipped with the controls. We rose with a disturbing jolt. The helicopter lifted and swiveled toward the south end of Silicon Valley. Beneath us lay the salt pools and the sewage dumps that used to upset local environmentalists—back before environmentalists were priced out of the local real estate market. From a height of three thousand feet the waste was the most beautiful thing in sight. The cop leaned out the window to stare, leaving Clark to fly his new machine. It was his sixth hour of flying a helicopter.

From where I sat, immediately behind Clark, I could see little of his expression beyond the pale yellow of the back of his head. But I could hear the cop shouting to make himself heard; he was singing the praises of the new helicopter. "We're at 140 knots," he hollered. "And we're not even breathing hard." Clark just nodded. "They say these things aren't capable of more than a forty-degree turn," said the cop. "That's just wrong." In a flash he resumed his grip on the controls and proved his point. The helicopter tilted over. We actually flew on our side, heads parallel to the ground. "You see," said the cop, "we're not even breathing hard." Then, without fully letting go, he loosened his hands on the controls and said, "She's all yours."

Clark looked down at the control panel. The gauges gyrated wildly. Dozens of circles and needles and lights and switches. About two people on the planet could know what it all meant. But the world breaks down neatly into people who can look at a control panel and know instinctively what it all means, and those who can't. And Clark was the king of control panels. "Don't even look at the little bastards," shouted the cop. "Just fly by the seat of your pants."

The machine tilted and rocked as Clark pushed the pedals and pulled the levers to lower it. He wanted to practice his takeoffs and landings; he wanted to know everything at once. He was not satisfied learning to fly a helicopter at the rate the cop wanted to teach him. Clark was teaching himself. The cop was a mere formality, the instructor required by law.

There's not much to say about a man who insists on learning all by himself how to fly, other than he has a tendency to terrify his passengers. Essentially, Clark taught himself by trial and error. He'd poke buttons and push levers, seemingly at random, to see what happened next. Each time he did this I flinched and waited for the inevitable tailspin. *There was nothing left but dust.* Oddly, the man who'd just a few minutes earlier spoken those words didn't seem to mind. While Clark poked and pushed, he just nattered on about the perils of helicoptering. "You have to be careful where you *land* a helicopter in Silicon Valley," the cop shouted over the racket. "A while back I had a guy take her down on a golf course. Landed on a *driving range*. Dumb bastards kept wacking golf balls at us. It was like Vietnam all over again."

Down below us a few people wandered in shorts and T-shirts doing the things people do on the fifth of July: mowing lawns, shooting hoops, washing cars. The overwhelming impression made by Silicon Valley at a distance of three thousand feet is one of newness. The houses are new, the grass is new, even the people are new. And not merely new: designed never to grow old. With the exception of Stanford University no structure on the horizon had been built to last any longer than it took some engineer to think up a good excuse to tear it down. Everything in Silicon Valley, including the people, was built so that no one would find it tragic, or even a little bit sad, when it was destroyed and replaced by something new. It was one great nostalgia-prevention device. It ensured that the greatest wealth-producing machine in world history was never gummed up by pointless emotions.

The McDonnell Douglas helicopter is supposedly known for its silence to those on the outside of it. On the inside, however, it makes a fearsome racket. *Whop! Whop! Whop!* it goes. I could only just hear the cop as he hooted with glee, "They don't even know we are up here! None of this whop whop whop crap." *Whop! Whop! Whop!* went the helicopter as we fell from the sky. Weekenders glanced skyward in terror. Somehow in the suburban sprawl Clark had found a field of alfalfa, and decided it was time to practice his landings. It was illegal for him to do it, but the cop bowed to the inevitable and said, "By the time they reach us, we'll be out of here." Clark set her down, sending alfalfa sprouts blowing every which way.

Clark still hadn't spoken much. From the moment we climbed into the helicopter, he had been perfectly silent, and concentrated on teaching himself how to fly his new machine. Now, for the first time, he turned his head slightly, and I had a glimpse of his face. His mouth was already in full pucker. He shouted over the whop whop whop to the cop, "Were you controlling it?"

Clark had one of those faces that virtually screamed what he was feeling. The pucker was its way of letting you know he was irritated. Irritation, for him, was not an ordinary low-level emotional event. Along with its brother, impatience, irritation was the sensation Clark felt most keenly. He was rarely irritated by machines, but he was often irritated by people, especially when they stood between him and what he was after. His face would redden, and his mouth would twist up into a mouth-of-the-volcano pucker as if it were trying to suppress the inevitable lava. The mood in the air once his mouth went into its full pucker was a bit like the feeling you might get when, climbing what you thought was a mountain, you looked up and saw smoke billowing from the top. When you spotted the pucker, you froze, turned, and scrambled back down to safety. You found another place to pass the afternoon.

The cop didn't know about the pucker. He shook his head pleasantly. He attempted to engage the volcano in conversation. The fool. "That was all you, Jim," he hollered with a big friendly smile.

"I felt you controlling it," shouted Jim, sharply.

"No, no," said the cop, taken aback, "it's been all you." It was hard to know if he was telling the truth. Probably not. The whole time Clark had been flying the helicopter, the cop had kept his hands on his own set of controls. From the back seat it was impossible to tell who was in charge. Apparently it wasn't much easier from the front.

"This really pisses me off," said Clark.

It was all I could do not to lean forward and scream, "Of course, he's been flying it, you idiot! You've been pushing buttons just to see what would happen! What, you want us all to be a pile a dust?" Instead, I sat quietly, sweat popping out of all sorts of unlikely holes, waiting for the conflict to reach its inevitable conclusion. I'd seen this too many times already to hold out any hope for the cop.

"I think you've been flying it," hollered Clark, unhappily. "I *felt* it." His ferocity astonished the cop. He shook his head again, this time not in disagreement but in shock. He was a small furry animal that realizes too late it has wandered into the jaws of doom. With a soundless sigh he removed his hands from the controls and let them lie limply at his side. The veteran of Vietnam helicopter warfare gave the machine over to the man with six hours of flight experience. "Let's go," he said.

In moments Clark had the helicopter back up at three thousand feet. There he stopped. The human mind—or my mind anyway—has come to associate flight with motion: as long as you're moving, you can be sure that you're not dead. There was no denying the fact that we'd stopped moving. We hovered three thousand feet above the earth, perfectly motionless. After a minute or so of just sitting there, drops of sweat ran down the backs of my legs. Then Clark began to twirl the helicopter, around and around. We pirouetted in the sky, like an ice skater at the end of a routine. "Good Jim," said the cop, a bit uneasily. "Always think of your hands and feet as an extension of your brain. Like a robot."

Immediately the robot pulled the helicopter out of its spin and raced forward to God knew where. Somewhere . . . anywhere . . . so long as it was . . . new. It was pure impulse. The cop resigned himself to letting him go wherever he wanted, since he was going there anyway. We crossed over a highway and into the golden Tuscan hills that rise along the east side of Silicon Valley. The cop sat with his hands in his lap and his eyes on these dimples on the horizon. He had nothing better to do than to enjoy the view—and that is what he did. Then he asked, "What's that shiny thing down there?"

Clark said he couldn't see anything. Neither could I. The cop pointed, "Take her that direction." Thirty seconds later we both saw what the cop had spotted, a glaring reflection coming out of a stand of oaks on the side of a nasty gully. "It looks like a plane," said the cop.

It *was* a plane. More perfectly preserved than any plane that had ever landed upside down in a tree. It jutted from the giant oak as if it had been placed there by a large, sensitive hand. "Take her down," said the cop. "Take her down *low*." Clark circled lower until we were maybe one hundred feet off the ground. The terrain offered no natural landing pad, and we were unable to come close enough to peer inside the plane's windows. But when it was clear beyond doubt that the shiny metal object was indeed a plane the cop phoned the tower at the San Jose airport.

"We have found an aircraft in an oak tree," he said. His tone suggested that an aircraft in an oak tree was perfectly normal, part of the guided tour.

Once that message had been digested, a new voice came over the radio. "You think they could be alive in there?" it asked.

"That's what I'm thinking," said the cop. "It looks like it could be a survivable crash." He leaned over to Clark, apologetically. "We're kind of stuck here," he said. "We've got to save those people down there—if they are still alive."

Clark just nodded. Then he said, "This makes no sense."

"Okay," said the cop. "Let's make ourselves safe. Jim, take it up. We're going to orbit until they arrive." Clark lifted the helicopter off the gulley, all the while complaining that the plane crash made no sense. There were open fields less than a mile away. "It's bizarre," he said. "Why would they have come here to ditch instead of an open area?" It was as if he was unhappy rescuing people until he found how they came to be in need of rescue. "Who knows what people do when they panic," said the cop. Soon we were high over the crashed plane and carving wide circles over the Valley. "It still doesn't make any sense," said Clark. "Well," said the cop, reaching into the self-help playbook. "Everything happens for a reason. We took off at exactly a certain time. The sun was setting at exactly a certain angle, so that we could see the plane . . ."

The control tower decided that we shouldn't land, at least not right away, for fear that we too might end up in an oak tree, and that there would be no one to lead the rescue effort. There was nothing to do but to wait for whoever it was who cleaned up after plane crashes, so that we might lead them to the oak tree. "I'll bet it was people up last night to see the fireworks," said Clark, after a bit. "They got over here and ran out of fuel. If it was dark and they ran out of fuel that would explain why they came down here." The cop shrugged and kept one eye on the plane below. It was small and white and fragile; it was hard to see how it hadn't collapsed on impact. For anyone still alive inside that plane, I thought, there was good news and bad news. The good news was that you'd been spotted. The bad news was that the man flying the helicopter leading rescue units to your aid had six and a half hours of flight experience and a hangover. And he was growing irritated at how little sense you made.

For the next hour Clark circled Silicon Valley, and I finally had a good look at the place from the perspective that Clark sought to maintain—the perspective of a man gazing down from a great height. It did not really look very much like a valley. It was more of a broad, watery plain, though if you drove far enough in any direction you eventually encountered some shy, self-effacing mountains. For that matter, it was as difficult to spot the silicon in Silicon Valley as it was to find the valley. The silicon had been Part One of the Valley's story, and Part One was over.

The Valley had a brief but curious commercial past, in which Clark showed no interest whatsoever. It ran something like this: The sunshine, the abundance of U.S. government research grants, the willingness of Stanford University to let its professors walk out the door with their inventions and start companies, the presence of a counterculture intent on arming the masses with new technology—all made the Valley the place to be for people with a knack for building new technology. Added to this was the absence of an Old World snobbery, still present back East, but nearly absent west of the Mississippi. Back East engineering had always been viewed as glorified manual labor. No one thought of Harvard or Princeton or Yale as a place you went to become an engineer.

The Valley was at least in part an attempt to reinvent the old social order. Out here engineering did not have the stigma of manual labor. Engineering was respected, maybe more than any other profession, perhaps because the original economic prospectors were mining engineers, and the lawyers and bankers came as an afterthought. In any case, by the mid-1950s technically minded people were aware that the region offered them a chance to do better for themselves than they might back East. "In 1955, I attempted to start a transistor business in California," a Nobel Prize winner, the co-inventor of the transistor, William Shockley, told a U.S. congressional subcommittee in the late 1960s. "One of my motivations was that I had come to the conclusion that the most creative people were not adequately rewarded as the employees of industry." The engineers Shockley talked into moving to the Valley and joining his company soon quit in a dispute with Shockley and created Fairchild Semiconductor; from there several moved on to create Intel; and from Intel an industry was born. Intel invented the microprocessor; the microprocessor made possible the boom in personal computing; the personal computer boom led inexorably to the Internet boom; where the Internet boom might lead nobody knew, though if Clark had his way, and history continued its trend, it would be bigger than the Internet. This mind-boggling chain of events had been triggered by the technical man's desire to find a place where he could take what he felt was rightfully his.

It wasn't until we hovered at three thousand feet over the Valley that I could actually *see* Clark's career. Unlike just about everyone else his age—fifty-four—Clark had made the leap from Part One to Part Two

of the Silicon Valley Story. Part One had been about engineers building machines, cheaper, faster, and better. They built them so fast and
so cheap that, commercially speaking, they made themselves uninter-
esting. Each new machine they built, sooner or later, became a commodity. Other people—usually foreign people—eventually figured out
how to build it more cheaply. The companies that made the machines,
such as Hewlett-Packard, remained viable. But they were as dull and
plodding and predictable as any other big American company.

Part Two of the Valley story was not at all plodding and predictable.
At some point in the early 1990s the engineers had figured out that they
didn't need to build new computers to get rich. They just had to cook
up new things for the computers to do. The thrill was in the concepts;
the concepts were the *recipes*. The notion of what constituted "useful"
work had broadened. All across Silicon Valley you found office buildings crammed with young technogeeks cooking up recipes that they
hoped would turn the economy on its ear. The role model for this activity was Jim Clark. This was due not so much to Clark's success as to his
talent for self-reinvention. Most other fifty-four-year-olds in Silicon
Valley had long ago been torn down and replaced. Not Clark. Other
people grew old, he stayed new. His psyche was a magic show, and this
was its favorite trick: no matter how long he'd been around, he could
behave as if he'd just arrived.

Clark's ubiquity was reflected in the landscape beneath us; every significant landmark below bordered on his life. Stanford University: he
had taught computer science there and was now paying to create a new
department within the engineering school, which he wanted to call biocomputing. Xerox PARC, birthplace of the personal computer: Clark
had built his Geometry Engine there, and the Geometry Engine had
changed computing. The great sprawling campuses of the old work station companies, Silicon Graphics and Sun Microsystems: Clark had created the former; some friends of his had created the latter. The dozens
of tiny ski chalets on Sand Hill Road, for which venture capitalists now
paid ninety dollars a square foot: they paid that money so that they
could be near Clark, and people like Clark, when they announced the
new new thing. The companies born on the Internet: Yahoo, Excite,
@Home, eBay, and so on: they derived, one way or another, from
Netscape, which Clark had founded after he left Silicon Graphics. The

Internet service companies now layering themselves over the old Internet software companies: Clark had created the most outlandishly ambitious, Healtheon, with which he hoped essentially to seize control of the $1.5 trillion-a-year U.S. health care industry. It was an extraordinary performance, and it wasn't over yet.

Clark's lack of nostalgia for the history beneath us was nearly complete. Actually, as we circled overhead, what he said was "They need to tear it all down and start over. It's a ridiculous waste of space." He pointed out that offices on Sand Hill Road were going for twice the rents of space in midtown Manhattan. Sand Hill Road had the most expensive commercial real estate in the United States. And they were still putting two-story buildings on it! "One day it'll all be skyscrapers," he said. The thought pleased him—he became less irritated by the crashed plane. The impermanence of the place allowed him, and it, to remain suspended in a state of pure possibility. He was fully occupied only by what had not yet happened. The part of his brain that kept him interested in being alive groped for what came next, after Healtheon.

We circled the Valley for another hour. The cop remained excited about the possibility that people inside the crashed plane were alive and upside down on top of the oak tree. Clark's interest in the plane in the oak tree had faded to nothing. Having led us into the excitement, he left us to enjoy it for ourselves. It was as if his job ended when he'd stumbled upon the plane; everything else was a mopping-up operation best left to others. Soon enough a convoy of eight cars, an ambulance, and a fire truck came up a highway in the distance, and we flew out to meet them. They spotted us in the air, and followed our lead down a dirt road. Twenty minutes later another helicopter appeared on the horizon. The voice of its pilot crackled over our intercom. "I tip my hat to you gentlemen," he said. "Quite a spot these fellows got themselves in."

From above we could just make out the rescue squad climbing the tree. They reached the door of the crashed plane. They opened it.

"It's empty," crackled the voice on the radio.

The cockpit was empty. An airplane upside down at the top of a tall oak tree. Eight, maybe nine, miles from the nearest road or house. And there was no one inside of it. Or, for that matter, anywhere to be seen.

## The Past in a Box

It wasn't until the next day that we learned what had happened. A few hours before we took off in Clark's helicopter, two guys had set out in their small white four-seater airplane, looking for goats to chase. Apparently people do this. They chase after goats in airplanes. They find themselves a big herd, come in low behind it, and frighten it into running off a cliff. Or something. Anyway, that morning the pleasure went out of goat chasing almost immediately, when the two men crashed into an oak tree, upside down. By some miracle of injustice neither one of them was killed, or even injured. The two men simply climbed down the oak tree and headed out to the highway to thumb a ride back to San Jose. They had some idea that they might return later with the necessary equipment and extract their airplane from the oak tree, real quiet-like. Unfortunately, almost as soon as they'd hit the ground, we'd shown up. The last thing the two men had wanted was to be saved. Rather than endure the embarrassment of explaining themselves to their would-be rescuers, they hid in the bushes until we left. Once the sky was clear they sneaked away.

We learned all that and more the next day. The afternoon after our helicopter ride, we hadn't the faintest idea what had happened. And we drove back to Clark's house in Atherton in radically different states of mind. I, for one, thought we had just had an unusual experience. We'd stumbled upon a plane crash, led a rescue effort, and wound up with a postmodern mystery: an empty cockpit. Here was the aviation equivalent of the authorless text. Clark, for his part, had little interest in any of it—not that day or any other. He never mentioned it again. When I said something about how strange it was to see an airplane sticking out of a tree, he said, "Oh, what did it look like?" For a full hour he had circled and dipped and swooped and plummeted over the wreck without once removing his eyes from the controls to glance at the crashed airplane. All of his attention had gone into learning to fly his helicopter.

At first I thought it was just coincidence that the most stupendously odd accidents befell Jim Clark. He was so wasteful of them, from a recreational point of view. Experiences from which most people could extract a life philosophy he glanced at once and discarded from his thoughts. He was the guy with a craving for sweets who'd been handed a huge bag of Snickers bars, which he worked his way through in an hour by eating a tiny corner off each one and chucking the rest. Eventually, I saw a kind of logic in his grazing: this was how he left himself open to accident. If nothing surprising or interesting was happening to him, he moved on until the situation corrected itself. This was as true of his work as of his leisure; indeed, it was hard to say where the work stopped and the leisure began. They formed a seamless, disturbing pattern of motion and change.

Clark's inability to live without motion and change had gotten him to where he was. In his world change and motion begat money, which begat even more change and more motion, and so on. "Change" was another word for wealth, and "wealth" was another word for money, and money was what he was after, or said he was after. My own view was that he needed change even more than he needed the money that came from the change. Different people have different words for this need for constant motion and change. "Despair" is one of them. "Impatience" is another. Impatience might be a social vice but, to Clark, it was a commercial virtue. "If everyone was patient," he'd say, "there'd be no new companies." The impatient man kept his own life in such a constant state of upheaval that neither his experience nor his immediate surroundings ended up meaning very much to him. He was keen on things only as they happened; after they had happened he lost interest in them altogether.

As a result, it sometimes felt that nothing had ever happened to him at all. Oh, every now and then he was seized by a sense that his past *should* matter, just as people who have lost a leg occasionally wake up thinking they feel it down there kicking. In one such moment he decided that since Netscape obviously had played some role in economic history he should record how it felt to create it. But almost as soon as he'd hired his ghost writer, he lost interest. It bored him to sit around answering questions about what had happened. His little contribution to economic history—called *Netscape Time*—though not without interest, wound up sounding as if it was written by someone else. Which, of course, it was.

As a practical matter, Clark had no past, only a future. That's when he really came alive: when you got him on the subject of what was going to happen *next*. Then he was full of ideas, and they would change from one moment to the next. This process bore no relation to the clichéd version of it offered up by more ordinary business people. Clark never used the words and phrases that we all have come to expect from the technology types who pretend to see the future. *Vision, the challenge of the next century, the new millennium, the road ahead.* That sort of grand talk struck him as perfect bullshit. In all the time I spent with him, I never once heard him refer to his ability to see the future. He couldn't see it—that's why he had to grope for it. He would be seized by some overwhelming enthusiasm—say, his ambition to create a new field of study that he wanted to call biocomputing, or his newest idea for snaring more billions in the World Wide Web—and he would be off and running down some long, dark tunnel leading God knew where. With him, enthusiasm was a physical event. He stood six feet three inches tall and weighed maybe two hundred pounds, but when he became excited about something he grew three inches and put on fifty pounds. It was as if someone had injected him with growth hormones.

Usually, after a week or two, Clark would decide there was something wrong with his new idea, and drop it. Moments after he'd exploded with his latest plan to create another multibillion-dollar industry, he would have forgotten about it. But every now and then the long, dark tunnel didn't come to a dead end. Whatever radar Clark possessed told him that it was okay to sprint into the dark. That's when he was most dangerous. It was also when he was at his best.

Anyway, it took some months before I realized that I was never going to hear about his past from him, at least not in the usual way that information changes hands. The few times I asked him directly how he had got from there to here—which, it was becoming clearer, was the same as asking how the modern world had got from there to here—he would offer some perfunctory reply and wave me away. "That's boring," he'd say. When I pressed he might say, "That's the past. I really don't give a shit about the past."

Then one day I discovered the cardboard boxes. They were stacked up in a closet in the guest bedroom of his house. It was, like most guest rooms, one of those rooms that looked as if they had been cleaned a thousand times and never inhabited. Since he first started out in Silicon Valley back in 1979 Clark had the same secretary, a woman named D'Anne Schjerning. After Netscape went public, in August 1995, she made so much money from her stock in various Clark-inspired enterprises that she bought herself a long gold Cadillac and retired. Up until then, bless her heart, she squirreled away Clark's notes and papers, and stuffed them into cardboard boxes. She kept the boxes at Netscape until the company outgrew its space, at which point she shipped them to Clark's home. The boxes had never been opened. They looked as new as everything else in the room. Clark had no idea what was in them ("It must just be some boring old stuff," he said), but he did not mind if I opened them.

At the top of the first box there was a yellowing clipping from the local newspaper in Plainview, Texas, where Clark grew up. The paper wanted to let the townspeople know that one of their own had gone to California and created a big company called Silicon Graphics. It played it as a straightforward local-boy-makes-good story, and made light of Clark's boyhood failure. It mentioned that he'd been expelled from the local public high school in his junior year. He'd been an indifferent student and a cutup—one of those great bad examples to youth who prove that if you really want to be a success in American life you have to start by offending your elders. The offense that got Clark tossed out for good was telling an English teacher to "go to hell." Before that he had exploded a small bomb on a school bus, smuggled a skunk, inside a horn case, into a school dance, and set off a string of firecrackers inside another student's locker, among other tricks. Once he left school—or school left him—he fled town.

The next clue folded neatly inside the cardboard boxes was a photograph of Clark circa 1970, having just received his master's degree in physics from the University of New Orleans, on his way to a Ph.D. program at the University of Utah. He wore thick dark-rimmed glasses, a crew cut, and an expression that approached, but did not quite achieve, innocence. In under eight years this person, considered unfit to graduate from public high school in Plainview, Texas, had earned himself a Ph.D. in Computer Science.

Actually, the story was more remarkable than that. His father abandoned the family when Clark was a small child. His mother should have taken welfare, but it never occurred to her. The home Clark went back to after a day of turning his school on its head was situated somewhere below the poverty line. When I asked him about the article in the Plainview paper, all he said was "I grew up in black and white. I thought the whole world was shit and I was sitting in the middle of it." At the minimum age of seventeen and a half Clark asked his mother to sign the piece of paper that permitted him to join the Navy. In September 1961, when the rest of his high school class returned for its senior year, he left Plainview for basic training just outside of New Orleans.

His career in the Navy started as badly as his career in high school ended. When he arrived at training camp, he was given, along with every other new recruit, a multiple-choice aptitude test. He had never seen a multiple-choice test, and he didn't know how to take one. To most of the questions several different answers struck him as at least partially correct. Instead of picking the one that seemed most correct, he just circled them all. The Navy assumed that he knew that circling more than one answer fooled the computer that graded the tests. They charged him with cheating, took him off the ordinary slow track for enlisted men, and put him on an even slower one for juvenile delinquents. Thus the first time Jim Clark ever heard of computers was when he was accused of trying to fool one into thinking he was smarter than he was.

The other recruits who took the multiple-choice test went into a classroom and obtained their high school equivalency diplomas. Clark alone found himself shipped out to sea. There he spent the next nine months, performing the most disgusting chores that need doing on a ship. Those nine months at sea have filled a lot of Clark's memory. He recalls officers telling him that he was stupid, and bullies tossing plates full of food on the floor just so that he would have to clean them up. He returned to the Navy's classroom convinced that Plainview, Texas, just might not be the world's capital of shit. He took his first math test and scored the highest grade in the class. He was unaware that he had any particular aptitude for math and didn't quite believe the result. Neither did anyone else. The Navy gave him another test. Same result. Six weeks later Clark was assigned to teach basic algebra to incoming recruits. A few after that, one of the instructors told him that it had been a long time since he'd seen someone so naturally gifted in mathematics. He suggested that Clark enroll in night classes at Tulane University with a view to getting a college degree after he'd finished his tour of duty. Within eight years Clark had his college degree, plus a master's in physics, plus a Ph.D. in computer science.

In the Navy, Clark said, he learned that his desire for revenge could lead to success. He was propelled in the classroom by his anger about the humiliation he'd suffered at sea. Thus success, for him, became a form of revenge.

I returned to the cardboard boxes. They suggested a turbulent early career. There were hints that between 1970 and 1978 Clark had married at least twice, sired at least two children, moved back and forth across the country at least three times, and held at least four different jobs, mainly at universities. He did postgraduate work at the University of Utah with the forefather of computer graphics, Ivan Sutherland. In 1978 he was fired for insubordination from a post at the New York Institute of Technology, at which point a wife, not his first, left him. "I remember her saying that she couldn't live the way I lived anymore," he recalled when asked. "She just wanted a more settled life."

When he said this, he was standing outside of his house, near his hill. Just a few years back, before the Internet boom, Clark's house in Atherton had been surrounded by empty fields. Now he was surrounded by new houses, many of them bigger than his own. One morning he looked up from his kitchen table and saw the neighbors looking back. He requested, and was denied, a permit to build a fence tall enough to screen them from his view. The city of Atherton, California, had strict rules about fences, and the fence Clark wanted to build was declared too high. So Clark built a hill, and put the fence on top of the hill. It did not occur to him that there was anything unusual about this.

As he stood beneath his self-made hill, he tried to explain this extraordinary leap in his career from thirty-eight-year-old unsuccessful college professor with a warning label on his forehead to a founder of a multibillion-dollar corporation. "It was one of those times when the whole fucking world went berserk," he said. "After my wife left I went into this spiral . . . six months of counseling. Then I said fuck counseling; it wasn't helping anything. There was all of this self-actualization stuff around, est and that kind of thing. I thought I don't need some guru to tell me how to find my way out."

"So it was as simple as that?"

He laughed. "No. For a year and a half I was in this kind of downbeat funk. Dark, dark, dark."

I said he still hadn't answered the original question.

"It's funny," he said. "One day I was sitting at home and, I remember having the conscious thought 'You can dig this hole as deep as you want to dig it.' I remember thinking, 'My God, I'm going to spend the rest of my life in this fucking hole.' You reach these points in life when you say, 'Fuck, I've reached some sort of dead end here. What was the point of getting here?' And you descend into this chaos. All those years you thought you were achieving something. And you achieved nothing. I was thirty-eight years old. I'd just been fired. My second wife had just left me. I had somehow fucked up. I developed this maniacal passion for wanting to achieve *something*." He paused. "I guess it was a little bit of self-imposed psychology." In something like an instant the man had changed his life. He reinvented his relationship to the world around him in a way that is considered normal only in California. No one who had been in his life to that point would be in it ten years later. His wife, his friends, his colleagues, even his casual acquaintances—they'd all be new.

The result of his self-imposed psychology surprised even Clark. He insists that the transformation occurred overnight and that he cannot really explain it. But all of a sudden the best graduate students at Stanford wanted to work with him on his special project—a computer chip he'd been tinkering with for nearly three years. Computer science became a formal academic discipline only in the late 1960s when an obscure subdivision of the U.S. government called ARPA (for Advanced Research Projects Agency) funded four university departments—at the University of Utah, the Carnegie-Mellon Institute, the University of California at Berkeley, and Stanford University. The best computer science students at Stanford were some of the best computer science students anywhere. Under Clark they gathered together into a new, potent force. "The difference was phenomenal, for me. I don't know how many people around me noticed. But my God I noticed. The first manifestation was when all of these people started coming up and wanting to be part of my project."

That project turned out to be Clark's first experience with the new new thing. It was 1979. Silicon Valley was chiefly a place where chips were made, though this new company called Apple Computer was having some success mass-marketing computers. Clark set to work turning his new interest in being alive into new technology. With his graduate students he created a chip that could do things no other computer chip could do. That much I knew from a fascinating new book, called *Dealers in Lightning*, about the role of Xerox's Palo Alto Research Center (PARC) in the modern computer industry. That day I showed Clark a passage from a chapter called "The Silicon Revolution":

Years later Lynn Conway [a PARC researcher] could still remember the moment she first laid eyes on the chip that would launch a new science. It was a week or two after Christmas 1979. She was seated before her second-floor window at PARC, which looked down on a lovely expanse of valley in its coat of lush winter green, sloping down toward Page Mill Road just out of the view to the south. But her eyes were fixed on a wafer of silicon that had just come back from a commercial fabrication shop.

There were dozens of chip designs on the wafer, mostly student efforts from a Stanford course being taught with PARC's technical supervision. They all strived toward an intricate machined elegance, comprising as they did tens of thousands of microscopic transistors packed into rectangular spaces the size of a cuticle, all arranged on a wafer that could fit comfortably in the palm of one's hand. A few years earlier the same computing power could not have fit on an acre of real estate.

One design stood out, and not only because it bore along its edge the assertive hand-etched legend: "Geometry Engine © 1979 James Clark." Where the others looked to be simple arrays of devices that formed simple digital clocks and arithmetic search engines and the like, Clark's was obviously something more—larger, deeper, more complex than the others, even when viewed with the naked eye.

. . . After the appearance of Clark's chip, the art and science of computer graphics would never be the same. The computer-aided design of cars and aircraft, the "virtual reality" toys and games of the modern midway, the lumbering dinosaurs of the movie *Jurassic Park*— they all sprang from the tiny chip Lynn Conway held by its edges that winter day.

Once again Clark's mind wandered out of the conversation. He had no interest in his Geometry Engine. He'd never heard of the book or its author, Michael A. Hiltzik, though he did, vaguely, recall Lynn Conway. "Kind of overblown title isn't it. *Dealers in Lightning*," he snorted, and then moved back to finding something in his house that needed to be changed. His ego was far too big for garden-variety immodesty, taking pride in his past accomplishment. He was actually irritated that he was somehow obliged to exhibit pride in something he had done; and he reacted by looking for something he might do. He'd pulled out the previous owner's idea of iron work and put up his own. He'd dug up his swimming pool and moved it across his yard. Twice. Now he cast around with the blank expression that always preceded a new plan.

I left him to it and returned once again to the room that had been cleaned one thousand times and cardboard boxes that had never been opened. They went silent. Right up until 1991 was a giant black hole. But after that the paper came fast and thick. First there was a big bill to Clark from a local hospital. "Motorcycle accident," read a scrap of paper attached to it. A note described an "interior tibia detached completely from bone." Beneath the hospital bill and the clinical description of Clark's shattered leg was a rough draft of a paper written by Clark, and dated just after his motorcycle accident. His paper was called "The Telecomputer."

## Disorganization Man

In 1956 a *Fortune* magazine writer named William H. Whyte published his classic study of American corporate life, *The Organization Man*. The book found its way onto the shelf crammed with evocative 1950s titles such as *The Lonely Crowd* and *The Man in the Gray Flannel Suit*. All these texts tried in one way or another to explain the strange uniformity of the American businessman. He commuted to work in his immaculate gray suit from his neat suburban tract house. He kept his front lawn and his hair trimmed to lengths tacitly agreed upon by his peers. He avoided high culture, or anything else that smacked of elitism. He worked for some enormous gray corporation such as IBM or AT&T that was more of a home to him than his house in the suburbs. The enormous gray corporation maintained a constant lookout for anarchists trying to pass themselves off as conformists. They devised clever multiple-choice personality tests, which they gave to anyone who applied for a job:

*Underline the word you think goes best with the word in capitals:*
NIGHT: (dark, sleep, moon, morbid)
NAKED: (nude, body, art, evil)

That question came from a test Whyte dug out of the archives of one of the enormous gray corporations. An actual human being read these tests, presumably looking for the fellow stupid enough to circle "morbid" and "evil." When the true Organization Man read NAKED, he underlined "nude," even if he thought "evil."

In any case, the Organization Man's taste for conformity led Whyte to a simple theory: the Protestant Ethic, with its emphasis on rugged individualism, had been displaced in American life by something else. "The Social Ethic" is the fancy name Whyte gave that something else. The Organization Man believed in the essential rightness of large groups—and the essential wrongness of the individual. He felt very strongly that people had a *moral* obligation to fit in. To Whyte this represented an important and possibly permanent shift in American values—a kind of loss of innocence. Americans were not merely working differently than they had in the past. They were voting, praying, dressing, buying, and loving differently, too. And all of it flowed from changes in the corporate culture. When Americans changed the way they made money, they changed a lot of other things too.

The character at the center of Whyte's wonderful psychodrama was "the well-rounded man." The well-rounded man was the ideal 1950s type. Whyte wrote his book in part as an argument against the well-rounded man. He believed that when society exalted the well-rounded it punished the truly talented: the scientists, the artists, the musicians, the engineers, the people who came at life from surprising new directions. The pressure exerted on the oddballs to be "normal" caused extraordinary products of the human imagination to be discouraged and suppressed:

Searching for their own image, management men look for the "well-rounded" scientists. They don't expect them to be quite as "well rounded" as junior-executive trainees; they generally note that scientists are "different." They do it, however, in a patronizing way that implies that the difference is nothing that a good indoctrination program won't fix up. Customarily, whenever the word *brilliant* is used, it either precedes the word *but* (cf. "We are all for brilliance, but . . .") or is coupled with such words as *erratic, eccentric, introvert, screwball*, etc.

Somewhere along the line the Organization Man passed from the American scene. Whether he was murdered or died of natural causes is hard to say; obviously, he had a lot of bad luck between the late 1950s and the late 1990s. One piece of bad luck was rapid technical change, which was a weapon that oddball upstarts could use against the enormous gray corporations. Another was Jim Clark or, more generally, the engineer with a taste for anarchy, who lifted one big middle finger in the direction of the enormous gray corporation. Silicon Valley hatched a lot of certifiable weirdos interested in getting their hands on money and power. These people became some of the most admired businessmen on earth. And yet, by the standards of the Organization Man, they were barely socialized.

Clark's quixotic bid for power and money began at Silicon Graphics. The company he founded with several of his Stanford graduate students was one of a handful that extended the reach of the computer and caused important people to rethink what the machine might be capable of. The chip Clark had designed, the Geometry Engine, was better able than any before it to process three-dimensional graphics in real time, and so create a simulation of reality on the computer screen. "Jim's logic was that the world was three-dimensional, and so the computer world would have to be, too," said Kurt Akeley, one of Clark's students. "He thought the right way to interact with the machines is the way you interact with the world." Clark had long been fascinated by virtual reality. The Geometry Engine made it possible to draw and redraw the real world inside a computer, which was the equivalent of bestowing upon the computer a sense of sight. When you turned on the computer in Clark's Stanford lab, you now saw a realistic, three-dimensional picture. "Computer graphics is as fundamental to computers as vision is to humans," Clark wrote back in his teaching days. That thought, strange at the time, soon became commonplace.

A lot of people who should have seen the importance of Clark's Geometry Engine thought it was a useless toy. Half the venture capitalists on Sand Hill Road who made their money, in theory at least, financing the future had failed to see its potential. So had the enormous gray corporations of the late 1970s. Clark had offered to license his invention to IBM, Apollo, Hewlett-Packard, and DEC. All turned him down. Even people whose work would be transformed by his invention were slow to grasp its importance. For instance, an engineer from Lockheed visited Silicon Graphics (SGI) soon after the company was founded. The SGI engineers offered him a demonstration: an automobile depicted and manipulated in three-dimensional space on an SGI computer. "That might be good for designing cars," said the man from Lockheed, "but I design airplanes." He essentially did not believe what he had just seen; he assumed Clark and his engineers had made a one-off trick of putting a picture of an automobile inside the computer. He didn't understand that Clark's new company had made it possible to design *everything* inside a computer. And that every new Lockheed airplane from now until eternity would be created by Silicon Graphics' technology.

The Hollywood people were shrewder about the possibilities, and it wasn't long before Steven Spielberg and George Lucas were banging on Clark's door and asking to be his first customers. The Silicon Graphics work station made possible a lot of new special effects. The spectacle that overran movies and television in the 1980s and 1990s, and kept viewers glued to bad stories, were all accomplished with SGI's technology. When a moviegoer rubbed his eyes and said, "What'll they think of next?" it was usually because SGI had upgraded its machines. Someone once said that the best technology is indistinguishable from magic. Clark now had the best magic act in Silicon Valley.

The best magic act attracted many of the best engineers. In the Valley it often did. The Valley had given engineers a place where they could make their living outside the enormous gray corporations that expected them to conform. It tended to attract the technologists who valued their freedom and wanted to live out on the edge. In any case, for a certain kind of engineer the chance to play with hot new technology offset the career risk of doing so. Clark gave them that chance.

In the early 1980s the labs that housed the world's finest technical talent—those of Hewlett-Packard, Bell Labs, Xerox PARC, Stanford, MIT—surrendered some of their best minds to Clark's new company. They came from all over, but they came for the same simple reason: they saw the possibilities in Jim Clark's silicon chip. Not all engineers were so adventuresome as Clark. Some of them probably wanted to linger back East and be given multiple-choice personality tests until they retired to Sarasota or St. Petersburg. But a lot of the smart ones were looking for the chance to show just what they could do. Greg Chesson, a young engineer at Bell Labs, recalls visiting Clark's Stanford lab in 1981 and seeing the Geometry Engine in action. He watched a computer-generated image of Snoopy flying his doghouse across Clark's computer screen—a sight that just a few years later would seem unremarkable. In 1981 it was a kind of miracle. Chesson knew instantly he was looking into the future. "There was no question in my mind," he says. "I just said, 'All right, here is where I work now.'"

Before long, Jim Clark's new company exerted a gravitational force on the technical mind. When you ask people who dealt with Silicon Graphics, or who worked for Silicon Graphics, or who bought machines from Silicon Graphics, or who simply observed Silicon Graphics from afar, they all say the same thing about it: "It was the smartest group of engineers I've *ever* seen in one place." Tom Jermoluk recalls his first encounter with the company. This was ten years before Jermoluk became, at Jim Clark's behest, the CEO of @Home Networks. In 1986 Jermoluk was an impressionable thirty-one-year-old engineer at Hewlett-Packard. Someone at Silicon Graphics called him up and said he should come over, just to have a look around. He met Clark. Within minutes they were off on an argument about the potential for computer-generated images. It lasted the afternoon. "I just joined literally on the spot: 'Okay I'm in,'" says Jermoluk. "Jim was building the coolest stuff. You wanted to be around just to see what was going to happen next."

What was going to happen next, just about everyone thought, was that Silicon Graphics would become a big company. And it did. Clark had invented the technology, bet his career on it, and been right. He had attracted the most talented engineers in Silicon Valley to his company, and they in turn created the most talented computers. But as a group, Clark began to complain, they had precious little to show for it. The lion's share of the equity and the power had been taken by others. Financiers and managers owned huge chunks of Silicon Graphics and had seized control of the board of directors, while Clark's engineers owned tiny slivers and watched the decision making from afar. Sure, they were doing much better for themselves than they would have done back East. But they did not do as well as people who had had no hand in creating the technology.

It didn't take long for Clark to become deeply irritated by the rules of American capitalism. In his opinion, the game was rigged so that the people who really mattered got the shaft. He believed in his bones that the people who mattered most were the brilliant engineers: the chefs who cooked up the new recipes. (Clark was a New Growth Theorist long before anyone in Silicon Valley heard of New Growth Theory.) This opinion was hardly surprising; he was one of them. What he did with his opinion, however, was astonishing. He forced it down Silicon Valley's throat. He left it to the Valley to take care of the rest of the world.

Of course, if the creator of the concept and the engineers who executed the concept were not getting what they deserved, someone else was getting more than he deserved. The first person Clark fingered was the man who lent him the money to build his new machine. When he set about to create his first company, Clark had no experience of the venture capitalists who back new enterprises. He wound up selling a 40 percent stake in Silicon Graphics to a man named Glenn Mueller at the prestigious Mayfield Fund for $800,000. Initially Clark kept a 15 percent stake for himself—which implied that he, his invention, and his ability to attract engineers were worth $300,000. He liked the deal when he made it; it took him about six months to change his mind. His original stake in his own business soon became a lot smaller; and he became irritated. His backers were about to discover what that meant.

Building new hardware costs a lot of money, much more than Clark realized. He and his engineers ran through their initial $800,000 of venture capital in less than a year, and were forced to return to the venture capitalists, hat in hand. Mueller and others put up another $17 million in exchange for another piece of the company. By the end of 1984 Clark's engineers had run through the $17 million and needed even more money, and so had to sell even more of their stakes in the business. As a result, before they'd made their first dollar, Clark and his engineers were largely squeezed out of their own enterprise. "I wouldn't be surprised if, of all the hugely successful companies in Silicon Valley, Silicon Graphics made the fewest millionaires out of the engineers who founded it," says Greg Chesson. The Mayfield Fund ended up making about $400 million on its investment.

Clark took this and almost everything else that happened at Silicon Graphics personally. At each step of the way it became clearer that

SGI would be a huge success; yet at each step of the way Clark found himself more at the mercy of his financiers, who had nothing at risk but their money. Six months after Silicon Graphics received its first infusion of capital, Clark decided somehow that he had sold too cheap. Glenn Mueller had cut a sweet deal for himself. Mueller was supposed to be a nice guy—everyone said so. The Mueller family threw the Christmas party each year that most everyone who was anyone in Silicon Valley wanted to attend. Clark had trusted him. He'd never do that again with a venture capitalist. And he never forgave Mueller for exploiting his ignorance. At board meetings Mueller often found himself subjected to Clark's fury. "Jim's face would get red and he'd start shouting that Glenn had cheated him and his engineers," recalls Dick Kramlich, a Silicon Valley venture capitalist who joined the board of Silicon Graphics in 1984. "Glenn would just sit there and take it."

Actually, the venture capitalists were just the first item on Clark's list of what needed fixing in American capitalism. One day in late 1984, just as Silicon Graphics was preparing to ship its first machines, Glenn Mueller called a meeting in his office. It had taken two years from the founding of the company to its first product. The new computers were not easy to sell, at least not at first. SGI delivered far more computer than most people could handle. A cheap one cost seventy thousand dollars. The founding engineer Mark Grossman recalls "endless meetings and debates about how to squeeze what we had into a smaller box. Basically we couldn't figure out how to make it cheap." But even a cheap one was complicated to use, even for someone who knew his way around a computer. People with modest programming skills in front of a Silicon Graphics work station sometimes felt a bit like a man in a Lamborghini on a two-lane road.

The result was a struggle between the engineers, who built ever niftier computers, and the managers, who had been brought in to market them. The managers wanted the engineers to make their products simpler to use. The engineers, like their leader, thought their managers were all idiots. "They were promising stuff we couldn't deliver," says the engineer Tom Davis, "and they didn't understand what we had. Of course, fifteen more years of experience showed me that this is the normal situation." At the time, however, the engineers were outraged. The managers would tell them to do one thing, the engineers would do the opposite, and, no matter how it turned out, the engineers thought they were right until someone proved them wrong. "It was like an especially contentious academic community," recalls Tom Jermoluk. "You were encouraged to shred each other's stuff. And everyone had an opinion about everything."

Glenn Mueller's meeting was an attempt to sort out the problem and to transform Jim Clark's company into a stable, well-adjusted, lasting institution. At the meeting were Clark, Vern Anderson, the CEO Mueller had told Clark he needed to have in order for the Mayfield Fund to supply him venture capital, a few other senior executives, and the venture capitalists bankrolling the enterprise. Dick Kramlich of New Enterprise Associates was the newest of these. It was Kramlich's first encounter with Clark's corporate culture, and it was the most contentious he'd ever seen. "People were yelling and screaming at each other, over the most petty things—not even business things," he recalls. "I waited until it was five o'clock, and then I got out. I told them that I really didn't want to go through any more of this and to call me when they'd worked out their emotional problems."

After the meeting Vern Anderson stepped down as CEO. This should have surprised no one: after Mueller had told him that, to obtain venture capital, he needed a CEO, Clark had literally walked outside, found Anderson on the street in Palo Alto, and asked him if he wanted the job. ("I bargained for a temperamental handful," says Anderson.) Clark never had any serious ambition to manage the company himself; even then he knew he'd be poorly suited for the job. He couldn't stand the small steps, the details, the tedium. He thought they should bring in some person to handle the details while he made sure that his beloved engineers kept on building the machine of the future. He didn't fully appreciate just how much power he had to relinquish for the detail person to do his job well. Soon enough, he found out. Mueller found another man to run the company. His name was Ed McCracken, a highly regarded vice president at Hewlett-Packard. When Mueller told Clark about McCracken, and explained that Clark would have to give up the illusion that he still controlled Silicon Graphics, Clark broke down and cried. "Jim always had a sense that we weren't doing things right," said Anderson. "He knew in his heart that we needed someone like Ed."

With the understanding that he would enjoy complete control, Ed McCracken left his safe comfortable job at Hewlett-Packard and took a risky one at Silicon Graphics. He and Clark taken together were proof of the limits of physiognomy. To look at them, they could have been brothers—tall and blond with wire-rimmed spectacles perched on surprisingly delicate features. To watch them in action, you would think they came from different planets. Hewlett-Packard was the closet thing in the Valley to an enormous gray corporation, and Ed McCracken was the Valley's version of the Organization Man. He had mastered the unnaturally sincere tone of voice of the Professional Man. When he wished to indicate seriousness, he dropped his chin down into his throat. When he took you aside to have a word, he looked and sounded as if he was giving a speech to an audience of a thousand people. To stress his points, which were rarely pointed or stressful, he'd press his thumb against his index finger as if he had just caught a fly by its wing. He wore suits. He hated strife. He loved consensus, or at any rate the idea of it.

For many of the founding engineers it was the first experience with a Serious American Executive, and with the vaguely phony emotional postures that seem to be, for whatever reason, necessary for the success of the leader of a large organization. "He came off as being awkward and manipulative," says Mark Grossman. "There was no idle chitchat." "He had a weird way of using silence in conversation," says Kurt Akeley. "Ed was one of those people who likes to design questionnaires for others to fill out," a third engineer says. McCracken liked to deal with people indirectly, through intermediaries. As yet another of the engineers who left Stanford with Clark to found Silicon Graphics puts it, "Ed had this phrase for all our problems. He said we were 'highly oppositional.'" It was that phrase—"highly oppositional"—that stuck in people's minds.

In late 1984 McCracken took over the company from Clark, who stayed on as chairman, whatever that meant. He looked at the books and discovered that the company had only seven million dollars left, and was running through money at the rate of two million a month, which meant it had exactly three and a half more months to run. He cast one long look at the contentious engineers and their warring opinions. He decided that Jim Clark's corporate culture needed more than a chief executive officer. It needed a therapist.

McCracken hired a corporate psychologist. The psychologist together with forty Silicon Graphics employees, including the senior engineers and their leader, Jim Clark, retreated for three days to a resort not far outside of the Valley. There they submitted to a battery of psychological tests designed to make them better Organization Men.

Before the retreat Clark and his engineers were required to find two people to fill out psychological evaluations on their behalf, and mail them to the corporate psychologist, confidentially. Once they'd gathered together at the resort, the engineers filled out two more forms. The first was designed to classify them into one of four psychological types. These types probably said more about psychology as filtered through the American business mind than about the engineers. At any rate, the tests broke the world down into introverts and extroverts, then into right-brained versions and left-brained versions. The four types were given the following names:

introvert + right brained = "supportive"
introvert + left brained = "analytical"
extrovert + right brained = "promoter"
extrovert + left brained = "controller"

Depending on the degree to which you possessed these qualities, you were classified as a "strong" or "weak" version of your type. Ed McCracken was a "weak analytical." Jim Clark was a "strong controller." (As Clark recalls it, "The psychologist determined that everyone else on the executive committee was passive aggressive and I was just aggressive.") The engineers Clark had hired all scored pretty much the same as he did. Of the thirty engineers who took the test, only two registered as "supportives" and two more were "analyticals." The rest were "controllers."

The second test required Clark's engineers to answer 250 questions designed to further parse their psyches. The results were laid out on a pie chart with twelve slices. Again, each slice of pie represented a different personality type. The psychologist had odd little names for these, too: "humanistic," "optimistic," "vague," and so on. When the chart was completely filled in, eleven of the categories remained empty. The names of all the engineers were crammed into a single sliver of pie.

"Highly oppositional," it was labeled. (That is when it occurred to the engineers where their new CEO got his lingo.)

Afterward each engineer was required to explain his psychological profile. That is where tempers finally flared: the charge that they were "highly oppositional" actually pleased a lot of Clark's engineers. *To this day* it pleases them. For instance, Tom Davis, one of the seven founding engineers who had followed Clark out of Stanford, says, "Their definition of oppositional was basically someone who stuck to his guns. That's clearly a bad trait if you stick to your guns when you're clearly wrong, but at the time it was probably the best group of engineers I'd ever seen assembled, and everyone knew that they were almost always right. From my point of view, they had exactly the right qualities to produce great products—they were almost always right, and if you disagreed, you had a big argument to change their minds. But if you were right, after some struggle they almost always would. If somebody insists that 2 + 2 = 5, I'll *never* back down, no matter how bad it makes them feel. I think that the shrink thought that you should. In nonengineering areas where things are a lot fuzzier, giving in more often is clearly a reasonable thing to do."

The psychologist ran the subsequent three-day drill like an AA meeting. He asked each of Clark's engineers to stand up, explain how he scored on his test, and tell everyone else how he planned to change. The second test, which the shrink kept calling "the instrument," had reduced each engineer's personality to a three-dimensional "shape," which turned out to be a piece of paper with warts and divots and ridges. One of the company's founders grabbed his shape and led off. He rose and said that he had spent his whole life getting himself to the point where he could tell someone he was an idiot and that he had no intention of changing that now. Did anyone want to fight about it? The other engineers cheered. Another engineer said that he had figured out how the questions related to the profile, and he wanted to take the test again so he could get a perfect score. The shrink insisted that there was no such thing as a perfect score. "He went on and on and on how there is no right answer," says Rocky Rhodes. "How this was just for us to get to know each other better. That there were no bad people and no bad shapes. That there was nothing judgmental about it. It was just a shape. You sat in front of the group on a little chair and held up your shape.

One by one. Then Greg Chesson walks up and the shrink almost gasps. He says, 'Wow! that's perfect!'"

One way of viewing Silicon Graphics in the mid-1980s is as an answer to a pair of questions. The first question was: If an extraordinarily willful human being with great technical aptitude is permitted to create a large business organization, how will that organization behave? By 1984 everyone understood that it would behave like Jim Clark, which is to say that it would behave as no big, successful American company had ever behaved. It would be a loose collection of argumentative, brilliant, bullheaded engineers who might or might not make money but almost certainly would build something wonderful.

The second question was: How would such a place ever grow old? The answer was: painfully.

After the retreat Ed McCracken quickly set about making his company less like Jim Clark. This is just how it always went with one of these new Silicon Valley hardware companies: once it showed promise, it ditched its visionary founder, who everyone deep down thought was a psycho anyway, and became a sane, ordinary place. With the support of Glenn Mueller and the other venture capitalists on the board of directors, McCracken brought in layer upon layer of people more like him: indirect, managerial, diplomatic, politically minded. These people could never build the machines of the future, but they could sell the machines of the present. And they did this very well. For the next six years Silicon Graphics was perhaps the most successful company in Silicon Valley. The stock rose from three dollars a share to more than thirty dollars a share. The company grew from two hundred employees to more than six thousand. The annual revenues swelled from a few million to billions. Therapy aside, the company remained the most desirable place to work if you were a certain kind of computer cowboy who wanted to live on the edge of the technology. The technology Clark and his brilliant engineers had invented turned out to be just what the world hungered for.

At the same time McCracken dealt Clark out of his own business. From McCracken's point of view Clark was just wildly disruptive. He'd wander around the company stirring up all manner of trouble and cause all the engineers to become even more highly oppositional than they were on their own. Senior engineers turned up in his office and told him that the chairman (Clark) had persuaded them they'd be better off quitting Silicon Graphics and starting their own businesses, and McCracken would have to spend hours talking them into staying. But he found outlets for his own frustration. When McCracken joined the company in 1985, Glenn Mueller had assured both him and Clark that they would be paid the same amounts each year. In late 1989 McCracken called Mueller, who now chaired the executive compensation committee, to complain about this rule. Mueller phoned the other members of the committee and changed the policy. The next year McCracken was paid hundreds of thousands of dollars more than Clark. Not long after that Clark ceased to be granted stock options in his company. He was the only member of the executive committee so treated.

Given what happened later, it is easy to feel sorry for Ed McCracken. At the time it was harder. Having established himself as the captain of the ship, he was doing what captains of industry have done since they were invented. He was transforming himself into an Important Person. He chaired conferences of the future of American industry. He hobnobbed with U.S. senators and testified before Congress. He encouraged the 1992 Clinton campaign to use Silicon Graphics as a backdrop for an important speech by Clinton on economic policy—only to find, too late, that Clark had decorated the halls that Clinton strode along with the *Fortune* magazine cover that featured Clark. Once Clinton was elected president, McCracken became a regular at White House dinners. Such highfalutin behavior might not sit well with Clark's engineers, who accused him of not paying attention to the business, but it had a purpose: it created an air of permanence not merely about Ed McCracken but also about Silicon Graphics. McCracken was trying to build something enduring.

Order and hierarchy were essential to this process. McCracken was uncomfortable with even the most trivial challenges to his authority—which is to say that he lived in a state of perpetual discomfort. The engineers, inspired by Clark, were constantly challenging his authority.

The practical jokes were a case in point. An engineer's idea of a joke is a practical joke, perhaps because a practical joke, unlike the less practical kind, needs to be designed. It requires the jokester to build the contraption to ensnare his victim. Silicon Graphics engineers loved their practical jokes. And they loved their chairman for the practical jokes he played, especially the ones he played on the boss. For instance, Clark had been struck by the inability of his teenage daughter to recall McCracken's name. She kept calling him Ed McMuffin. So one day Clark bought one of the thin name plaques that were affixed to the doors in the executive suite, stenciled with the name ED MCMUFFIN. He replaced McCracken's name plaque and waited for the response. For three days the new CEO walked in and out of an office with a door marked ED MCMUFFIN. The engineers would sneak up from their labs to watch him do it, then run back giggling to their work.

Everyone waited for the glorious moment when the victim of an engineer's practical joke realized what was happening and blushed and smiled and stammered and told everyone what a good joke it had been. It never came. On the fourth morning of the joke, the ED MCMUF-FIN plaque was gone. McCracken never said a word about it. Along with a lot of other pranks Clark played on McCracken, it festered in company lore. One day, years later, at a meeting filled with Clark's engi-neers and McCracken's managers, Clark told the story of how for three whole days McCracken was McMuffin. McCracken reddened, the man-agers swallowed their laughter. "It was like someone had played a joke on the dictator and you weren't allowed to laugh," says one of the engi-neers who was there.

Ed McCracken was Jim Clark's first intimate encounter with the American professional management class, and its politics. From it was born his conviction that there was a whole layer of people in American business who called themselves managers who were in fact designed to screw up his plans. Life was unfair: Jim Clark wasn't the first person ever to feel that way. What is more surprising is that a man who grew up, as he put it, "sitting in a large pile of shit" would be as convinced as Clark was that life *should* be fair. He was so convinced of this that he set out to correct the problem, and to take what rightfully belonged to him and to his engineers. Of course, it took people a while to realize that the new rule in Silicon Valley was that Jim Clark always got his way. It took ten years, to be exact.

Right through the golden years of Silicon Graphics, as McCracken took over the company and made it his own, Clark fought a civil war. He persuaded his fellow engineers that they should feel as mistreated as he did. "Tom [Davis, another founding engineer] and I would go in and talk to Jim," recalls Rocky Rhodes, who had left Stanford with Clark to create SGI. "And we'd learn how shitty life was. When we'd leave his office, we'd say, 'Yeah, I guess we really have been mistreated. I guess we should have been paid millions of more dollars.' Before that, I had no idea. I walked into Silicon Valley with $500 a month from the government. I was a twenty-seven-year-old with essentially no computer experience. Now I had stock options that Jim said would one day be worth a million dollars. Plus I now had a big salary. Before I learned from Jim that I'd been mistreated, I was quite pleased."

A whispering campaign wasn't Clark's style. Anything he said to his engineers he also said directly to McCracken. Dick Kramlich recalls a meeting between Clark and McCracken, attended by himself and Glenn Mueller. "Jim just ripped Ed apart. He explained to Ed everything that was wrong with his character. Jim can be truly brutal—unfairly so. And that day he just took Ed apart into pieces. By the time he was finished, Ed was crying. No one knew what to say." Clark's friends who did not know McCracken came to believe the man's name was Fucking Ed McCracken. "Fucking Ed McCracken," Clark would say, "he may have helped to stabilize the company, but now he's destroying it. He can't see what's happening."

What was happening was the personal computer. When Clark created Silicon Graphics, the computer world was a pyramid. At the top were people like him and his engineers, who played with the fastest machines. At the bottom was the personal computer. The PC had been created in Silicon Valley as a toy for hobbyists, a joke technology derided by the sort of hotshot who worked for Jim Clark. Now it had found a market for its services. Moore's law, which stated that the price of computing power would fall by half every eighteen months, implied that the pyramid must collapse. The PC would soon be able to perform all the functions of a Silicon Graphics work station. Microsoft controlled the market for personal computers through its operating system, and so Microsoft would displace Silicon Graphics. Microsoft and Silicon Graphics sold shares in themselves to the public the same year, 1986. Silicon Graphics might have been stunningly successful, but Microsoft was taking over the world. "You could see a time when the PC would be able to do the sort of graphics that SGI machines did," says Clark. "And SGI would be toast. Eventually, Microsoft would take over its business."

The falling price of computing power was leading the computer into new markets. Moore's law came with a social corollary: high-tech could not remain high-tech for long. You might be the smartest engineer in the Valley, and you might have built the most sophisticated computer, but it was only a matter of time before some schlepp with a PC wrote a program that let him do everything you could do, at a fraction of the cost. Technical vanity did not pay. If you wanted to make a great deal of money and acquire a great deal of power, you cultivated a more egalitarian outlook.

In the late 1980s and early 1990s people with a reputation for inventing the future spent a lot of time talking about where the trend might lead next. Jim Clark was one of these people. In December 1990 he joined a discussion at a conference called PC Outlook. One of the questions the panel considered was "Will personal computing and personal communications be combined, or will it just remain as science fiction?" In 1990 the idea that people would use their PCs to communicate with one another was outlandish. Yet it was still worth discussing, for if the computer ever did become a communications device it might transform not just the Valley but the economy. It would plug the masses into the thinking machine, and the thinking machine into the masses. At the conference Clark predicted that this would happen once the computer became fun to use. For the preceding two years he had argued that the new new thing was computer games, like Nintendo. He was wrong, but in an interesting way. He was groping toward a mass market. "Jim always was looking to democratize the technology," says Dick Kramlich. "He was always thinking about how to make some high-end technology accessible to a larger audience. That's what he'd done with the Geometry Engine. His chip cut the cost of real-time computer graphics from millions of dollars to tens of thousands."

Clark saw only one solution: Silicon Graphics had to build a cheap computer to compete with the personal computer. Cheap machines meant mass markets, and mass markets meant great sums of money. In early 1987 he started arguing, in characteristically undiplomatic fashion, that SGI was doomed. "Jim was probably two or three years ahead of the rest of us in seeing what was coming," Ed McCracken says. "He could see problems down the road and the problems become *emotionally* important to him." "I was saying, 'Goddamn we're out of our minds,'" says Clark. "I was so worried about the PC. I was adamant that we had to build a low-end product, and that it had to be something that sold for under five grand." It didn't happen—largely because McCracken did not share Clark's view. Fred Kittler, then an analyst with J. P. Morgan, recalls visiting Clark in his office at SGI in early 1990. "I was out here with a couple of analysts, and he was pacing back and forth like a man in a prison cell complaining about how his board wouldn't let him create his cheap computer. It was clear by then he had no real power."

Clark thought that Silicon Graphics had to "cannibalize" itself. For a technology company to succeed, he argued, it needed always to be looking to destroy itself. If it didn't, someone else would. "It's the hardest thing in business to do," he would say. "Even creating a lower-cost product runs against the grain, because the low-cost products undercut the high-cost, more profitable products." Everyone in a successful company, from the CEO on down, has a stake in whatever the company is currently selling. It does not naturally occur to anyone to find a way to undermine that product. Clark thought he knew how to become the agent of his own creative destruction, and he was prepared to do the deed. He wanted Silicon Graphics to operate in the same self-corrosive spirit.

More to the point, he wanted Ed McCracken to operate in this way. But Ed McCracken was not the man to roll the bones on the future—for which he could hardly be faulted, since as CEO he would get a lot more of the blame for any gamble that went wrong. Still, he manufactured a kind of contradiction in the heart of his company. All the good things that happened at Silicon Graphics happened because Clark had guessed that computer graphics had a commercial future. The company had been built entirely on Jim Clark's foresight. But once it became a big company it had no room for Clark or his hunches. A big company—even a big company as highly charged as SGI—needs to believe its own internal propaganda: that its products are the best, that its technology will win, and so on. It has trouble entertaining the thought that it is doomed.

When it became clear to Clark that he could not force his own company to reinvent itself and lead this charge, he went into another dark hole of despair. He'd just married for the third time, and his new wife, the journalist Nancy Rutter, had started to complain about his behavior. He had to find something else to occupy his turbulent mind. He hired people to renovate his house. He bought a motorcycle and rode it too fast. He discovered model helicopters. At first, he was embarrassed at the mere possibility that someone would see him—it was such a typical technogeek thing to do. But they had these fantastically elaborate kits that let you assemble a machine that you could fly by remote control. So he would wait until the middle of weekdays, when the neighbors were all at work. Then he'd take out his helicopter kit and fly.

Soon enough Clark had become obsessed with his little choppers. He would put them together in the garage, then take them out and fly them around the neighborhood. He'd buzz other people's homes. Nancy would come out to the garage and see this six-foot-three-inch, forty-seven-year-old man bent over the ground piecing together a toy designed for a small boy—at least in the beginning the choppers resembled children's toys. Clark started with the small models; once he got the hang of it, he moved on to the bigger, more realistic machines. The bigger machines kicked up huge clouds of dust in the front yard, so naturally he built a landing pad in his driveway. He'd stand out there for hours in the middle of the day in the middle of the week, executing takeoffs and landings of these giant toy helicopters.

One day some workers he'd brought over to move a swimming pool, or build a hill, made the mistake of parking their cars near his landing pad. Clark went over to them and told them, in a slightly embarrassed tone, that they might want to move the cars, as he planned to fly his helicopters. The workers laughed, and went about their business. Clark seized the controls of his largest helicopter and sent it up, up, up over the neighborhood. And then something went terribly wrong. As he guided it down toward the landing pad, the controls ceased to function, and instead of gliding backward and down the helicopter came zooming straight for his head. Clark dropped the remote control and dived out of the way just in time. The helicopter whipped along the side of the workers' cars with a horrible *whack whack whack*, as it dented the doors and peeled the paint.

Obviously, he couldn't spend all of his time flying toy helicopters around his neighborhood. He wrote the workers a check for the two grand to cover the damages, and took up computer programming.

## Inventing Jim Clark

When I asked Kittu Kolluri what he thought of his first encounter with Jim Clark, he thought for a moment and then said, "So . . ." This was not unusual. When a computer programmers answers a question, he often begins with the word "so."

"Why did you come to Silicon Valley?"

"So . . . I'm from this small town in Iowa . . ."

"So" cuts across the borders within the computing class just as "like" cuts across the borders within the class of adolescent girls. It's the most distinctive verbal tic manufactured by the engineering mind. Silicon Valley engineers for whom English is a second or even third language acquire it as readily as native speakers. Nobody knows why. Some say that "so" imposes the semblance of logic on an essentially illogical event, human conversation. After all, "so" implies that the answer follows directly from the question. Others claim that "so" just buys you time to think.

"So," said Kittu Kolluri, who learned to speak English where he learned to program computers, in Hyderabad, India. "Jim Clark walks into our office at Silicon Graphics. It is 1990. I have just joined the company. And I'm thinking: *This could not be! The chairman of SGI has just walked into our office! He walked right by my cube! He's standing right there next to Pavan!*

[Pavan is Pavan Nigam, the Indian man who hired Kittu to work at Silicon Graphics]. Jim Clark didn't say anything; he was looking at our group. Finally, he turns to Pavan and says, 'Pavan, we got to get some more Indians around here.' I was so shocked. I am thinking: *You cannot say such a thing in California. It must be against the law!"*

Clark then asked to see what the Indian engineers were working on. Pavan and Kittu showed him. Silicon Graphics was still having problems making its machines easy for people to use. Clark could relate. Looking for some way to occupy himself, he had taken to programming at home on a Silicon Graphics work station. He was experiencing some of the same frustrations as SGI's customers and was hungry for anything that made it easier for him to write programs that worked. And that, it turned out, was why he had paid his call on Pavan and Kittu. Clark was a physicist by training. When he returned to programming computers again, he wrote his code in the language of physics, mathematics. The Silicon Graphics machine required the programmer to translate his math into computer language. For example, if you wished to square a number ($x^2$) in a program, you needed to write it as $x**2$. "Jim was speaking German, and the machine only knew Spanish," said Pavan Nigam, "so there was this extra layer of thought required to turn Jim's German into Spanish. This drove Jim crazy; he thought the machine should bloody well know German, since German was the language of first principles. Since he was the chairman, we would say, 'Good idea, Jim! Good idea, Jim!'—and then we would talk to product development people, and they would say, 'Why the hell do you want to do that? That is about number 300 on a list of 300 things we need to do right now.'"

Clark turned the young Indians into his private software tutors. The young Indians were both flattered and impressed. Two minutes with Clark and the young wizard always fell under his spell, as many engineers before them had done. They felt that Jim Clark understood their value as no other important person did. "Jim Clark is not one of these flakes who starts companies," said Kittu. "He's not some manager who doesn't know what he's talking about. When he first saw the tools, he knew exactly what they meant. He knew we were onto something." But it was a few months before Kittu discovered why Clark had taken up computer programming, which seemed a rather odd activity for such an important man. Then one day Kittu's phone rang. He picked it up, and a female voice on the other end of the line told him that Jim Clark was calling. Kittu felt a surge of excitement. He pictured Clark sitting at his fine desk in his fine office in the finest of the dozen red brick buildings on the Silicon Graphics campus. There was a long pause and then came Clark's voice, distant and crackling. He sounded as if he was in Outer Mongolia.

"Kittu," Clark said, "I have this bug I can't find." He described the problem he was having. Kittu could barely hear him, he sounded so distant.

"Jim," he asked, "where the hell are you?"

Long pause. More crackling on the line. Then Clark's deep voice, "I'm not sure."

"What do you mean you're not sure?" asked Kittu.

Nervous laughter. "Off the coast of New Zealand somewhere."

"Jim, what are you doing off the coast of New Zealand?"

"I'm on my boat." Clark had bought a second-hand sailboat. The boat came equipped with a personal computer, which Clark had chucked over the side, on principle. In its place he'd installed a Silicon Graphics work station.

"Jim, what are you doing programming a goddamn computer off the coast of New Zealand?"

More nervous laughter. "I'm programming *the boat.*"

And this was the first inkling that Kittu, and so also Pavan, had that all was not right with Jim Clark. Soon Kittu figured out that Clark called him from everywhere *except* his fine office in his fine building at Silicon Graphics. The man had stopped showing up for work. He spent all of his time writing a navigation program for the sailboat he had just bought. He was doing this, he once told them, because he had ideas about the future of high technology that no one would listen to. Teaching his boat to sail itself diverted his mind from the fact that others, not he, were about to inherit the earth. On his boat he could think about how to inherit the earth from its current heirs.

For about nine months Clark called Kittu and Pavan regularly to pester them about his software. Then he went silent.

About that time—late 1990, early 1991—the cardboard boxes in his guest room stuffed by his devoted secretary with his old papers suggested, his life took another unexpected turn. Clark's motorcycle skidded out from under him as he rounded a bend near his home in Atherton.

It crushed his leg against the street and laid him up in bed for six weeks. It gave him another reason to be angry with Ed McCracken. If McCracken would do what Clark told him to do, he, Clark, wouldn't be forced to amuse himself by riding around on motorbikes on wet city streets in the middle of the week.

In bed waiting for his leg to heal and with nothing better to do but curse McCracken, he wrote a paper. It summarized his thinking of the past few years, as he groped for a solution to what he viewed as Silicon Graphics' inevitable doom. He was right about the future of the company. Through its monopoly of the operating system Microsoft already controlled the personal computer. Microsoft would one day overrun the high end of computing where Silicon Graphics made its money. Microsoft had made it clear that the only way to preserve your station in Valley life was to create a monopoly. If you created a monopoly, you were at least partially exempt from the ordinary rapid cycle of creation and destruction. In computing, a monopoly took the form of a toll booth. Bill Gates had his toll booth, the PC operating system. Jim Clark wanted his own toll booth.

In 1991 people who had computers on their desks used them mainly for financial analysis and word processing, but that was sure to change as the price of computer memory fell. For the moment, though, the reach of the personal computer was nothing like that of the television set. About 95 percent of American households owned at least one television set; only one in ten owned a computer. To Jim Clark this looked like a huge opportunity: turn the television set into a computer. He finished his paper in bed and called it "The Telecomputer."

Technically, the telecomputer was feasible. The United States had a tantalizing new infrastructure into which such a device might plug. In the preceding decade the cable television industry had laid pipes leading into 75 percent of all American homes, and those pipes could carry information into and out of a telecomputer. The question was: Could you make a telecomputer cheaply, and persuade ordinary people to buy it? If so, you could control an exciting new chunk of the American economy. The computer had an important trait that the ordinary television did not: it could interact with the viewer. You could tell it what you wanted, and it could go out and fetch it for you. You could shop through it. You could send instant messages through it, and receive messages back. You could order up local news from anywhere in the world. You could order any movie you wanted, when you wanted it, and pause it when you went to the toilet. The machine could be the conduit for all information into and out of the home.

The general idea hardly originated with Clark. Back in the late 1970s the corporate ancestor of Time Warner, called Warner-Amex, had created a pilot for an interactive television in Columbus, Ohio, called Qube. Qube was supposed to let cable TV viewers send messages to the networks, and request the programs they wanted to see, via remote control. But the machine didn't work particularly well, and it cost a fortune to build. The company spent $30 million trying to build it, and then quit. Then there was an idea, called Videotext, cooked up by researchers at the British post office, also in the 1970s. It hooked a black box between the telephone line and the television set and enabled people to send messages to each other while they watched the BBC. Nobody wanted that either. A few years later AT&T and Knight Ridder came together to deliver the newspaper each morning to the masses on their television set. The masses yawned and went back to bed.

In every case, at least a part of the problem was that the wires entering and exiting the average home were unable to transmit data with sufficient speed. The wires could handle printed text, which required much less "bandwidth," but they could not send moving pictures. Moving pictures contained a lot of digital data, and so required vast computing power. Never mind. The engineering problem was so interesting that it seemed rude to spoil it by asking who, exactly, wanted to read text on his television.

A stunning ignorance of mass tastes was a common problem in high technology. When a brilliant engineer dreamed up a product, he tended to build the sort of things only a brilliant engineer would appreciate. Typically, he overestimated the average person's willingness to learn how to use some new machine and underestimated the cost of making the machine. When you page through the history of computing, you find a lot of very weird examples of just this. In a warehouse behind the Computer Museum just north of San Jose, for instance, stands a gleaming red four-feet-high computer built by Honeywell in the mid-1960s. The Kitchen Computer, it was called. The Organization Man's housewife was meant to program her recipes into it. "If only she could cook as well as Honeywell can compute," read the ad in the Neiman Marcus catalog. The computer was premised on the dubious assumptions that every American housewife would (a) want a massive computer in her kitchen and (b) know how to program it. Neiman Marcus failed to sell a single unit.

The idea Clark became wedded to, albeit briefly, was that the computer would become the most important household appliance. Information appliance, was one term used to describe it back then. The company that built the first information appliance would sit in the middle of all human communication; it would be the McDonald's of information. It could play the same role on the television that Microsoft played on the PC. "The telecomputer was a direct result of the frustration I felt watching Silicon Graphics continually fall behind the PC in market share," Clark says. "I was trying to do an underbelly thing with Microsoft—come in under their monopoly and take it away." The telecomputer would be the most fabulous toll booth ever built. But before it happened, a question needed answering: Why would people rush out to buy a telecomputer? What would a telecomputer do that people simply could not live without?

Clark had no great hope that Americans wanted their computers to educate themselves. He assumed they wanted their computers to play Nintendo and otherwise divert themselves from the poverty of their existences. The answer he finally came up with was that people wanted to watch any movies they pleased, whenever they pleased. The telecomputer would be many things, but at first blush it would be a virtual VCR.

Of course, Ed McCracken wanted nothing to do with a virtual VCR, at least initially. It was just another flaky idea from his flaky chairman, who refused to leave him to run the company alone. And so Clark found another outlet for his ambition, the media. Once he'd recovered from his motorcycle accident, he shared his thoughts freely with journalists. "I might not have any power at Silicon Graphics," he says, "but *they* didn't know that. I was still called the chairman. And most journalists think a chairman of a big company is an important person." He knew perfectly well that McCracken disapproved of his talking to the press. But hype had its own wonderful generative power: the more he talked about his telecomputer, the more people wanted to hear about it. It was almost as if by talking about the telecomputer he made it happen. "I would go out, and I would just say all this shit to reporters," he recalls. "And they'd print it! And people inside SGI started to talk about it. And I thought, 'Fuck Ed McCracken. I can say whatever I want. And by God if I go out and talk about it enough, Ed won't have any choice but to build it.'"

Clark's opinions found their final published form in 1992 at the annual trade show for the computer graphics industry, called Siggraph. Clark delivered as a speech the paper he'd written while he was laid up in bed recovering from his motorcycle accident. The paper described "the consumer's computer." Clark guessed it could be built in "two to three years." He explained that, although computer memory in 1992 made such a device too costly to be mass-marketed, computer memory in 1995 would be a different story. He outlined the basic technologies—digital audio, digital video, transmission-reception decoupling, resolution decoupling—all of which existed in one form or another. But he dealt with the technical side of things in only the sketchiest form. Mostly his paper was a bit of political propaganda, aimed at raising the heat on McCracken. In Silicon Valley political propaganda took the form of futurology. "Over the next four to five years," Clark told his audience,

> unprecedented change will occur in the computer, telecommunications and television industries as Multi-Media technology enters the home via the telecomputer. . . . The present "local loop" of the telephone system and the "cable franchise" for television will become one Multi-Media server loop. Each loop will represent tens of thousands of clients, each using a telecomputer. In the loop will be high-speed computer systems for serving audio and movies on demand, virtual reality games, digital forms of daily newspapers, weekly and monthly magazines, libraries, encyclopedias and interactive books. In time, all media will be available in dynamic form.

He was wrong about all of this, at least in his timing. He was off and running down a dark tunnel that ran directly into a brick wall. But at least he was running.

Clark's paper attracted a lot of attention from everywhere except Silicon Graphics' boardroom. The cardboard box in Clark's guest room contains a tall stack of fan mail and his responses. For instance, on August 4, 1992, he replied to a letter from Lance Glasser at the U.S. Department of Defense, who agreed with Clark and wanted to know why he didn't just build his new machine. "Silicon Graphics Management considers pursuit of Digital TV a distraction," Clark wrote. "I am the driving force but . . . left to its own, SGI will not pursue this for at least four or five years. . . . I believe the solution is to form a new company."

By far the most important letter he had came from Jim Chiddix. Chiddix was the chief technology officer at Time Warner Cable. Chiddix told Clark that he had heard his talk and that Time Warner shared his interest in the telecomputer. He agreed with Clark that now, at last, the world was ready for the new machine. Time Warner had just decided to yank out all of its copper cables and replace them with fiber-optic cables, which transmitted data much more efficiently. In other words, the infrastructure would be laid for a telecomputer to traffic in moving images. More to the point, Time Warner was willing to pay someone to build a telecomputer. Chiddix suspected Clark was just the man for the job.

The deeper Chiddix dug into the problem, the more certain he became that Clark was the only man for the job. Or, at least, the company Clark had founded was the only company for the job. In late 1992 Chiddix toured the companies that might conceivably build the black box he needed: Microsoft, Oracle, Sun Microsystems, Silicon Graphics. They contained the biggest egos and brightest minds in technology. They sold themselves as hard as they could to Chiddix, and yet Chiddix came away with a very clear opinion: the engineers Jim Clark had brought together were in a class by themselves. "It was clear that Clark himself had no power in the company," says Chiddix. "But it was also clear that if anyone could build an interactive television it was Silicon Graphics. Everyone at all these companies was smart. But the engineers at SGI, they were the real cowboys."

In October 1992 Clark finally made his pitch for his telecomputer to the Silicon Graphics board of directors. He opened with a slide that read "How We Can Be to Entertainment Computing What Microsoft Is to Productivity Computing." He laid out his view of the market, which he thought could be as big as 10 billion dollars a year. He discussed potential competitors—Sun Microsystems, IBM, DEC. And then he pulled a kind of bait and switch: rather than create the telecomputer inside SGI, he suggested, SGI should finance a new company to do it. In exchange for money and technical support, SGI would be granted a large equity stake in the new enterprise, which Clark would control. No more Fucking Ed McCracken. Clark called his new company an Entertainment Computer Company. As a kicker he mentioned that Time Warner was willing to pay for the telecomputer to be built.

Not long after Clark's presentation to the SGI board, Pavan Nigam was called in to see Tom Jermoluk—T. J. as he was called. Improbably, T. J. had been able to win Clark's friendship without alienating Ed McCracken. While McCracken was off playing corporate statesman, T. J. ran the company; and it was through T. J. that Clark exercised what influence he had on SGI. "When I got the call that T. J. wanted to meet with me, I thought he wanted to complain about the bugs in our software," says Pavan. "He was always complaining about our bugs. So I brought a list of the bugs and what we were going to do about them." Instead T. J. had an offer for Pavan. "How would you like to build the world's first interactive television set?" he asked. He explained that Ed McCracken had come around to Jim Clark's way of thinking, but did not like the idea of Clark's having his own company. Time Warner was willing to pay SGI $30 million to build what it was calling an interactive television (ITV). Whatever SGI built would be installed in four thousand homes that Time Warner was wiring for the occasion in Orlando, Florida. And on the recommendation of Jim Clark it wanted the thirty-three-year-old Pavan Nigam to run the project.

The minute Time Warner announced that it had chosen Silicon Graphics, just about every big company that had anything to do with information or entertainment leaped into action and hired its own engineers to build them a telecomputer. "There was a mad scramble," recalls Chiddix. AT&T and Viacom announced that they were building their interactive television pilot in Castro Valley, California. TCI and Microsoft announced their pilot in Seattle. The phone company U.S. West, the computer company DEC, and the computer animation company 3DO announced their own project in Omaha, Nebraska. Oracle announced its vague intentions to get involved. When you added it all up, it implicated thousands of people and hundreds of millions of dollars. The telecomputer was the first big step in a new direction. Very large companies, and a lot of important investors, became swept up in the idea of an intelligent home appliance. They bought into Clark's notion that people would shop, communicate, and amuse themselves through their televisions.

It took about three days for Ed McCracken to make the telecomputer his own and for the Orlando project to become the place to work at Silicon Graphics. Before long, Michael Douglas and Arnold Schwarzenegger had dropped into SGI's offices to hear about the technology that would change their business. The CEO of Time Warner, Gerald Levin, rolled up to the front door of Silicon Graphics in the longest limousines anyone had ever seen. The scramble to get assigned to the project became so vicious that McCracken sent out an e-mail warning engineers about sabotaging each other's careers. At the same time he let Pavan Nigam know that the project was critical to the future of the company. "'Spend what you need to spend; the thing must work,' was what Ed said," recalls Pavan. "All of a sudden everyone thought ITV was the future of the company. All of us thought it was going to be the next big thing." Pavan believed that "a thousand people don't build anything; if you need to build something really complicated really fast, you hire fifty of the smartest people you can find." That is exactly what he did. He started by hiring Kittu Kolluri. The telecomputer had been entrusted to Clark's private software tutors.

To the engineers the main appeal of the telecomputer was its complexity. This was in itself an ominous sign. It's a good rule of the technology business that the more intellectually appealing a machine, the less likely anyone will pay for it. It was not trivial to rig a system so that the fat guy on the sofa with the beer in his hand no longer needed to drive to Blockbuster to get the movie he wanted. Every fat guy required his own video stream, and a single video stream contained a huge quantity of data. The computer needed to process information more quickly than information had ever been processed. "The Orlando project turned out to be the most aggressive supercomputer project ever put together in the history of the world," says Jim Barton, one of the senior engineers on the job. "As a pure engineering challenge," says Marco Framba, another engineer on the project, "it was more difficult than any I've ever heard of." Jim Chiddix at Time Warner says, "It required more lines of computer code than was required to put a man on the moon."

Pavan and Kittu were told that they had eighteen months to build the new machine. They said it would take them twenty-four. It took them twenty-three. On December 12, 1994, the press piled into Orlando for the demonstration. Other companies had spent more money and employed more engineers, but none of them got a system that worked. Time Warner's Gerald Levin sat on the stage with Ed McCracken and a couple of other suits. Their presence was a kind of assurance that technology moved in a stable and predictable manner, the way the men in suits directed it to move. "Never in the history of telecommunications," Levin said, "has a medium of such complexity been designed, developed, and given its debut in such a concentrated space of time." Then he picked up the remote control and pressed a button and . . . it worked! ("Like a charm," says Pavan.) The engineers received standing ovations. Levin cut the tape and announced that Time Warner intended to spend five *billion* dollars to deploy this fantastic new technology. All Americans would one day live even more of their lives than they currently did through their television sets. The new technology would change the way people shopped, voted, worked, and loved.

Ed McCracken followed Gerald Levin onstage. Without once mentioning Jim Clark, he explained to the audience how his team at Silicon Graphics was now poised to control the future.

From their seats in the crowd Pavan Nigam and Kittu Kolluri looked up, and they knew it wasn't true. They had spent the last eighteen months pulling off one of the great engineering feats of the century, and they had nothing to show for it but black boxes that cost five grand apiece. Few would pay that much for the technology, and the value of the technology depended in part on a lot of people's owning it. A VCR was as valuable if one person owned it as it was if a hundred million did. But a television that interacted with other televisions demanded an audience. "ITV was one large academic exercise," says Kittu. "We solved a problem that was not that important to many people. I'm not terribly proud of what we accomplished. We started out to change the world. Did we change the world? No fucking way."

There was another bad sign—though just how bad they didn't fully appreciate. Jim Clark was gone. He'd up and left the company he'd created and said he was going to start another. "It was good that Jim left," says Ed McCracken, in what must rank as one of the troughs in a career of understatement. "No big company could accommodate such financial ambition." Clark's lawyer had advised him to quit bitching and moaning about McCracken for six months, and then walk into a board meeting and quit. And that's what he did. Publicly, he said he was leaving on the best of terms. Privately, he told friends that he was going to show Fucking Ed McCracken that it was he, not McCracken, who had been responsible for the success of Silicon Graphics. He told the engineers who had helped him create SGI that he was going to get rich. Rocky Rhodes recalls him stopping by to talk about his future plans: "Jim said right out, 'I'm going to make $100 million.' And I said, 'That's great, Jim,' and also something about how pleased I was with the way SGI had worked out. And *then* I said, 'But even if it hadn't worked out, I've had a great time, met great people, learned a lot.' And Jim got mad. He said, 'No! If I go and do this next thing and don't make $100 million, it'll be a failure. I'll be a failure.' And that's kind of the way I remember leaving it with him."

Pavan and Kittu knew most of this, and it troubled them—but not nearly as much as it should have. They still believed that economic history was moved along slowly, by big companies like Silicon Graphics.


By the time Clark walked out of SGI in early 1994, the list of grievances he was nursing had grown too long for anyone but him to keep track of. First Glenn Mueller screws him. Then Ed McCracken takes full credit for things he was at best partially responsible for. Then Mueller and the other board members conspire to shut him out of the company while McCracken fucks it up. Then Mueller and McCracken cut him out of the stock options pool. Then he puts the company right out in front of the future—arranges for Time Warner to pay for them to be there!—and is then promptly shut out of all further discussion. The minute Time Warner's limousines turned up at Silicon Graphics, Ed McCracken had taken over the project. There was so much ill will between him and McCracken that when he found his image missing from a picture in the SGI annual report of the founding engineers, he assumed McCracken had ordered it removed.

Success was his chosen form of revenge. Clark was intent on inventing a new role for himself that would not allow the Muellers and McCrackens to take advantage of him. In retrospect, there are many ways to describe this new role. But maybe the simplest is the way Clark described it to himself: the guy who finds the new new thing and makes it happen wins. The engineers who help him to do it finish second. The financiers and the corporate statesmen, the sucker fish of economic growth, finish a distant third. Clark intended to sit on top of Silicon

Valley as surely as Microsoft sat on top of the personal computer. Of course, he was not the first engineer with a taste for money and power. He was just the one who finally said, "Now's the time to take it."

But that version of events is misleadingly neat. Clark didn't conceptualize his new role: he groped for it. He had an animal desire to have what he wanted and not to have what he did not want. He wanted Silicon Valley to be even more suited than it already was to his talent for anarchy. He wanted to harness the forces of creation and destruction. He did not want to manage a large company. He did not even want to be a venture capitalist who vetted thousands of business plans, backed dozens of companies, and then sat back with Olympian detachment and hoped that a few became big. He wanted to create *the* company that invented the future. Once he'd done that, he wanted to do it again and again and again and again. For his services he wanted to be treated better, and paid more, than anyone else.

A few people sensed exactly how potent Clark was once he'd spun himself out of Silicon Graphics. The venture capitalist Dick Kramlich assigned a young man named Alex Slusky, whom he had just hired out of the Harvard Business School, to follow Clark wherever he went. "I told Alex to sleep under Jim's bed if he had to," recalls Kramlich. "Jim's a revolutionary, you know. He's out to revolutionize whatever needs to be revolted against." Slusky was a bit like one of those janitors at the Institute for Advanced Study in Princeton who trailed around after the aged Albert Einstein and took down his random scribblings on the off chance they turned out to be important. His job was to stick to Clark and take notes. When Clark finally decided on his next venture, Slusky was to insist that Dick Kramlich at New Enterprise Associates be allowed to buy a piece of it. "Dick was a little unusual in this view," says Slusky. "Some of his partners didn't want to have anything to do with Jim Clark. They thought Jim Clark was a bit of a crazy guy."

But Slusky did as he was told. After four years at Harvard University, two at the Harvard Business School, he found himself dining with Clark two or three nights a week. Slusky was small and mild mannered and polite as a choirboy. He was unused to grown men flying into rages for no apparent reason. He listened to Clark rant about Ed McCracken, moan about Glenn Mueller, and think out his next move. At first Clark believed that the Orlando project might end well. He tried to buy the rights to the operating system from Time Warner, and set himself up as the Microsoft of the new technology. Time Warner declined to sell. Next Clark talked about creating new applications for the telecomputer—there was a lot that could be done with the device, once a lot of people owned one. To do that he needed young software talent, and to that end he called a twenty-two-year-old not long out of the University of Illinois and new to the Valley named Marc Andreessen. Clark had seen a piece of software that Andreessen had helped write in college, called Mosaic. Mosaic enabled its user to travel around the Internet. Why anyone would wish to do so was at the time unclear.

About the first thing Andreessen said was that he didn't want to make a business of Mosaic. Clark didn't care. His ambition was more inchoate than that. He needed to find some more software cowboys to replace the ones he'd left behind. "I was desperate to find some smart engineers because I knew I wanted to start a company," he says. "And Marc knew a bunch of them from school." For the next month or so Alex Slusky ate his dinners with Jim Clark *and* Marc Andreessen. Clark would spew ideas; Andreessen would jot them up in a business plan. Almost all of these ideas assumed the telecomputer under construction in Orlando, Florida, was the future. After all, Time Warner said it would spend five billion dollars to make it happen. By that point every big media and software company in the United States was intoxicated by the idea. Even if people weren't quite ready for the technology, the technology would be forced upon them. This wasn't the Kitchen Computer.

Then one day, as Andreessen and Clark sat at Clark's kitchen table, Clark announced that he'd changed his mind. This wasn't unusual: Clark was always changing his mind. Now he said that his telecomputer was ahead of its time. It was too expensive to build. "We could always build a Mosaic killer," said Andreessen. "What do you mean?" said Clark. Andreessen said that the software he'd written had been appropriated by the University of Illinois but that he felt sure the university would bungle any subsequent attempt to commercialize it. He mentioned again that 25 million people were now using the Internet, and that their numbers had been doubling every year for a long time. Clark recalls, "I thought, Jesus, those are big numbers. I've never been in a business with those kind of big numbers. Eventually you were talking about all the people on earth."

The whole time he'd been stewing with Andreessen about what to do, the solution was right in front of them. The Internet. "All of a sud-

den it was clear to me when I looked at the Internet that I was looking at the personal computer in 1985," Clark says. "It was this slow
clunky technology, but people were using it. And it would get faster.
I realized that this was the thing I'd been groping for." He and
Andreessen hired Andreessen's college buddies who had written the
code for Mosaic, which permitted a user to browse the Internet, and
Clark had yet another team of young engineers to lead into battle. He
called the company Mosaic Communications, then changed the name
to Netscape.

This time Jim Clark was right. He was off and running down the dark
tunnel with no end. Within eighteen months the world's biggest technology companies realized they'd been trumped. Bill Gates sent a memo
to his employees saying that the Internet now posed the greatest threat
to Microsoft's control of the computer industry. The one thousand
Microsoft employees dedicated to building a telecomputer were reas-
signed to compete with Jim Clark's start-up. Thousands of others at
Oracle and Sun and even Time Warner were similarly redirected. "Jim
put the whole of ITV out of business." says Pavan Nigam. "Everyone at
once realized that the next big thing was not the television set but the
personal computer hooked up to the Internet." If you page through his
talk on the telecomputer, you can see just how chance favors the prepared mind. The presentation Clark made to his board back in 1992 is
a fair blueprint for the Internet boom. All of the ideas (e-commerce, e-
mail) and some of the technology he dreamed up for his beloved telecomputer were grafted onto the Internet.

You have to sit down and think for a bit to realize what that means,
not just for Clark but for anyone with the slightest interest in how
economies and societies are nudged from one place to the next. A company dreamed up by a technical man a lot of big shots thought was
slightly unhinged, with a twenty-two-year-old who didn't want to do
it in the first place, and another twenty-two-year-old assigned to sleep
under his bed, did not become merely a success. It torpedoed investments of hundreds of millions by the world's biggest corporations and
putatively smartest minds—SGI, TW, Microsoft, Sun, Oracle, AT&T.
Thousands of people had more or less wasted billions of dollars and,
whether they knew it or not, had been *following his lead*. Then, just as
they all ran as a herd in one direction, he took off in another. And
within six months he made them all look like fools. It was one of the

great unintentional head fakes in the history of technology.

Soon enough, Clark's opinions reached the venture capitalists on Sand Hill Road, who started calling and asking if they might invest in his company. Alex Slusky told Dick Kramlich that Clark was about to make his move—that he had invested three million dollars of his own money, a substantial chunk of his total worth, into the venture. Kramlich called Clark, and Clark said that this time any venture capitalist who wished to back him would do so on new, unprecedentedly harsh terms. He was valuing the newly named Mosaic Communications, which consisted of three million dollars of his money and seven new graduates of the University of Illinois, at eighteen million dollars. He would permit venture capitalists to purchase a stake in the new company, at three times what he had paid. Or, as he put it to Kramlich, "My dollars are worth three times what yours are worth."

This was about three times what Kramlich expected to pay. Kramlich called John Doerr, who worked a few yards up Sand Hill Road, hoping that Doerr might help him talk some reason into Clark. Instead, Doerr invited Clark to his office and gave him exactly what he asked for. His firm, Kleiner Perkins, purchased a 15 percent stake in Netscape that valued the company at $18 million, and left Clark still holding 25 percent of the company. "That moment," says Alex Slusky, "was the defining moment for this period in the Valley. No engineer had ever cut such a deal." (Clark, who had grown fond of the young man assigned to sleep under his bed, offered Slusky a job at Netscape. Slusky turned it down. "He was just too volatile for me," he says. "I couldn't live like that.")

Dick Kramlich, who came up empty-handed, was upset. But the venture capitalist up on Sand Hill Road who called Clark most often, and who sounded the most upset, was Glenn Mueller. Throughout March 1994 Mueller called Clark repeatedly and pleaded to be let in on Netscape. He apologized for the way he'd treated Clark at Silicon Graphics. He said that he agreed with Clark. The Internet, not ITV, was the future. On April 1, 1994, Clark told Mueller for the last time that he would not be permitted to invest in Netscape. Mueller was calling from his sailboat, off Cabo San Lucas. He pleaded with Clark one last time, and Clark rebuffed him. On April 4, 1994, the day Netscape was incorporated, Mueller picked up a gun and shot himself through the head. He died instantly.

It took a while for the people who thought they knew Glenn Mueller to find an explanation that put their minds at rest. Mueller's wife let his colleagues know what they had not known, that he suffered from intense fear that people were out to destroy his business. In other words, he suffered from an extreme version of a mental disorder that many Silicon Valley tycoons prided themselves on, paranoia. The genealogy chart of Silicon Valley companies that decorated the walls of every office—Shockley spawned Fairchild, Fairchild spawned Intel, Intel spawned . . . ) was a cheery face on a violent truth. The new companies often put the old ones out of business; the young were forever eating the old. The whole of the Valley was a speeded-up Oedipal drama. In this drama technology played a very clear role. It was the murder weapon.

For the next few weeks, until the tragedy passed from people's minds, a lot of people told Clark that Mueller's suicide wasn't his fault: no human being killed himself simply because he was shut out of a business deal. They did this because in the back of their minds they suspected that maybe Mueller's suicide *was* Clark's fault. And so did Clark. Two thousand people turned out for Glenn Mueller's memorial service. Jim Clark read a poem he wrote for the occasion. Then he moved on and, maybe for the first time in his life, actually had to try to forget.

It took a few years before Ed McCracken realized that he, too, would be excluded from the future Clark was inventing. But the process by which he was excluded began immediately. Six months after he founded Netscape, Clark agitated for the company to go public. The company had few revenues, no profits, and a lot of new employees. No one else inside the company thought it should do anything but keep its head down and try to become a viable enterprise. "Jim was pressing for us to go public *way* before anyone else," recalls Marc Andreessen. It turned out there was a reason for this. He'd seen a boat called *Juliet*. He wanted one just like it, only bigger. To get it he needed more money.

By then the decision was not Clark's alone to make. The company had hired a big-name CEO, Jim Barksdale, and had a proper board of directors. Barksdale didn't want to go public. He thought the company had enough problems trying to figure out how to turn a profit without having to explain itself to irate shareholders. But this time Clark had power, through his equity stake. He called a meeting to discuss the initial public offering (IPO), and stacked it with lawyers and bankers who stood to reap big fees from a public share offering and who were, as a result, enthusiastic about his initiative. At that meeting Barksdale finally capitulated. Eighteen months after Netscape was created, and before it had made a dime, Netscape sold shares in itself to the public. On the first day of trading the price of those shares rose from $12 apiece to $48. Three months later it was at $140. It was one of the most successful share offerings in the history of the U.S. stock markets, and possibly the most famous.

There was only one explanation for its success: the market now saw the future through Clark's eyes. "People started drinking my Kool-Aid," says Clark. "Netscape obviously didn't create the Internet. But if Netscape had not forced the issue on the Internet, it would have just burbled in the background. It would have remained this counterintuitive kind of thing. The criticism of it was that it was anarchy. What the IPO did was give anarchy credibility."

In the frenzy that followed, a lot of the old rules of capitalism were suspended. For instance, it had long been a rule of thumb with the Silicon Valley venture capitalists that they didn't peddle a new technology company to the investing public until it had had at least four consecutive profitable quarters. Netscape had nothing to show investors but massive losses. But its fabulous stock market success created a precedent. No longer did you need to show profits; you needed to show rapid growth. Having a past actually counted against a company, for a past was a record and a record was a sign of a company's limitations. Never mind that you weren't actually making money—there'd be time for that later, assuming someone eventually figured out *how* to make money from the Internet. For the moment you needed to plow all of your revenues back into growth. You had to show that you were the company not of the present but of the future. The most appealing companies became those in a state of pure possibility. Which is to say that the U.S. capital markets acquired the personal predilections of Jim Clark.

Another old rule that changed was the rule that the financiers who backed the company, and perhaps the CEO who steered it to success, made the most money and accumulated the most power. Anyone who bothered to read Netscape's prospectus discovered a curious fact. The venture capitalists on Sand Hill Road and the new CEO, Jim Barksdale, owned a few million shares each. In the end they made hundreds of millions of dollars from Netscape, and so had no reason to complain. But the young engineers whom Clark had pulled together to create the company also became rich. An engineer who joined Netscape in July 1995 was, by November, worth ten million dollars. Clark made certain that Marc Andreessen, the young inventor, did not suffer the same fate at the hands of the venture capitalists as he himself had twelve years before. After the IPO Andreessen, by then twenty-four, was worth eighty million dollars.

Clark also made certain that by far the biggest stake in the company—nearly one-quarter of the whole—belonged to Jim Clark personally. Clark became the Valley's newest billionaire.

The speed with which Clark had made himself and a lot of other engineers rich created new forces of greed and fear in Silicon Valley. Microsoft was twelve years old before people started talking about Microsoft millionaires; Netscape was one and a half. Up until then the typical engineer's decision about where to work turned on old-fashioned considerations, like salary and benefits and the inherent technical interest of the work. Suddenly, all of these were overshadowed by stock options. The engineers who went to work for Netscape were no different from you. And yet . . . they—not you!—were getting rich. Worse, they were the B team. The A teams of engineering had been, in general, too well treated by their companies to take a flier on what appeared, from a distance, a doubtful new venture. Netscape ushered in an age of doubtful new ventures. Whether he liked it or not, every day he went to work the engineer was making a huge financial gamble. Silicon Valley laid itself out before him like one giant high-stakes roulette table, and the engineer had to decide on which number he should place his services. Guess wrong and he'd miss the boom; guess right and he'd be rich.

Most people don't enjoy making huge gambles on the future. They would just as soon have someone else tell them what to do. And that is what Jim Clark did. From the moment Netscape made him a billionaire, he acquired a new form of power: the power of being Jim Clark. Half the engineers in the Valley wanted to work for whatever company he started, on the assumption that if anyone was going to predict the future it was Jim Clark. All Clark had to do was announce how he next planned to invent the future, and huge sums of money and vast reservoirs of engineering talent came pouring in, intent on proving him right. The question was: What would he do next?

In late 1995 a lot of Silicon Graphics engineers were asking that question. The company had the smartest engineers, and the smartest among them had just wasted two years of their time and hundreds of millions of dollars. From the moment Netscape went public, Silicon Graphics was officially unwell—a company of the past rather than the future. The company's stock peaked at $44 a share the week after the Netscape share offering and then fell steadily for the next four years, right down to $8 a share. In 1997 Ed McCracken was fired from Silicon Graphics. He left Silicon Valley and took a job running a foundation in upstate New York. Many of the people who thought him a genius just a few years earlier now thought him a fool. "At the time I thought Jim was just brutal with Ed," says Dick Kramlich, who negotiated McCracken's golden handshake. "Now I think Jim was just right."

A lot of the engineers at Silicon Graphics promised themselves that whatever Jim Clark did next, they would do it with him. Word spread that Clark was off building a new boat. A boat! His boat is where he always went when he was stewing on the new new thing! His old friend Forest Baskett, who had followed Clark from Stanford to Silicon Graphics, received a phone call from Clark. It was late 1995, just after Netscape went public and Clark became the Valley's newest billionaire. Yet Clark did not sound satisfied. He sounded agitated, the way he did when something came between him and what he wanted. He wanted to talk to Forest about his new boat. As it happened, Forest had introduced Clark to sailing in the San Francisco Bay. Now, just a few years later, Clark was trying to figure out whether the boat he wanted to build could fit into the San Francisco Bay.

"Forest," he asked, "how high is the Golden Gate Bridge?"

Once a month, sometimes more often, Clark would crawl out of bed at four in the morning, drive down to the private air terminal in San Jose, California, climb aboard his new jet, and fly to Amsterdam. The plane couldn't make it without refueling. At some point he had discovered a strip of tundra north of the Arctic Circle with a tiny village that consisted of not much more than a tarmac, a gas pump, and an emergency medical station for Eskimos. He'd dive down out of the sky, pull up next to the pump, pull out his American Express card, buy two thousand gallons of gasoline from an Eskimo, and shove off. Once he arrived in Amsterdam, he'd drive an hour and a half north to Wolter Huisman's boatyard in Vollenhove. Vollenhove felt only slightly less remote than the Eskimo town.

Clark made this trip sixty times between the Netscape public offering, in August 1995, and the launching of the boat that the Netscape public offering had paid for, in December 1998. One of those times came in late January 1998, five months before *Hyperion* was scheduled to be finished and eleven months before it actually was finished. The boat perched like a beached white whale on a dolly in the hangar beside

Wolter Huisman's office. There was, as usual on these visits by Clark, the tingle in the air that precedes bad news.

Inside the office Clark settled in at a conference table across from Wolter Huisman, several of Wolter's underlings, and the captain of *Hyperion*, Allan Prior, and waited to hear what that news might be. Replicas of wooden boats and sepia-toned photographs of Wolter's ancestors surrounded the table. It was a working office but also a shrine to the Huisman sailing tradition—a tradition that Clark now threatened.

A bookmaker not intimately familiar with the characters would probably say that the odds were against the challenger. Traditions are more easily preserved where the risks of changing things outweigh the rewards, and a sailboat is one such place. A sailboat built by Wolter in 1992 had a great deal in common with a sailboat built by Wolter in 1972 or a sailboat built by Wolter's father in 1932 or a sailboat built by Wolter's grandfather in 1892, for the very simple reason that the Huisman way of doing things had kept a lot of people dry. For better than a hundred years now, the Royal Huisman Shipyard had churned out lovely wooden boats not so very different from the original Dutch pleasure craft of the seventeenth century. Normally, the Glorious Dutch Boatbuilding Tradition was what Wolter was selling. When a rich man turned up in the Royal Huisman Shipyard, among the first things he was shown were the charming old black-and-white photographs of the thirteen-year-old Wolter building a dinghy with his father. The rich man was allowed to finger the lovely old wooden models of yachts built long ago, and to hear about the fires, and the floods, and the various occupying German armies that the Huisman Shipyard had survived.

Then, in 1993, the odds shifted dramatically, when a new kind of sailboat customer showed up. He was American. An entrepreneur, from San Francisco, a friend of Jim Clark. He wanted a yacht bigger than any Huisman had ever built, 142 feet. To make certain he got exactly what he wanted, he made dozens of trips to the Dutch village of Vollenhove. Occasionally he slept on the floor of Wolter Huisman's office. He was, in the way that the English disapprove of, aggressive. In late 1993 the boat was finished. It was christened *Juliet*. *Juliet* marked a shift in the demand curve, at least in Wolter's newly unsettled mind. His business, which had been 60 percent German, became 75 percent American. The rich, and especially the new American rich, suddenly acquired a taste for obscenely big boats and for the high technology required to run them. The boats had ceased to be merely boats. They were tiny floating city-states. Wolter kept his objections to his customers' tastes to himself, at least until they were out of shouting range. But after they left, he'd explode. "Always, bigger, bigger, bigger!" he'd shout. "If someone has duh 90-foot boat, dey want a 95-foot boat. If someone else has duh 95-foot sailboat, dey want a 100-foot sailboat. It is normal, ya?" He left it open whether he was making a simple statement or asking a question.

Either way, Wolter was not entirely at ease in the new climate. Before *Juliet* the official slogan of the Royal Huisman Shipyard had been "If you can dream it, we can build it." Now a new sign hung in one of Wolter Huisman's offices: "Their Dream Is Our Nightmare."

At his most pessimistic, Wolter could have had no idea what strange forces *Juliet* would unleash. When she left the Huisman Shipyard, she made her way back to San Francisco Bay, where she was seen and admired by technically minded people poised to create one of the loudest explosions of wealth in economic history. In the summer of 1995 the first of these people walked into Wolter's office at the Huisman Shipyard. He said his name was Jim Clark, and he had just created a new Internet company called Netscape. To buy the yacht of his dreams, he explained, he had persuaded his board of directors to take Netscape public—that is, sell shares in the enterprise to investors. (He often did the right things for the wrong reasons.) Wolter called around to find out whether Clark's money was real and . . . he came up empty. No one he knew had ever heard of Netscape. It turned out the company had existed for a bit more than a year, had made huge losses, and had no concrete plans to make profits, and . . . well, Wolter couldn't begin to say what it actually did. Then, a few months later, Wolter found himself reading magazine articles about Jim Clark. Netscape had made Clark a billionaire.

Wolter's role in the creation of Clark's computerized yacht had been to suffer ironically. It was a role for which he was poorly suited. Clark and his new ideas were actually very stressful to Wolter. He'd spent two and a half years with this contradiction squarely in the middle of his life: a customer who wanted to grope for the new new thing in his old old place. Wolter woke up in the middle of the night imagining the headlines in the newspapers. World Famous Huisman Yacht Sinks! Huisman Owner Unable to Explain Computer Boat! He'd aged visibly—a few months into the work on *Hyperion* his heart went bad, and he was taken away to a hospital bed. After a few days he emerged with a doctor's order to take it easy . . . and found Jim Clark and his computer programmers waiting for him in his boatyard.

On this particular visit of Clark's, Wolter opened the conversation with one of his pet themes, the wisdom of letting a computer sail the boat. A recent article in one of the yachting magazines pointed out that Jim Clark's new sailboat would "learn" to sail itself, in all conditions. *Hyperion* was, in fact, a learning machine. It contained thousands of electronic sensors capable of measuring everything from the pressure on the sails to the temperature in the fridges. They would feed a continuous stream of data into twenty-five industrial-strength computers. Over time the computers would acquire the information they needed to cope with every possible sailing condition. If he wished, Clark could connect to *Hyperion* over the Internet from his living room back in California, seize the computer from the captain, and sail it from a keyboard. That particular point had caught Wolter Huisman's eye. "I don't believe in that," he said, brusquely. "You need a captain on board, ja?"

"I don't believe in it either," said Clark. In the past year, perhaps as a concession to Wolter's weak heart, Clark had taken to claiming that never in a million years would he try to sail his boat from his computer back in California. "But," he continued, "it's a nice thing to have cruise control on a car, you have to admit. You may or may not use it. But it's a nice thing to have."

Wolter thought about that for a second or two as if deciding whether Clark had conceded his point. He concluded that he had. "The boat is just another thing for Yim to write software for," he said to the others, with a great big laugh.

"Well," said Clark, pressing. "You wouldn't want to do any accidental jibes in a boat this big." This was an understatement. Clark was building the world's tallest mast. The world's tallest mast supported the world's largest sail. The world's largest sail implied the greatest wind ever collected in one place. By eliminating the problem of handling the sails manually, the computer had made this ambition feasible.

"Ja," said Wolter, "this is true."

"And you wouldn't mind having the boat set off an alarm to warn you when you are sailing dangerously close to the wind," said Clark, running down his mental list of the many feats the computer might preform better than a fallible human being.

"Ja," said Wolter, less happily, "this also is true."

The yachting magazine had pointed out, too, *Hyperion* would not have only a brain but also a voice. Rather than sound an alarm, the computer would actually holler at the captain. If the captain ignored the warning, the computer would shout at him again. "Watch out, you bloody fool!" was Clark's suggestion for a second-warning sound.

"Yes," said Captain Allan Prior, uneasily, "I heard there will be a voice."

"A millennium voice," grumbled Wolter. Wolter was not entirely comfortable with the idea of a talking boat.

"A *German* voice," said Clark, laughing at the idea of it. He put on his best Third Reich accent and boomed, "Allan! Zee boat is zinking! Get out uff your bunk!"

Clark enjoyed the joke more than Wolter, and Wolter enjoyed the joke more than Allan, but then Allan had heard why Clark had decided to computerize a sailboat in the first place. This particular brain wave washed over Clark back in 1991, when, in despair over what was happening at Silicon Graphics, he had retired to the high seas to stew over the telecomputer. No matter where he turned, however, he had trouble with his captains. The captain of the boat Clark then owned had sailed one evening from St. Bart's to Anguilla. On the way back he ran the boat quietly up onto a coral reef; just as quietly he slipped the boat off of it. He never told Clark, who spent that night ashore, of the mishap. But Clark's wife, Nancy Rutter, who was aboard, was partially awakened by the sound of the scraping. That his captain kept this piece of data from him five years before has infuriated Clark *to this day*. From this he drew the lesson: the captain needs to be watched. And from this he had the idea to write a computer program to watch him. A computer could monitor everything that happened on board the boat. Clark had only to keep an eye on his screen and he'd know most of what his captain got up to when he was away.

Allan Prior knew the story. And so he also knew that the computer software was aimed at *him*.

Putting the computer to one side, Wolter then finally broke the bad news. "Yim," said Wolter, "this boat they are building in New Zealand. It will have a mast that is maybe bigger than yours."

Clark leaned back in his chair.

"Maybe more than 200," said Wolter.

"More than 200 feet?" asked Clark.

Wolter nodded.

"And we're only 197," said Allan. Sometimes they said it was 189 feet, other times 197. Whatever. It was big.

Actually, one hundred and ninety seven feet was an important number, in Clark's mind. It was the maximum height for any boat that wished to pass at high tide beneath the Balboa Bridge in the Panama Canal. Clark assumed that any boat big enough to support a 197-foot mast would want to be able to pass through the Panama Canal. If he was right, his 197-foot mast would be not merely the tallest built to date but the tallest built *for all time*.

"How tall exactly is this other mast we are dealing with here?" asked Clark, but before they could answer he was up and pacing. I take that back. He wasn't actually standing and walking around. I call it pacing because I can think of no other way to get across the effect he had on everyone else in the room. In fact, he merely altered his facial expressions. His mouth squinched up into its tiny pucker, his face reddened slightly, and his head bobbed like a boxer's between punches. But to judge from the faces across the table from him he might as well have risen from his chair and marched back and forth across Wolter's office while hollering at the top of his lungs. Wolter looked stricken.

Soon enough, Clark actually was on his feet and leading the others out of Wolter Huisman's office. They left the back way and crossed the catwalk that snaked around *Hyperion*, four stories off the ground. At that point *Hyperion* was a skeleton of its future self, and you could see all of its baffling complexity. There were twelve refrigerators, a water maker, a sewage treatment plant, three generators, an engine the size of a Volkswagen beetle, an endless number of hydraulic-powered winches, and several thousand electronic sensors affixed to everything that could be measured by a computer. There were sixty *miles* of electrical wires running from the sensors to twenty-five Silicon Graphics computers, which stored and manipulated the data. They collected and analyzed forty thousand separate pieces of information. The boat had been reduced to the sum of its digital data.

Clark and Wolter and Allan and the Royal Huisman executives walked past all this marvelous complexity, down the steps of the catwalk, and through a shop floor teeming with the fifty woodworkers crafting the boat's teak and mahogany furnishings. These people were as different from Clark as Maori tribesmen. Many of them had learned their craft in the Huisman Shipyard from their fathers, who in turn had learned their craft in the Huisman Shipyard from their fathers. Generations of Dutch boatbuilders lived and died without giving a passing thought to leaving. There was never a question when they got out of bed in the morning what they would do that day, or the next, or the next. They were the tiny figures in the middle ground of the Dutch landscape who, after digging a few canals and erecting a dike or two, were content to leave the world as they had found it.

The group of executives, led by Clark, entered the shed at the end of the yard. Before Clark arrived on the scene, there was no building in the Huisman Shipyard that could house a 197-foot mast. Clark had waved that objection to one side, and said he would pay for a new building. The new building in the old boatyard was long and low and light. From a distance it appeared to be an enormous greenhouse. It wasn't. It was an oven.

Once finished, and well before it impaled the boat, the mast would acquire its slick white veneer. But now it was a long black rod stretched out across the floor. No one who didn't know what it was would ever guess; it could be, perhaps, the Alaska Pipeline. When finished, tilted upright, and sealed onto the boat, it would fail to fit beneath the Sydney Harbor Bridge, the Coronado Bridge in San Diego, or the Triborough Bridge in New York City. Even now a dozen workers were gradually thickening its girth by wrapping layer upon thin layer of black carbon fiber. After they laid each layer, the workers heated the building to the material's melting point. The black layers melded together into a blacker whole. Blacker and blacker the mast grew. It wasn't built, it was cooked.

And until ten minutes earlier it was the world's tallest mast. That this might no longer be true distressed Clark. Of course, he knew as well as anyone how ridiculous it was for him to make a big deal about having the world's largest mast. That was one of many odd things about him. One minute he could say, "Who cares which rich guy has the tallest mast?"—and actually believe every word of it. The next minute he would be standing at one end of the shed with his arms outreached as if he was Moses parting the Red Sea and the mast jutting out from him like an enormous black phallus and booming, "Mine's sixty meters. How long is yours?" Inside him a quality and a chemical—intelligence and testosterone—wrestled for hegemony. At the moment the chemical was winning on points.

The chemical gave rise to a certain unease in him. Journalists were forever describing Clark as "a tall, lanky Texan." The picture this conjured up of a big easygoing fellow loping through town with a sloppy grin on his face was completely false. He was big, and he could fake a certain relaxed quality for just long enough to fool a stranger, but there was nothing easygoing about him. His temperament did not belong in a man of his size. He was as agitated as a mongoose eyeing a cobra. This agitation could be deeply unsettling to others. Rich Karlgaard, the publisher of *Forbes* and a longtime observer of Silicon Valley, once said that there were only three men in the Valley who were physically intimidating. Larry Ellison, who ran Oracle, Gerald Saunders who ran Advanced Micro Devices, and Clark, who ran himself. That statement was both strange and true. It was strange because though Clark had a temper he was never violent. It was true because people often were terrified of Clark, even if they didn't fear being hit. Clark let his anger rage freely inside of him. Once it had reached a boiling point, he choked it off. The object of his anger looked into Clark's face and saw a blast furnace that was about to blow up. Hence the pucker.

In any case, on that morning in the Huisman Shipyard, Clark did not have to say why he was a bit upset, because everyone in the shed knew why he was a bit upset. He had gone to some trouble to determine the rules for boats that wished to pass beneath the Balboa Bridge in the Panama Canal. Now Wolter tells him that he missed a trick. At low tide, and with special permission from the U.S. government, which owned and administered the Panama Canal, boats that rose 200 feet over the water were allowed to sail through. Worse, in the year 2000 the Panamanian government gained control of the canal from the U.S. government. And the Panamanian government was now saying that it might extend the height limit from 200 feet to 204 feet. The owner of the New Zealand boat, an Atlanta real estate man, figured he could suffer the inconvenience of waiting until low tide to pass through the canal for a year. After the canal became Panamanian in 2000, he could pass through anytime he pleased.

Standing on one end of what was now clearly only temporarily the world's longest mast, Clark thought about his own private Y2K problem. He asked Wolter what he thought about adding an extension to the mast. Wolter muttered that he did not think it was a good idea. Finally, Clark turned to Allan, his captain, and said, "I think we should challenge this Atlanta guy to a sailboat race."


Clark's life always had a topsy-turvy quality, but from the moment Netscape went public and he became Silicon Valley's newest billionaire it grew more reversed than ever. His play took on the intensity of work, and his work acquired the flavor of play. His play was his creation of the world's first computerized yacht, and the yacht more than anything else kept him up all hours. Many nights he lay awake thinking up mathematical solutions to *Hyperion*'s software problems.

For instance, one problem that irked him was how to create a gauge on a computer screen that had the look of a mechanical gauge. Mimicking reality inside a computer was his career-long obsession: his Ph.D. thesis at the University of Utah had been about virtual reality. One day he created a fuel gauge in the normal fashion, using the new computer language C++. That night he lay awake torturing himself over the sloppiness of the work. He disliked the imprecision of computer language, which he thought of as an inexact science. He became more and more irritated that the gauge did not look exactly like a mechanical gauge. There was no shading around the edges, for instance, and the needle clicked along like a digital tool rather than smoothly gliding along like the analog speedometer on a car.

At three in the morning he finally gave up trying to sleep. He slipped out of bed without waking his wife, got in his car, and drove to his office three miles down the road. The problem was the fucking computer language. One of the reasons the software business favored the young is that every so often the language changed. It was as if you announced to the population of France that everyone would be speaking Esperanto instead of French. Old people with their old language were shoved aside by new people who, with nothing invested in the old language, picked up the new language more easily. That Clark, in the late 1980s, had bothered to teach himself C++ was itself a triumph of character over condition; in the Valley anyone over forty tended to fade into technical irrelevance. "I'm an old dog who taught himself a new trick," Clark would say. He was an old dog who taught himself so many new tricks that he was a threat to the reputation of old dogs.

This particular trick did not exactly do the trick. And so there, at three in the morning, in his dingy little office over the Jenny Craig weight loss center, Clark solved his problem with mathematics, then translated the solution back into computer code. When he was finished, he had a gauge he liked. A few hours later I plucked his work out of the garbage can, as a memento of how the late twentieth-century American technology billionaire spent the hours between midnight and six in the morning:

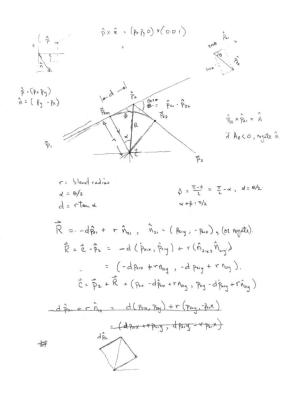

The truth was that no casual observer could say when Clark was working and when he was playing. In part this was because, to Clark's way of thinking, the big distinction wasn't between "work" and "play" but between "creating new technology for money" and "creating new technology for pleasure." In part it was because there was no distinction at all.

By the fall of 1995 Clark had finished with Netscape. Having learned from Silicon Graphics that he did not really belong inside a large organization, he designed all future large organizations without a place for himself inside. He kept the title of chairman, and sat on the Netscape board, and held on to most of his nineteen million or so shares (the stock had split), but really he didn't do much but attend a few meetings and trouble the company's new chief executive, Jim Barksdale, with his various premonitions of what was about to happen.

To Clark it seemed clear that the Internet browser business would one day be devoured by Microsoft. Microsoft had devoured SGI slowly; it would devour Netscape quickly. Microsoft's monopoly in the PC operating system gave it two big advantages in the battle for the Internet. The first was billions of dollars in profits; it could outspend any rival. The second was leverage over every company that intended to sell anything to the user of the PC. Netscape already was at Microsoft's mercy. There was no point in designing newer and better versions of its Internet browser that were not compatible with each subsequent version of Microsoft Windows. And it could not do this without receiving early versions of Windows from Microsoft. Microsoft had done a good job marketing itself as a dynamic young company intent on changing the world. And to many people that is what it was. To Clark it was a force for slowing change, so that change did not disrupt its monopoly. It was bigger than General Motors and, in its way, just as stodgy.

And so Jim Clark set out thinking about how to make himself another billion dollars, to replace the billion he might lose to Bill Gates. That was the starting point for Clark after Netscape: how to make not millions but *billions* of dollars. Quickly. When he cooked up his plans, it never occurred to him that he was an outsider with no experience in the industry he planned to invade. He felt that pretty much the entire American economy was up for grabs, thanks to the Internet. No, the problem was that any computer-related market that was big enough to enable Clark to become much richer than he already was would be a market Microsoft itself would covet. When he asked himself, "How do I make another billion dollars for myself?" he was really asking, "How do I make another billion dollars for myself before Microsoft notices what I'm up to?" It took him four months to come up with an answer.

In late 1995 Clark was diagnosed with a rare blood disease, hemochromatosis. Essentially, his blood produced more iron than his body needed. The disease required Clark to visit the hospital once every few weeks, where he was subjected to an old medieval panacea, bleeding. It was the first time he'd visited a hospital since he'd crashed his motorcycle and shattered his leg. The blizzard of forms and the bureaucracy was more than any new billionaire could be expected to tolerate. It got him thinking of a solution.

By early 1996 Americans were spending $1.5 *trillion* a year on their health care and about a third of that was pure waste. Much of the waste could be avoided simply by eliminating the paperwork. Since much of the paperwork seemed designed to prevent the patient from getting what he wanted when he wanted it, eliminating it would please the customer. The Internet was made for such tasks: in effect, the Internet enabled all of the many parties of any health care transaction to be present in the same room. The patient could walk into the office of a doctor he'd never met, supply the doctor with a password, and a few seconds later the doctor would have his medical record and insurance coverage. A few minutes after the patient left, the doctor would bill the insurer over the Internet, and be paid by the insured over the Internet. If the patient needed drugs, those too could be ordered from the screen, right in the doctor's office. No forms, no papers, no hassle.

Clark sat down with a piece of paper—a piece of paper!—and drew this little diagram:

PAYERS
*

DOCTORS   *                     *  PROVIDERS

*

CONSUMERS

The way he drew it, it came out a neat little diamond. The Magic Diamond. Clark thought a minute about the spot in the middle (*), which is of course where he assumed any company he would create belonged. Say, there was maybe one-third of a trillion and a half dollars a year of pure waste. Say, he cut out half of that and kept the rest as profit. He'd still be bigger than Microsoft, and Microsoft was on its way to becoming the most highly valued company on the New York Stock Exchange. If he was going to create the most valuable company in America, the company would need a name. He might as well have written in "Jim Clark Enterprises," for that is what it amounted to. Instead, he wrote "Healthscape."

Any other human being would have been tossed into an asylum for thinking such grandiose thoughts. Clark had invented Jim Clark, and so he was taken seriously.

## Throwing Sand in Capitalists' Eyes

Not long after he drew the Magic Diamond with himself at the center of the U.S. health care industry, Clark drove up to Sand Hill Road to see the venture capitalists. The venture capitalists advertised themselves as the great financial risk takers of the Valley, but you could learn everything you needed to know about their attitudes toward risk, simply by driving up Sand Hill Road. Sand Hill Road was where the venture capitalists clustered together for safety, like ducks in a park waiting for the bread crumbs to fall. Each time Clark made this trip, the ducks came out of it worse than the time before. The price of the crumbs rose; and they had to quack louder for them. When Clark had gone to see the venture capitalists about Netscape, it was with the understanding that he would act as the CEO until the company was up and running. This time he proposed not only that he take home the lion's share of the stock in the new company but that the venture capitalists do all of the actual work. Clark had no plans to spend even a day in the Healthscape offices. He had ceased to be a businessman and become a conceptual artist. Having articulated the new new thing, Clark intended to return to the important work of teaching his computer to sail his new boat.

Amazingly, the question in his mind was not whether a venture capitalist would accept this deal, but which venture capitalist he would grace with his presence. The venture capitalists had learned a hard lesson from Netscape. Before Netscape went public, a lot of venture capitalists had thought John Doerr and his firm, Kleiner Perkins, had been mad to agree to Clark's terms. Clark had charged Doerr three times the going rate for start-up capital. Doerr had cleared $500 million or so in eighteen months, or thirty times his original investment, and become the most talked-about venture capitalist on Sand Hill Road. The other venture capitalists were forced to concede the point: the new, higher price for concepts, and the people who dreamed them up, was obviously worth paying.

Dick Kramlich from New Enterprise Associates (NEA), the Valley's biggest pile of venture money and health care expertise, made the strongest pitch to Clark. Clark still complained about the way Kramlich had joined forces with Ed McCracken to muscle him aside at Silicon Graphics. But Kramlich was one of those gentle souls who just want everyone to get along, and he was, at least on the surface, willing to subordinate his ego to others. "If there is crow to eat and groveling to do," says one of his colleagues, "Dick is the first in line to do it." Kramlich had turned up at one of Netscape's meetings with investors immediately before the IPO, and told Clark how happy he was for his success. This act of self-abasement—a formal acknowledgment that Clark was too important to ignore—encouraged Clark to rethink his opinion of Kramlich. He still hadn't forgiven Kramlich for siding with Ed McCracken, and he never would, but he was, let us say, touched by the gesture.

As it happened, Clark had a motive for reconsidering his irritation with Kramlich: he was now even more irritated with John Doerr. Whenever Doerr's name came up, Clark's mouth went into full-pucker mode. When Clark had offered Doerr the chance to invest in Netscape, Doerr had been rather down on his luck. Between 1991 and 1993 Doerr had persuaded a lot of people, himself included, that the future of the Valley was in pen computing. Pen computing was a version of the Palm Pilot, ahead of its time. Doerr had burned tens of millions of capital on a dramatic failure to stuff computers into ordinary people's pockets called GO. After GO, Doerr seized on interactive television. He took to making futuristic speeches the theme of which was that interactive television would transform the world. (He'd give the same speech right through to the end of the decade, simply replacing "interactive television" with "the Internet.") Clark had rescued Doerr from that particular blind alley, and then helped him to cook up other new Internet companies. One of those companies was @Home. Clark and Doerr shared an obsession with Microsoft. Both felt that the Internet would be too big for Microsoft to ignore. They assumed, further, that a few years down the road the Internet would enter people's homes through their television cables, which could transmit data much faster than phone lines. Ergo, Microsoft would seek to dominate the cable Internet industry. @Home was designed to secure the cable industry for Silicon Valley.

The important work was in the concepts, so far as Clark was concerned, and the concept for @Home had been at least as much his as Doerr's. And yet Doerr's firm, Kleiner Perkins, had denied Clark the chance to buy a piece of @Home, at least at first. Kleiner Perkins hewed to the old venture capital model, which relegated entrepreneurs like Clark to the sidelines of any business they did not explicitly create. They declined to pay Clark at his new conceptual-artist rates. Clark responded by telling Doerr that he planned to go elsewhere with his concepts.

Now he had one: the Magic Diamond. Once again he had put his name on a concept and was off and running down his long, dark tunnel. A few weeks after he saw Kramlich at the Netscape gathering, Clark drove up Sand Hill Road and paid a call on NEA, Kramlich's venture capital firm. Kramlich finally seemed to understand that the world had changed, and that the engineer with the beautiful concept was its natural ruler. That was a big point in Kramlich's favor. Kramlich gathered his partners into the conference room. Clark drew the Magic Diamond with Healthscape at the center of America's only $1.5 trillion industry, the world's single largest market, and announced he was going to "fix the U.S. health care system." Of course, no one who actually understood the U.S. health care system would have dared to make such a grandiose statement. And, of course, Clark knew he did not understand it—and knew also, or at least sensed, that his lack of understanding was a psychological advantage. No one who understood the U.S. health care industry would bother to try to fix it.

Kramlich and his partners responded just as Clark assumed they should. They wanted a piece of the action. They asked him to come up and talk to them again. Soon. The failure to land Netscape had already cost Kramlich half a billion dollars. That failure was in part blamed on Alex Slusky, the young Harvard Business School graduate who had been assigned to trail behind Clark after he quit Silicon Graphics. Slusky had been forced to move on from NEA shortly after Netscape went public. ("They 'fired' Alex because he didn't land Jim," says another former NEA employee. "Fired in this case just means they made Alex's life so miserable that he left.")

To handle Clark this time around, Kramlich lined up two senior partners, whom I'll call Phil and Bill. Phil and Bill were NEA's health care specialists. Phil and Bill were also pretty much everything Clark hated about venture capitalists. Both were self-consciously "professional" men who knew how to dress down for meetings with engineers and how to dress up for meetings with Wall Street financiers and never said anything in any of these meetings that surprised anyone. They were conventional people who assumed that conventions made the world go round, which, of course, they usually do. In any case, they didn't really believe in the possibility of change, and so did not bring the passion of revolutionaries to their work. As one of their NEA colleagues explains it, "Phil and Bill were totally unwilling to work nights and weekends, to write a business plan, brainstorm, spend time with Jim during the off hours, etc." Phil and Bill, even more than Dick Kramlich, viewed Clark as a dangerously volatile, perhaps even mad, character who needed to be "managed."

Clark looked around Dick Kramlich's conference table filled with NEA partners and said he wanted nothing to do with Phil and Bill. He wanted Hugh.

Hugh was Hugh Reinhoff, a young doctor with little business experience who had just quit one job at Johns Hopkins and taken another in NEA's Baltimore office. So far as Phil and Bill were concerned, Hugh was an interloper. So far as Clark was concerned, that was fine. Clark often preferred young, inexperienced people over older, more experienced ones. Even if they didn't quite know what they were doing, at least they hadn't learned the wrong things. They hadn't lost their passion; they hadn't become Business Bores. And so, in September 1995, at Clark's fierce insistence, Hugh took over where Alex Slusky left off. He became Clark's personal minder on the sprint down the long, dark tunnel. "My job," Hugh later said, "was not to leave Jim's side—to make sure that NEA got a piece of whatever Jim created."

Improbably, Clark had been catapulted to the top of the capitalist food chain. Once there, he insisted that the people who had spent their careers there act more like him. He expected the venture capitalists to join him in throwing money at the idea and letting his engineers work out the details. Up until then the businesses funded by Silicon Valley venture capitalists may have been adventurous by the standards of American commerce, but the adventure was well planned. Now the adventure was reckless; Clark was making it up as he went along. Deep in his intuitive soul he thought "business plans" and "business models" and "management structures" were a waste of time. Time was the one commodity you could not waste if you wanted to make a billion dollars from the Internet. Once he had identified the new new thing, all he needed was some really smart, passionate engineers to chase after it and make it happen. After all, the idea was simple: eliminate the paperwork, the waiting around, and the market illogic from the U.S. health care system by bringing all the people in that system together on a single network.

The idea was not nearly as astonishing as Clark's audacity in putting it across to the venture capitalists. At the same time that he was telling them how to invest their money, and plotting to take over the $1.5 trillion health care industry, Clark was working nearly full-time as a computer programmer. He took on the world's single largest market as a part-time job. When he woke up in the morning, he wrote code for his boat; when he went to bed at night, he stared at the ceiling and thought about the bugs in the boat's code. He communicated with the venture capitalists chiefly by e-mail—which is to say that he rarely actually had to see them anymore.

A chapter could probably be written on the effect of e-mail on the American business imagination. Within about eighteen months it had gone from being exotic to essential. Those businessmen who were uncomfortable with computers cheated and pretended to use e-mail. Netscape's CEO, Jim Barksdale, for instance, did not actually fetch his own e-mail but had his secretary type it up for him. But all of the peo-

ple with whom Clark dealt were now available at his fingertips whenever a whim might strike him at three in the morning. He had a lot of
whims.

Most of Clark's early missives betrayed his concern with finding people he liked to run Healthscape. He wanted to hire people he trusted
rather than people the venture capitalists recommended. For instance,
on October 24, 1995, Clark wrote to Hugh Reinhoff,

> "TJ [Clark's old engineering buddy Tom Jermoluk, now president of
> Silicon Graphics] could absolutely do the job of CEO [of
> Healthscape] but I doubt he's interested because although he'd like
> to make more money, he's not risk oriented. I also met with the best
> software manager at SGI and he is interested . . . keep this highly
> confidential, because while he expressed interest in going, I don't
> want anyone else to get wind of this.

Clark didn't want anyone else to "get wind of this," because it was a
breach of his contract. The moment Netscape went public, it started
getting résumés from Silicon Graphics' engineers. Already Clark had
received letters from Ed McCracken's lawyers threatening to sue him if
he recruited engineers from Silicon Graphics.

The Valley's leading venture capitalists did not instantly adopt all of
Clark's assumptions about work and life. But they entertained them. And
they tended to let Clark have his way. Clark now possessed a new kind
of power—he could go anywhere he wanted with his precious concepts,
and if the venture capitalists did something he did not like, he would.

Inevitably, the venture capitalists did something he did not like.
Toward the end of October, Dick Kramlich invited Mark Perry, the vice
chairman of Silicon Graphics and an Ed McCracken sympathizer, to
become a partner at NEA. In theory, this should have been none of
Clark's business; in practice, Clark now had a lot to say about what happened inside any venture capital firm that wanted his concepts. On
October 31, 1995, Clark fired off an intemperate e-mail to several NEA
employees:

> Dick is nuts for getting Mark Perry as partner of NEA. Your firm went
> down a notch when I heard that. [It] calls into question Dick's judge-

ment. . . . Quite an insult to the rest of the partners. Sorry to be so blunt.

With that out of his system, he made some small attempt at conciliation:

> I do like Mark, but he is still Vice Chairman of SGI, which when added to Dick's role there [Kramlich remained on the board of Silicon Graphics] makes me very uncomfortable that SGI will hear that I'm talking to TJ . . . and this would not be good. I intend to recruit heavily from SGI.

Then he gave up being sweet:

> Anyway, I think you'll probably have to co-invest with KP [Kleiner Perkins], and if I detect any problems with these guys hearing about my recruiting, I will move away from NEA pronto.

Breaking up was never all that hard for Clark to do. E-mail made it easier. As he was well aware, the whole point of Hugh's shadowing him was to prevent him from drifting into the arms of other venture capitalists. Kramlich's nightmare was Clark wandering up the road to John Doerr at Kleiner Perkins—who simply by following Clark's lead was already being treated as the venture capitalist of the future. Clark's tiff with Doerr had given Kramlich his opening; now Clark was saying that his new irritation with NEA exceeded whatever lingering resentment he felt toward Doerr.

Inside NEA the situation quickly went from bad to worse. One of NEA's partners, who called Clark a "psychopath," took to pasting magazine photos of him on the office walls, with homemade captions that cast Dick Kramlich as "the unfortunate father" and Clark as "the troubled son" in an Oedipal melodrama. Another partner complained regularly that Clark was mucking up their entire investment portfolio by persuading them of his latest ideas about the Internet, which he often himself abandoned. Half the firm was furious that Kramlich had done a deal with the devil; the other half was furious that the deal had not been fully consummated. And once it was clear they might lose control of Clark to John Doerr, all hell broke loose. Kramlich tried to pull Hugh Reinhoff off Clark and slide in, once again, the older and more established pair, Phil and Bill. Phil wrote Hugh, instructing him to back away from Clark. Hugh wrote Phil and said he'd do so, gladly.

The trouble was that, whether or not Hugh knew it, Clark now was in control of Hugh. And Clark didn't like being told that he had to deal with Phil. He wanted Hugh and, as was now abundantly clear, what Clark wanted Clark got. He shot off another e-mail that found its way to Dick Kramlich:

> I'm really pissed at Phil's attitude. He is a fucking partner there. . . .
> I'm not going to let NEA have as much of the deal because of his childish behavior. That is a fucked up partnership, with babies like him as General Partners.

Within days Clark had called a meeting with NEA that included John Doerr. Within weeks he had agreed to split the equity into eleven parts, he and Kleiner Perkins each taking four parts and NEA getting only two. In mid-November 1995 the Kleiner employer David Schnell, writing "on behalf of NEA and Kleiner Perkins," sent Clark an e-mail, "reviewing our discussion on your business model."

> Thanks for getting the NEA and KPCB groups together to share ideas. Like Netscape we believe [Healthscape] should be built first by capturing all the plans, employees and employers in enterprises (eg. corporations, universities, non-profits) with services they demand now and will pay for. Establishing that beachhead then allows [Healthscape] to attack other opportunities.
>
> P.S. John Doerr's now predicting that you may be the only entrepreneur on the planet to found THREE ventures worth more than a billion $.

Schnell was yet another medical doctor who had decided that he wanted to be a venture capitalist. He was now a Kleiner employee who had been told by his bosses that, if he wanted to make partner, he needed to prove himself. The bosses' idea of how Schnell might prove himself was to become a captain of one of Jim Clark's ships. If Schnell went out with Jim Clark's imprimatur and came back with a few hundred million dollars in profits, he could be a partner at Kleiner Perkins. Schnell, who knew perfectly well what it meant to be a captain of Jim Clark's ship, politely declined. In the end, he was given no choice, and he became, reluctantly, Healthscape's acting CEO.

The sycophantic tone of his e-mail to Clark suggested that Schnell, like every other venture capitalist, felt Clark needed to be "managed." He sought to give Clark the feeling that he was in control of what might become the world's largest company without giving him actual control. As a result, it wasn't long before Clark found fault with Kleiner Perkins—or at least with David Schnell. Schnell, together with Hugh Reinhoff at NEA, kept trying to pin Clark down, by offering up various "business models" and "business plans" for Healthscape. In early December, Clark wrote to both,

> The problem I have with the way this discussion with KP/NEA and me has been going is that it is more or less in the abstract—that is, we're cooking up a business plan without a management team. This may be the way some companies are formed, but I'm more interested in finding bright people with a passion to change the way things are.

Clark had required only about six weeks of very part-time work to sow strife inside Dick Kramlich's partnership. He required only a few weeks more to disrupt John Doerr's. A month after his first e-mail to Clark, David Schnell sent another e-mail to everyone but Clark who was even slightly involved with Healthscape to complain about "JC's behavior here." David Schnell had new fears. The guy inside the venture capital firm who worked with Clark, he grumbled, was always the guy who got fired. He was more prescient than he knew.

That was how it was now with Clark and the venture capitalists who now sat on top of American capitalism, funding the many people newly engaged in the search for the new new thing. Clark was at best ambivalent about young men in suits who had gone to business school and never run a real risk in their lives. He certainly was never going to let them have their way, unless their way happened to be his way. This raises an obvious question: Why did the world's most important venture capitalists put up with Clark? Surely, it would have been easy enough for Kleiner Perkins or NEA to announce that they were backing someone else to do the same thing as Clark. Valley venture capitalists stole each other's ideas all the time. Right from the start Clark put much less effort into his enterprise than they did—though even they did not know that he was spending most of his time computerizing a boat. ("I knew Jim was doing this on the side," Reinhoff said, much later. "He had the big vision . . . the details fell to those in the company. I really didn't know what else he was doing. I assumed it was Netscape that took up most of his energy.") And yet not once did anyone dare to suggest that Clark was not carrying his load, or that the business would be better off without him.

That was the miracle of Jim Clark: by the end of 1995 he had created a money-making machine in which he was the least easily replaced part. The venture capitalists, the investment bankers, the CEOs—they were all fungible. If you were going to seize control of a $1.5 trillion industry you needed a certain authority with the engineering class. In the fall of 1995 no one in the Valley had the same authority with the engineers as Clark. That aura was why every one of the e-mails sent from Kleiner and NEA to people who might come to work for Healthscape boasted right up front that the Magic Diamond was Jim Clark's idea. In late 1995 a new kind of faith was in the engineering mind. Engineers believed that if Jim Clark said he was going to do something new, however outlandish his proposal, he would do it. And Clark responded to the faith by cooking up ever more outlandish new things to do.

The software that was required to link the entire U.S. health care industry was not trivial to design. The land-grab logic of the Internet meant that it had to be thrown together about three times as fast as it should. To build a complicated piece of software so quickly you needed engineers—and not just any engineers. You needed the smartest engineers. By late 1995 the smartest engineers in Silicon Valley had a lot of choice in how they spent their time. The Valley was booming. A lot of people were claiming to have stumbled upon a great new business opportunity. To attract the smartest engineers you needed to persuade people that you had the new new thing.

Clark figured that there were about three software cowboys who could pull off what he had in mind, as quickly as it needed to be pulled off. All worked for Silicon Graphics. He knew them all and spoke to them all, and they were all more than a little interested in working for him. In the end, he decided that one more than the others "had the passion to change the world." On Christmas Eve 1995, Clark's final choice arrived at Kleiner Perkins for his interview with David Schnell—which even Schnell knew was a formality. On Christmas Day, David Schnell wrote to Clark, "I spent several hours yesterday with Pavan. I think he's great, and I believe he wants to join."

## The Great Brain Quake of August 9, 1995

Like a lot of software engineers in Silicon Valley, Pavan Nigam can recall where he was when he heard about Netscape's initial public offering. Or, at least, he can figure it out. He was in India—he's sure of that. He couldn't have been in Kanpur, his hometown. Kanpur was a squalid, fly-specked, death-drenched city overrun by cows and pigs and chickens. When a person with Western standards of hygiene stepped off the train in Kanpur, his first thought was to get right back on. Even Pavan now found it repellant. More to the point, Kanpur did not receive American newspapers. And Pavan distinctly recalls reading the front page of *USA Today*. So he must have been in Delhi, which means he was in a hotel. So in a Delhi hotel he picked up the August 10, 1995, edition of *USA Today* and read that Netscape had risen from its offering price of $18 a share to a high of $171.

By late 1995 Pavan's mental state was not good. In the fifteen years since he had come to America from India, he had risen to what he thought was fantastic heights in Silicon Valley. He had just finished eighteen putatively spectacular months at Silicon Graphics, where he had been the boss of the most glamorous engineering project in the

Valley: the creation of the world's first interactive television. He'd hired fifty of the smartest engineers ever assembled under one roof. He'd spent three hundred million corporate research dollars. He'd had his name and his picture in the newspaper; famous businessmen had told him that his work was important. And all he had to show for it was a black box that was supposed to sit on top of people's TVs but was as hopelessly out of touch with the market as the Kitchen Computer. Not a single one was ever sold.

That experience had pretty much shattered Pavan's faith in pure technical virtuosity, or what he called "the religion of technology." Great technical success had proven to be a great commercial failure. "Just a bunch of engineers solving problems," as Pavan put it, derisively.

Anyway, by the time he left for India and a few weeks of serious self-examination in August 1995, Pavan suspected that Jim Clark was always right, except, of course, when he was wrong. And when Jim Clark was wrong, he wasn't around to suffer the consequences. The lesson Pavan extracted from the bitter experience was to watch what Jim Clark did, not what he said. Before he boarded the plane, Pavan called his stock broker and left an order to buy Netscape at the opening. Reading USA Today in a Delhi hotel, he calculated that he must have bought at $50—the price of the first trades—and sold at $100—the price at which he'd instructed his stock broker to sell. He never seriously believed that Netscape's share price would reach $100. It was, he says, "the easiest money I ever made in my life," but even so it was bittersweet. Netscape had gone to $171 a share! He'd left $71 a share on the table!

With that and many other thoughts on his mind, Pavan returned to the squalor of Kanpur. "I remember sitting there in my parents' house for two weeks with all these cows running around me," he says. "I remember that I decided right then whatever I did next it was going to be with the Web." Pavan had learned enough about American capitalism to know that where the stock market went the opportunity followed. That thought was followed pretty quickly by a second thought: "I remember thinking that if I could find out whatever Jim Clark planned to do next I would do that."

The Silicon Valley labor market was one of the many new joys in Jim Clark's new life. Having decided that the $1.5 trillion health care industry was the new new thing—and, in so deciding, having transformed it into the new thing—Clark needed to hire a lot of smart people quickly. There was no easier place on the planet to do that. Silicon Valley engineers had long treated the companies they worked for with less than the usual fidelity to the corporate cause. Their bosses, of course, disapproved of those who defected, and so there was a running debate about what was simply the proper workings of a free market and what was an unseemly breach of loyalty. The steady stream of engineers out of Silicon Graphics and into Netscape just before Netscape went public prompted Ed McCracken's lawyers to write Clark nasty letters. With Healthscape, Clark figured he needed even bigger brains, and planned to poach them from Silicon Graphics—only he couldn't be seen to do it. His solution to the problem was to sneak in and hire one fine software cowboy and let him be the Pied Piper. If he hired the right person, the rest would beg to follow, and Ed McCracken could do nothing to stop them.

The moment of conception was, to Clark's way of thinking, the critical moment of any new enterprise. At that moment it was important not merely to hire the people bent on changing the world but to avoid hiring the people bent only on changing jobs. "There are all sorts of guys who will show up because they can't think of anything else to do," he said. "Those are exactly the people you don't want. I have a strategy for dealing with these people. When they come by to apply for a job I tell them, 'We're all confused here. We don't know what we're going to do yet.' But when you find someone you want, I tell them, 'Here's exactly what we're going to do and it is going to be *huge* and you are going to get very, very rich.'"

For engineering talent Clark looked to Silicon Graphics. In particular he had his sights on the Indian engineers who had taught him to write the code for his boat and then built the interactive television. Clark had a thing for Indians. "The Indian outcasts of Silicon Valley," he usually called them; "my Indian hordes," in less sober moments. He thought of the young Indian men who had taught him the tools he needed to program his sailboat as some of the sharpest technical minds he'd ever encountered. "As a concentrated group," he said, "they were the most talented engineers in the Valley . . . *and they work their butts off!"*

As it happened, the Indian education system had been built to find and to cultivate precisely those skills Clark, and people like Clark, valued most. Of course, that isn't how it was originally conceived. The Indian educational system was conceived by Nehru in reaction to the British colonial experience. Nehru believed that India was more likely to remain an independent country if it made itself technologically equal to its former rulers. To that end he created a ruthlessly efficient mechanism for finding and exploiting Indian technical talent. It was called the Indian Institute of Technology. The IITs were created in the early 1960s with foreign aid. The first two, at Kharagpur and Madras, were funded by Germany; the third, in Bombay by the USSR; the fourth, at Kanpur, by the United States; the fifth, at Delhi, by the United Kingdom.

The IITs became the funnel through which young Indians who finished high in a national standardized test passed on their way into Nehru's game of catch-up ball. The force of their attraction was spectacular. It was as if a nation of 900 million people had set out to find the few among them most able to program a computer, and leave nothing to chance. By the time the Nehru regime finished engineering Indian society, every parent in the country wanted his son to become either a doctor or an engineer. By the early 1970s hundreds of thousands of Indian seventeen-year-olds were sitting for the annual two-day engineering exams. A few weeks after the exam the results were posted in the newspapers. The two thousand students with the highest scores won admission to the IITs and had their names printed in the newspaper. Imagine the thrill of gaining entrance to Harvard. Multiply it several times. That gives you some idea of the sense of destiny that accompanied admission to an IIT. "If you could make it into an IIT, the rest of your life was guaranteed," says Pavan Nigam. "If you don't make it into an IIT, there are no guarantees about anything. And I mean *anything.*"

But the exam was just the beginning of India's search for its own technical aptitude. The two thousand students who passed the test were further ranked according to their scores. Beginning at the top, they selected the schools and the departments they wished to enter. These schools and their departments had their own informal hierarchy. For instance, by the early 1980s the most desirable place to study in the

whole of India was the computer science department at IIT Kanpur—
the school funded by the United States. The Kanpur computer science
department had only fifty places. By the time the student who had
placed 100th in the exam wandered in to make his choice, the places
were already taken by others who had done better on the exam. Out
of the 150,000 Indian high school students who took the national exam
in 1975, Pavan Nigam finished 91st. He took one of the last places in
computer science at Kanpur.

He couldn't have known it at the time, but his success put him on a
collision course with Jim Clark. A system designed to churn out engineers for a Third World economy would soon be used to its greatest
effect in the quest for the new new thing. The talent that the government had gone to such trouble to find and cultivate wound up being
some of the most sought-after corporate employees on the planet. All
these bright young men spoke English. They could quite easily pick up
and go to America, which was paying the highest price for their talent.
And, in massive numbers, that is exactly what they did. Indian engineers flooded Silicon Valley in the 1980s and 1990s. By 1996 nearly
half of the 55,000 temporary visas issued by the U.S. government to
high-tech workers went to Indians. In early 1999 a Berkeley sociologist
named AnnaLee Saxenian discovered that nearly half of all Silicon
Valley companies were founded by Indian entrepreneurs. The definitive smell inside a Silicon Valley start-up was of curry.


So one day when Jim Clark had finished writing his code for the boat,
he picked up the phone and called Pavan Nigam and told him about
his idea for making him rich. When Pavan asked for a business plan,
Clark simply revealed the Magic Diamond with Healthscape at the center. Pavan was at first very excited; then he was very nervous. Software
engineers went hunting in packs: he couldn't do such a big project
alone. Where would he find the engineers he needed to help him? Pavan
often said that "the difference between a great software guy and an okay
software guy is *huge*. A great software guy is worth ten times an okay
software guy." Software wasn't like hardware; software was more like
art. Clark was thrusting a project on him that required the very best
artists. True, a lot of those people worked with him at Silicon Graphics.

Like Clark, though, Pavan knew that Ed McCracken's lawyers would not put up with a systematic raid on the staff. And if he couldn't actively recruit from Silicon Graphics, where would he find the brilliant engineers he needed to succeed?

"You won't have to recruit," said Clark. "They'll follow you."

Clark's confidence finally swayed Pavan. Then he hung up.

An hour later Pavan's anxiety came storming back. After all, he was at that moment a very senior guy at Silicon Graphics, and Silicon Graphics was a very well-established corporation. It was a big risk for him to jump to running a start-up. He knew exactly nothing about the U.S. health care system. He had never been inside an American hospital, or visited an American doctor. He wasn't even sure what his own health insurance covered.

Pavan phoned Clark back. "I thought about it, and I don't think they'll follow me," he said. Clark said, "Pavan, just trust me on this one."

But how could Pavan trust anyone with a decision of such importance? Clark was already a billionaire. ITV had demonstrated Clark's ability to lead Pavan and a lot of other people down a blind alley and into a brick wall. What if Clark changed his mind again? What if Pavan left Silicon Graphics and announced that he planned to "fix the American health care system," and no one showed up to help him? Where would he be then? He'd be the thirty-six-year-old Indian immigrant who had built a black box no one had bought, sitting alone in an office while everyone he knew laughed at him behind his back—that's where he'd be. *Fix the U.S. health care system.* Right.

Pavan knew well that it was possibly illegal and certainly immoral for him to recruit from Silicon Graphics. But surely he could pick one person and have a . . . chat. There was one person above the rest who would considerably ease Pavan's anxiety, Kittu Kolluri. Kittu was both the smartest engineer he had working for him and a trusted friend. Surely Pavan had a right to confide his discussion with Jim Clark to his friend.

For a few years Kittu Kolluri had been the chief target of Jim Clark's weird phone calls. Clark called him KEE-TOO, when the correct pronunciation was KIT-TOO. Never mind. Whenever Clark was floating off the coast of Tahiti or Borneo and needed a bit of advice on the computer program he was writing for the yacht, he could not afford he called Kittu. Kittu could not understand why the chairman of a big American corporation would spend his time writing computer code. He understood very well, however, why a man writing computer code would call him for help.

Kittu was another fine example of the power of Indian society to ferret out its technical talent and catapult it in the direction of people like Clark, who knew how to use it. "There are these definite moments in my life," Kittu says. "When I know that things changed and I became an engineer." The first such moment was when his cousin from Bombay came one summer to visit his family in Hyderabad. Kittu was in the sixth grade, and his cousin was a pretty young woman. "She described this guy she had fallen in love with," recalls Kittu.

> She was completely in love with him because he was so smart. She talked about how she loved his *brain*. He went to an Indian Institute of Technology. That was the first time I ever heard of an IIT She spoke to me about him for two straight hours! I was captivated. Totally. I mean, what she was describing was a complete geek. She talked about how he had these twelve-inch spectacles and so on and so forth. He sounded like a pretty grotesque-looking guy when you thought about it. But she kept saying how brilliant he was. And he's all she talked about. And I fell in love with the image my cousin had of Mokund Thapa. I wanted to be like Mokund Thapa.

One evening the next year, when Kittu was in the seventh grade, he fought with his father—about what he does not recall. But he had gone off to a corner of the house and curled up to sleep. "Then my father comes over and is being very friendly. He is smiling. And I say, 'What the fuck is wrong with this guy?' An hour ago he was being an asshole! And he says, 'Swaroop—that was what I was called then—the principal just called and said they want to take your picture for the newspaper!'" In the general tests administered to Indian seventh-graders, Kittu had come in first in his region. His region contained eighty million people. "It was one of those moments," said Kittu. "When you say, 'Whoa! I knew I was good. But I didn't know I was *this* good.' After that it became a complete obsession for me. I was going to go to an IIT. My dad would come into my room at three in the morning, and I'd be studying! He would say, 'Swaroop, you must go to sleep, you know.'"

Kittu, like Pavan, left India the minute he graduated from his IIT. After the requisite two years inside some American graduate school, which the Indians treated as a weigh station en route to Silicon Valley, Kittu had landed his job at Silicon Graphics. Not long after that he met Clark. And not long after that he found himself a kind of professional observer of Clark's quest for the new new thing. Jim Clark's mind was Kittu's hobby; Kittu was fascinated that such a technically minded person could be so happy groping blindly toward big piles of money. "Jim Clark has a clarity of vision that is prompted by the purest form of greed," says Kittu. "Nothing clouds it."

Like the other young programmers in the ITV department, Kittu could have had himself a job at Netscape the day the company was founded simply by turning up at the front door. "I knew that I was making a mistake by not joining Jim at Netscape," he says. "So many times Jim has said, 'I told you so.' And I assumed he would say, 'I told you so,' again. But I didn't know how loudly he would say, 'I told you so.'" His failure to join Netscape was the biggest financial mistake Kittu hoped he would ever make. In December 1995 he remained a Silicon Graphics employee earning a salary of $89,000. Had he followed Clark into Netscape, he would have been worth $20 million.

Like Pavan Nigam—like pretty much every engineer at Silicon Graphics—Kittu saw a certain injustice in this. He viewed the computer engineers at Netscape as ever so slightly second-rate. Certainly, the best and the brightest had not left Silicon Graphics to join Clark. "Technically the Netscape browser was not much of an accomplishment at all," Kittu says. It did not belong on the same page with what he and Pavan and the others had achieved in Orlando. Kittu could rattle off all the technologies brought together to create the world's first interactive television: 3-D graphics, 2-D graphics, ATM, frequency modulation, IMP1, IMPEG2, switching, infrared, a blizzard of baffling terms that leaves the outsider with the clear opinion he does not want to know any more than he needs to. "We got all wrapped up in the technology," Kittu says. "We all thought, 'Dammit this technology is so *cool*. It must bring so much value to *someone*.'"

This puts a fine point on a painful truth: the purpose of that technology was *to make money*. The higher purpose of the interactive television was to facilitate the stupor of the guy on the couch with the beer in one hand and the remote control in the other—which is to say that it had no higher purpose. Its lack of any higher purpose made its ultimate failure even more absurd. "ITV was, from a technical standpoint, as challenging as putting a man on the moon," says Kittu, "and in the end, it was one great academic exercise. A waste of fucking time."

Netscape, on the other hand, was clearly not a waste of time. "The trick to Netscape was *markets*," says Kittu, "being at the right place at the right time. And that was all Jim Clark. If Jim Clark had not been there, Marc Andreessen and his friends would still be working for their Ph.D.'s at the University of Illinois." Thanks to Jim Clark the B team had got rich while the A team stayed middle class, at least in Kittu's view. Some engineers, especially the older ones, passed this off to the different "risk profile" of engineers who created new companies. The implication was that really brilliant engineers like Pavan and Kittu did not have the taste for risk required to take a flying leap into one of Jim Clark's fantasies.

Only now they did.

Clark was onto something when he went looking for Indians. It wasn't just that half his work had been done for him by the Indian government. It wasn't just that, next to the sifting mechanism through which Pavan and Kittu had passed, the Harvard admissions office was a kind, forgiving place. It was that any person with the brains to get into the IIT's *and* the gumption to get himself to the United States was capable of all manner of miracles. The Indian engineers had the lust for the kill that Clark loved. They were ferociously, recklessly competitive. Pavan and Kittu had finished in the top one-hundredth of one percent on the test taken by bright young Indians who probably were already in the top one-hundredth of one percent on the national brainpower scale. Yet about twice a week Pavan found a way to remind Kittu that he had finished 250 places behind him.

To Kittu the suggestion that he was too smart to take risks was "total bullshit." In the first place, how much risk was there in working for a Silicon Valley start-up? The worst thing that happened is that the start-up failed, and you went back to your old job and your $80,000 a year.

Silicon Graphics or any other big company would have hired them back the instant they applied. In the second place, his life had been nothing but risk: the risk of growing up in a Third World hellhole, the risk that he wouldn't get into a decent school that might catapult him out of the hellhole, the risk that he wouldn't find work in the United States, the risk that ITV, the highest-profile engineering project in Silicon Valley, would flop. So far as Kittu was concerned, he'd lived his life on a high wire without a safety net. Watching the B team of computer science whooping it up down the road after the Netscape public offering enraged him. "I'll tell you what I knew on the day Netscape went public," he says. "I knew two things. I knew my next company would be a start-up. And I knew that anything smaller than Netscape was unacceptable."

That day in December 1995, after Jim Clark showed him the Magic Diamond with Healthscape at the center, Pavan went back to his job at Silicon Graphics. He asked Kittu to take a walk with him. The two men spent several hours walking along the manicured lawns of Shoreline Boulevard, down by the marshy reaches of the Bay where they were less likely to be seen. Pavan told Kittu about the Magic Diamond. Kittu had only one clear thought about it: "No freaking way I was going to miss this one."

Of course, Pavan was not supposed to tell anyone about anything. When that afternoon he confessed to Clark that he'd spoken privately to Kittu, he also confessed his new problem. Tom Jermoluk (T. J.), the CEO of Silicon Graphics, had come to him and asked him to promise he would not steal any Silicon Graphics employees. T. J. had himself just decided not to jump to Clark's new venture. And so, strictly speaking, Pavan could not recruit Kittu without breaking his promise. But there was nothing other than the fear of Ed McCracken's lawyers to prevent Clark from calling Kittu on Pavan's behalf, just to get things rolling. And so Clark did. And so once again Kittu found himself the surprising recipient of a call from Jim Clark. Clark asked Kittu to stop by his house as soon as possible.

Kittu stopped by the next day. He'd already made up his mind, the instant Pavan told him about the Magic Diamond. So far as he was concerned, all that was left was to negotiate the number of stock options he would receive. Moreover, he was thrilled by the invitation to visit Clark at his home. "But you know something," he says, "I was not nervous at all. I could have gone to work *anywhere*. The fact that Jim Clark wanted me was enough. There's no way you can't follow Jim Clark." Like Pavan, Kittu had absorbed the essential lesson of interactive television: do what Clark did, not what he said to do. Kittu rolled into Clark's blond pebbled driveway and gazed up at the big house with the man-made hill at the back and the cardboard boxes in the guest bedroom and the old tuba beside them. There were about six shiny sports cars in the driveway; it could have passed for a small dealership. Clark ambled out of the house to greet him. He had his easy manner on.

Clark was fond of saying that "there's nothing that gets you interested in money like having some of it." Now that he had a billion dollars, his life had become a great deal more . . . financial. He truly loved money, money truly loved him, and he wanted all the people he liked to be a part of the new relationship. He had just himself reached the point where he associated the word "dollars" not with "millions" but with "billions." He wanted to help Kittu get over his old habit of thinking "thousands" and into the new one of thinking "millions." Soon enough he was telling Kittu his favorite parable of missed opportunity. He had bought his house with the blond pebbled drive right after Silicon Graphics went public, back in 1986. To pay for the house he had sold one million shares of Silicon Graphics stock at $3 a share. The stock was now at $30 a share. "You see that house," Clark said to Kittu, making the obvious calculation, "that's my $30 million house."

Kittu didn't miss a beat. He turned around and pointed to his dusty Toyota and said, "Jim, you see that car. I sold two thousand shares of Silicon graphics at $10 a share to buy that car. So that's my $60,000 Toyota Camry."

That day Kittu returned to SGI to give notice. He was willing to stick around a few weeks and help his managers smooth the transition. But already his managers were in a state of high paranoia: people had heard that Jim Clark had a new start-up and that he had spoken about it to Pavan. Kittu's manager accused him of plotting to steal other engineers. "And so," recalls Kittu, "I just said, 'Fuck you, I resign.'"

Pavan Nigam resigned from Silicon Graphics on a Friday afternoon in February 1996. He had no idea who might join him, aside from Kittu. He still suspected that *no one* would join and that he would become a Silicon Valley laughingstock. So far as he knew, the only people aware of what he was up to were him, Kittu, Clark, and a few of Clark's venture capitalists.

When he arrived home that evening, he found that several dozen people had faxed their résumés to his home machine. On Saturday morning his phone began to ring. It never stopped. The first callers were engineers Pavan knew from Silicon Graphics. Within a few hours the callers were complete strangers, who worked for companies Pavan had never heard of. By late afternoon the calls were coming thick and fast: the moment Pavan ended one conversation, the phone rang and he started all over again. All the callers wanted one thing: a job with Pavan's new company.

Soon enough it was clear to Pavan that he was in a buyer's market for engineering talent. He needed only a dozen or so extraordinarily talented people to get the company off the ground. Once he realized how many people wanted to work for him, his manner became noticeably more gruff. When he'd pick up the phone, he wouldn't even bother to say hello. He'd say, "Why are you calling me? What can you do for me?" By Sunday morning the engineers who had been unable to get through to Pavan on the phone started turning up at his front door. By Monday morning more than three hundred engineers had faxed résumés to his home machine, and countless others had phoned, to apply for a job with Healthscape. And none of them had the faintest idea what Healthscape was.

From this initial group of three hundred—a *far* bigger group stormed the gates later—Pavan culled his favorite Silicon Graphics engineers. After Kittu he picked Shankar. After Shankar he picked Motasim. After Motasim he selected Flavio. After Flavio he picked . . . well, you get the idea. Soon he had ten of the smartest engineers he knew, all of whom had built the world's first interactive television. Two were Italian, one was Chinese, most of the rest were Indian.

Pavan and Kittu and the others assembled on February 19, 1996, in a dinky office in downtown Palo Alto. It was a year or so after Hillary Clinton finally abandoned her hope of reforming the U.S. health care industry from the White House. Six Indians, two Italians, a Japanese, and a Belgian were going to do it from Northern California. Of course, none had the first clue what it was they were meant to be doing. "It was very, very fuzzy," says Motasim Najeeb. "We didn't have a single line of code. We had nothing, really. HMO. PPO. All these names!" "I was asking for a business plan," recalls Shankar Srinivasan. "And there wasn't one! Pavan's notion in general was just to get enough bright people and throw them at the problem, and something good will come out of it." As Kittu puts it, "No one knew a fucking thing about health care." The thought clearly pleased him.

On February 19, 1996, the ten young engineers came to work; on February 20 they flew to Boston to meet with Blue Cross/Blue Shield. Most of them had never heard of Blue Cross/Blue Shield. Here's how Shankar Srinivasan recalls his bizarre first brush with a tiny appendage of the U.S. health care industry: "The first day was for them to tell us what they did and what they needed. The second day was for us to tell them what we were going to build. In between the first day and the second day, we had to figure that out. We sat up all night reading all this literature about health care. We asked, 'What is the problem we are going to solve here?' All we had was Jim Clark's concept."

Pavan's engineers had no experience and no knowledge. But they had arrogance, ambition, and a blissful ignorance of the magnitude of what they were aiming to achieve. They had something else too: the faith that they could impose technology on others. In short, they behaved as people always have at the cutting edge of capitalism, with the conviction that they could remake the world in their image. They worked mad hours—many of them sent their families back to India. One morning at eight Clark showed up on his motorcycle to have a look around. He noticed Panos, a Greek engineer, tucked behind his computer work station. He said, "You're here early." Panos looked up and said, "I never left," and went back to work. "The passion, the fire was there," says Kittu. "There was a feeling that we were about to change the world. And we all now knew that was how you made money, by changing the world."

Theirs was a sunny aggression, propelled by Clark's will, his money, and his expectations. Any hope Pavan harbored that he might be permitted to fail quietly was quickly dispelled by a rearguard action of Clark's with the journalists who covered Silicon Valley. Although Pavan knew that Clark spent a surprising amount of his time on the phone with business journalists, he thought they had agreed that for the first six months, until they had something to show people, they wouldn't talk to the press. A couple of days after that conversation Pavan sat on the company toilet skimming the *Wall Street Journal* or *USA Today* or some other newspaper and saw a short article that began, "Jim Clark, founder of Silicon Graphics and Netscape announced today that he plans to remake the U.S. health care industry . . ."

The more interesting truth was that ten engineers in a small office in Palo Alto intended to remake the U.S. health care industry, with a bit of guidance from a doctor who had agreed to be their CEO only because he wanted to make partner at Kleiner Perkins, and an older man who was interested mainly in writing the code to computerize a yacht. And most of the engineers were not even citizens of the United States.


Stuart Liroff was a short, bearded American man with big, clean-shaven manner. Stuart was open, relaxed, friendly, large-spirited—and eager to be a part of the new new thing. He had joined Silicon Graphics back in 1990, and gone to work building interactive television in April 1995, after the Orlando trials but before the technology was unveiled in Japan. Several times Pavan hinted to Stuart that he thought Stuart was a cut above the average member of his team. Like a lot of other people, Stuart had been converted to entrepreneurship by the Netscape IPO. "That was the defining moment in all of our lives—'Ah shit, why didn't I do that?'" he says. "Every one of us had it." And so when Stuart saw a certain change come over Pavan, he asked Pavan if he had plans to leave Silicon Graphics and start a new company. Pavan became agitated and told Stuart, "I can't approach you about it, but there is nothing to stop you from calling me. Do you understand what I am telling you?" Stuart said he understood. And he did. The day Pavan announced his resignation Stuart faxed over a letter to Pavan's house. It sat in the stack along with the three hundred other faxes Pavan didn't read.

A few days later Stuart called Pavan and asked to talk. Pavan told him to wait two weeks and call back. Stuart waited two weeks and called again. Pavan failed to return his call. Stuart waited some more and then became irritated. "I called every day and I couldn't reach him," he says.

"I left message after message. Now I'm getting bitchy. Finally I just said, 'I'm going down there.'"

Stuart found out that Pavan had rented offices in downtown Palo Alto and drove over. "I walk in. And there are all these people I know. There's Motasim! There's Kittu! And Shankar!" Ten engineers were crammed into a bit less than two thousand square feet, beavering away on some mysterious new project. "I see Pavan," Stuart recalls, "and he says he never even saw my letter, he had so many letters." When Stuart asked Pavan what the hell he was up to, Pavan drew a picture of the Magic Diamond. All the engineers loved the Magic Diamond, which Stuart remembers as "a picture with Jim Clark at the center of 15 percent of the U.S. economy." It was like one of those cave paintings at Altamira, used by the hunter to secure his prey in advance, simply by depicting it on the wall. The engineers were hexing their prey.

Anyway, once he caught the drift, Stuart was even more eager to be a part of the new company. He asked Pavan for a job. "And Pavan says, 'I want to know what you're going to do for me?'" At which point Stuart did a kind of double take: *Pavan, it's me, Stuart.* "In the end I just sort of made something up." Stuart knew that Pavan was an engineer's engineer. The most gifted people wanted to work for Pavan because he didn't waste time on the details. "He focuses on engineering the design of the product," Stuart notes. "He says, 'Screw the details . . . for the moment.' It's aggressive, but it's not stupid." Stuart realized Pavan wasn't thinking about how to test the product, how to record the work. "He assumed other people would take care of that stuff. I said I was other people. And he said it sounded good."

And then Pavan, busy trying to make himself an expert on the U.S. health care system, promptly forgot. "So two days later," recalls Stuart, "I drove up there *again* and ambushed Pavan. We went over to a coffee shop and in a few minutes figured out my salary and stock options. That's how I got my job at Healthscape."

It wasn't quite as simple as that. Pavan explained to Stuart that the usual American standards of diligence no longer applied. To work for Healthscape meant more or less abandoning his private life. Stuart took the job anyway. As he wrote to me later,

The potential for making a lot of money was always there, implicitly. But when Pavan and Jim negotiated my compensation the only explicit articulation of it was a 35% pay cut! The rest was funny money, in the way of stock options, and I had absolutely no frame of reference to base the value of these options. So my wife and I made the decision to quit SGI and join Healthscape based on my belief that P, J, and KP [Pavan Nigam, Jim Clark, and Kleiner Perkins] were going to do something great and I was just going to be a part of it. She asked me how much I could make and I remember saying something about "never having to work again." I remember telling someone, rationalizing why I had just quit SGI, "'Never in my life will I find all of these stars lined up at the same time: P [Pavan], J [Clark], KP [Kleiner Perkins], the diamond with the H in the middle."

Stuart Liroff was the eleventh person, and the tenth engineer, and the second native-born American, to come to work for the new company. He joined at the end of February 1996. He was given a desk in the canteen bordered by the refrigerator, the sink, and the fax machine. He worked one hundred and twenty hours a week—so many hours that the notion of "work" and "home" was absurd. Life *was* work—or at least being in the office. "Pavan in his inimitable wisdom grabbed a date out of the air and said, 'We can deliver a product on October 1, 1996." And no one had a *clue* what the product was. All we knew is that it had to be a really huge piece of software—so that it would look right in the middle of this huge diamond."

In spite of the obvious stress that came with his new situation Stuart was delighted. "It was three am," he recalls. "I'm sitting there drinking espresso, listening to music, and writing up some notes about the software and . . . I could never explain this to anyone . . . not even my wife . . . I was *so* happy. I just laughed to myself."

That's how they all felt that first nine months, as they rushed to complete their first piece of software, for Blue Cross/Blue Shield. They felt they were doing something important. Blue Cross/Blue Shield was just the initial foray; soon they would sit in the middle of the Magic Diamond. Other engineers begged to join them! Journalists came from afar to interview them! Jim Clark rode into their lobby on his motorcycle! Before long *Fortune* magazine was ready to go to press with the first article on the company—before Healthscape was even really a company!

Just then the engineers were told that some enterprising person, on the heels of Netscape, had bought the rights to all sorts of names ending with "-scape,' including "Healthscape," and wanted a fortune for its use. The engineers already had their logo, a big blue sign with "Health" in the middle. So they sat around thinking up names starting with Health. Health Now. Health-O. Health-a-Thon. In the end Healthscape became Healtheon. And they were on their way.

In short, Clark's latest little act of nerve triggered such a violent wave of talent and money to come washing his way that within a few months a lot of serious people were saying things like "Health care's the biggest market, but Jim Clark already controls that." But by then Clark was fully aware that all he had to do was announce to a few journalists that he intended to insert himself in the middle of the world's largest industry, and all sorts of serious people were off and running down his long, dark tunnel.

That's where his job ended, so far as Clark was concerned. After he'd drawn his little diagram of the world's largest market with himself in the middle, he was finished. Other people could take care of the messy details of turning Healtheon into a giant corporation. That's what he always said just after he had disgorged the new new thing, and the new new thing became, simply, the new thing. He was not finished, however. The one hard rule in Jim Clark's life was that he must always pursue the new new thing. Three multibillion-dollar companies was not enough for one lifetime. Once when I'd asked him how he planned to convert his wealth to leisure, he said, "You've got to figure out something that is out of the path of Microsoft. You can forget building a big software business. If it is going to be big and it is software, then it will be controlled by Microsoft." Another morning he went off on an old-fashioned tear the point of which was that Healtheon would prove that he had nothing more to prove. "They can say that Silicon Graphics and Netscape was just luck, but when I do it again, and Healtheon will do it, they can't say it was just luck," he said. "I don't have to do it again." Not long after that he said, "But it would be something to do a fourth, wouldn't it?"

Well before Healtheon became a success, he was groping. He programmed his boat and he groped. Each time was harder than the time before because each new idea had to be bigger than the one before. Netscape had been bigger than Silicon Graphics; Healtheon he felt sure would be even bigger than Netscape. What was bigger than Healtheon? "I could always make fifty million dollars," he explained to me once. "But who needs that?" He didn't have time to create companies that were worth only fifty million dollars. Fifty million dollars didn't count. Hell, his boat had cost fifty million dollars, when you added in the tax bill. When he groped, he groped big. He was a multibillion-dollar corporation perpetually waiting to happen.

He was also a rare case of a man with the Chinese curse: he had gotten what he wished for. He was treated better, and paid more, than anyone else in the Valley. He owned three times more shares in anything he dreamed up than anyone else, and other people did most of the work. And now—this was the curse—he couldn't stop. Even if he wanted to, which, occasionally, he claimed he did, he couldn't stop trying to force the hand of the future. He was doomed to be forever searching for the new new thing. If nothing else, he now had an audience to play to. It was as if he had sold ten thousand tickets to a one-man show and now found himself standing on a stage, wondering how to keep the people in their seats. Venture capitalists lingered at his feet like Labrador retrievers watching their masters dine. Bright young people streamed out of Netscape and Silicon Graphics and a lot of other companies, begging for Clark's help. Clark's enthusiasm for his calling was almost viral. Young people didn't need his money—they could get money from venture capitalists. They needed his imprimatur on their new ideas. Some of them didn't even have an idea, just an idea that they might like to have an idea. All of these budding entrepreneurs wanted to be around Clark in the same way normal people wanted to be around at sunrise, just to see where the light came from. They wanted to see Clark stand up and say, "Behold, the new new thing."

The whole situation was preposterous, or would have been at any other time and any other place. But, as Clark himself realized, a number of things had changed that made his approach to business, and to life, viable.

The first and most obvious change was the miracle in the U.S. stock market. From the launching of Netscape to the launching of *Hyperion* the Dow Jones industrial average ran up more than 5,000 points. More

to the point, the Nasdaq stock exchange, which listed most new technology companies, quadrupled. The market paid people a great deal of
money for technology companies that made only losses. The American
public decided that it was willing to take a flying leap into the future,
which is to say it was willing to take a flying leap on whatever Jim Clark,
and entrepreneurs like him, were willing to take a flying leap on, at ten
times the price.

The second thing pushing Clark on was the nature of the software
business. Netscape and the companies that followed it were in important ways different from Silicon Graphics. The most important difference, at least from the financial point of view of those who dreamed up
the companies, was that they cost almost nothing to start. All you needed was an idea, some excellent engineering talent, and a pair of big brass
balls to execute that idea. You didn't need to raise millions to build your
product and in the process whittle your stake down to almost nothing.
You found the concept, you wrote the software to exploit the concept,
you sold the company to the public.

All of this caused, and was in turn caused by, a subtle but important
shift in the Silicon Valley value system. And that was the last reason
Jim Clark was the man of this particular moment. "Silicon Valley has
more in common with Hollywood than it does with Detroit," says Vern
Anderson, the first CEO of Silicon Graphics and thus the first captain
of the first ship built by Jim Clark. "The venture capitalists are the studios. The managers are the directors. The ordinary engineers are the
writers. And the entrepreneurs are the stars." What happened in Silicon
Valley is a lot like what happened in Hollywood once the studios lost
their clout. The stars seized power. And once they'd seized power they
raised their price and demanded the right to direct their own pictures.
And very great stars like Jim Clark cut deals worthy of Marlon Brando.
They showed up on the set for a few days then strolled away with half
the budget.

And so, even after he'd drawn the Magic Diamond, Clark groped on.
For a couple of months during the summer of 1998, there was a fellow
named Greg Kovacs, whom Clark had somehow gotten to know at the
Center for Integrated Systems at Stanford University. Clark had walked
into Kovacs's lab, peered into a microscope, and found himself staring
at what appeared to be an ordinary computer chip. The chip began to

pulse, as if it had a heartbeat. Kovacs had grafted the cells from the heart of a chicken onto a chip. The egg cartons were piled up behind Kovacs's door, as if to prove it. The electrical impulses of the cell "spoke" to the chip. The chip was alive!

For maybe eight weeks the idea of a living computer chip had Clark's mind racing down its long, dark tunnel. Kovacs already had a deal with the Defense Department, which thought the chip might come in handy in biological wars. Clark thought about other applications. Actually, he thought back to his graduate work at the University of Utah, where he had become fascinated with the idea of recording the electrical impulses in the brain and creating a kind of library of thoughts and sensations. If you could graft a cell onto a chip you could graft a chip onto a cell. "I'm sure in some way the neurosystem will one day be integrated with the computer," said Clark. "Wouldn't it be great if you could neurally integrate, say, the number 500342?" Chips could be planted inside the human body. Clark went to his friend John Hennessey, the dean of electrical engineering at Stanford, and offered to pay for a new field of study, which he wanted to call biocomputing.

Then one day Greg Kovacs disappeared, and Clark never mentioned him again. In place of Kovacs came a steady stream of young people, toting their inventions and ideas. There was FM and AM radio on the Web. There was local news on the Web. There were the countless fruits of the Human Genome Project. It wasn't uncommon to find Jim Clark talking to someone with a glass of wine in one hand and a petri dish in the other. They came to his house. They came to his office. But if they were smart they came to the boat. The boat was where all serious gestation occurred. The boat was where he kept his mind alive to the possibilities.

*Hyperion* was not merely a technologist's utopia or a budding new new thing. It was both of those things. It was also a place where Clark could remain apart from the environment he was continually reinventing. He could never become one of those ordinary people—a venture capitalist or a chief executive or a member of a museum board or anything else that required him to behave in the way important businessmen are meant to behave. Circumstance had made him an insider, but temperament kept him forever an outsider. He was like the man who threw the world's biggest bash and failed to show up for it.  This outsidderliness was what gave him his unusual view of the world. His talent for groping the future was generally viewed as a supernatural gift, but it was a matter as much of his limitations as of his strengths. He could see human society in ways that most businessmen could not, because he was not very much a part of it. And consciously or not, by retiring to his floating island, he preserved this precious limitation.

The next time he and some new technology entered the larger society, he would be on his boat. He did not walk into other people's lives; he sailed into them.

## The Home of the Future?

Ａnd so to the boat we went, at least until the time came for the new new thing. What links Clark maintained from there to the world outside ran through twenty-five computers manufactured by Silicon Graphics and an Internet browser created by Netscape. "There is nothing more satisfying to me," he said, "than to create a complete self-contained world when a computer is controlling it." It took a while before anyone saw the full implications of that statement, especially for the less technical people who lived in that self-contained world. The first inkling came just after the tumultuous trial in the North Sea.

By the end of December 1998 the damage caused to *Hyperion* during its trial in the North Sea had been repaired, and the crew and the computer programmers moved on board and prepared for the Atlantic crossing. Soon enough it became clear to them that if you lived on board you either programmed the computer or were programmed by it. Either you were Steve and Lance and Tim, or you were not.

Steve and Lance and Tim each had, at one time or another, worked for Silicon Graphics; they had quit whatever they were doing to be involved in whatever Jim Clark was up to. Clark called this new enterprise Seascape. By the time of the sea trials the Seascape programmers had spent more than two years cobbling together the code required to control a sailboat. Right from the start they had assumed that Clark wouldn't bother to yoke his yacht to a computer unless there was money to be made from it. They had no real reason to think this except that Clark was incapable of creating new technology without finding a way to make money from it. Any one of them could easily have found jobs, and stock options, with Yahoo or Cisco or even Microsoft. Yet they preferred to toil in relative commercial obscurity, building a system that any intelligent, uninformed person—that is, anyone who did not know Clark—would view as a rich man's folly. To them Clark's commercial life was a magic act.

Oddly enough, by December 1998, and before the software even had been tested, the programmers' instincts were looking less like blind faith and more like prescience. One of Clark's business ideas had them excited: the boat's software could be adapted to the home. The American Home of the Future, it went without saying, would be controlled and monitored by a computer. The computer would permit the owner to enter into a new, fantastic relationship with his dwelling. Indeed, one way of viewing *Hyperion* was as a test of the technology. Clark had served up his sailboat's captain and six-person crew as guinea pigs: they would see how life would be in a computerized home. By the end of 1998 Steve Hague, whom Clark had designated Seascape's programmer in chief, was trading e-mails with corporate executives and venture capitalists who might become involved, then passing on the results of his discussions, also via e-mail, to Lance and Tim. The general idea was to sell their software first to rich technophiles and then, gradually, infiltrate the minds of the middle-class owners of suburban tract houses. In one of his messages written about the time *Hyperion* left its dock, Steve informed his fellow programmers of a big-time CEO who might want to help create, as Steve put it, "a package which he can sell as part of a big custom installation to the Larry Ellisons of the world [i.e., rich technologists]. Ultimately I think this technology could be sold as more of a standard product, maybe via franchises. One interesting example was big vacation homes in Hawaii where the owners would like to log in to the house over the web and see if the pool's warm and the cleaners are not fucking in the master bed."

No doubt the Home of the Future was only one of several possible uses Clark would find for their work. That was Clark's job—to imagine a future for their software. *How* he did this Lance and Tim and Steve could not have cared less. Like a lot of the smart engineers in Silicon Valley, they had given up trying to figure out how Clark's mind worked.

And so they wrote the code to control Clark's boat and waited to find out what Clark's next trick might be. Mainly, they tried to ensure that the first Home of the Future did not wind up on the ocean floor. They set up their machines on a long grade school cafeteria table in *Hyperion*'s main salon. Everyone else working on the boat—and along with the eight full-time crew members there were still dozens of boat-yard workers—swirled around them. In context the computer programmers appeared idle. They sat quietly, stared into their screens and sipped cappuccinos. And yet they were by far the most important people on board *Hyperion*.

Steve Hague was the project manager, which is to say that he was supposed to stitch the patches of computer code written by different people at a furious speed into a perfect, seamless quilt. Many of the biggest patches were written by Clark himself, of course. This put Steve in the delicate position of supervising his boss. He acquired, as a result, a superhuman ability to sit still and be hollered at. His life had prepared him for the job. Raised in a working-class family in Leeds, a dreary city in the north of England, he had emerged with one of those wry, self-effacing personalities that have existed in England at least since Shakespeare wrote his comic relief. Steve was Rosencrantz and Guildenstern and Bardolph and Pistol rolled into one. When he claimed that his childhood had been so dull that he didn't recall anything of it except that "a cat died once," he was so perfectly droll that you didn't stop and think about what that meant.

Although Steve's skill with computers had been his ticket out of Leeds to Silicon Valley, he regarded the machine as, at best, an unsteady ally: it was always laying traps for the programmer. He thought of the computer as a less than straightforward tool for controlling and manipulating the world around it, like a shovel with a loose blade. He had little patience for the mystical, spiritual approach of computer programming. That is to say, his patience often was tried by Lance.

Lance was Lance Welsh, who, in the days leading up to the ocean crossing, sat beside Steve at the long cafeteria table in the boat's main living room. Together with Steve and Jim Clark, he wrote the parts of the computer program you could see and touch. Typically when Lance set out to write a piece of code, he started with a complicated solution and made it even more complicated. Sometimes it worked, at other times it didn't, but in every case no one else could figure out how Lance did what he had done. Lance was to computer programming what Joyce was to literature, possibly profound but also baffling. The trouble was that clarity and simplicity were more important in computer language than in human language. A programmer brought in from the outside to fix a bug in the code needed to determine quickly how it worked. With Lance's code this was impossible. When something went wrong in it, which it often did, there were only two things that could be done. Either Lance had to go in and fix it himself, or someone had to start from the beginning and rewrite the program.

Lance was, in a word, a romantic. The nostalgia the romantic feels for the past Lance felt for the code he had written. For instance, editing computer code, like editing written English, often requires the programmer to remove extraneous lines. Lance refused to do this. Instead, he instructed the computer to preserve his old lines of code. When he came upon a passage that needed deleting, he wrote,

```
#ifdef

—

(Lance's old code)

—

#endif
```

The computer took this to mean: ignore the old lines of code, but preserve them. In this way a lot of useless code written by Lance was entombed in *Hyperion*'s computers. This attempt at preservation was only mildly irritating to Steve; it drove Clark wild. Whenever Clark ran across one of these tiny electronic mummies, he'd redden and squinch up like the mouth of Mount Etna before an eruption. Then he set about deleting everything Lance had done. Lance often became upset and complained to Steve that "Jim has no feeling for the code."

It didn't help Lance's political situation that he was handsome—and not just a little handsome. He was Last of the Mohicans handsome, all long dark hair and smoky features. Those assigned to open up Lance's code and find a bug often assumed that Lance, at that very tedious moment, was out somewhere being chased by packs of randy women. Lance had the aura of a man who spent a lot of time being chased by packs of randy women. "Lance has some strange effect on females," Steve explained. "Since I started on this project I've had more of my female friends ask me whether he was married than asked me whether Jim was married." Every man who worked with Lance suspected that there must be some connection between his excessively romantic attitude toward computer programming and his appeal to women. Lance might not be proof that a male computer programmer, to be desirable to women, had to completely overhaul his attitude toward his machine. But he was terrifyingly suggestive evidence.

Tim Powell was the third man on the *Hyperion* job. He was built like a football tackle and thought of himself as the programming equivalent of one. If you asked him which part of the software he was responsible for, Tim would look away and blush. If you pressed the point, he would say, "If I do my job well, you'll never know about it." Possibly he had seen enough of the ongoing struggle between Jim and Steve and Lance to know he wanted no part of it. In any event, Tim lay low and worked hard and said little. Tim was the only reason I had to suspect that *Hyperion* would not wind up on the bottom of the ocean floor.

Steve and Lance and Tim and Jim; Jim and Tim and Lance and Steve. They had spent two years bouncing back and forth between Wolter Huisman's boatyard and the single, stultifying room on top of a Jenny Craig weight loss center. Now on a dock outside of Amsterdam, they sat center stage. With every stroke of their keyboards they hacked a path through the forest that others would be required to follow. The computer programmer creates the only path available to the computer user; the effect of his decisions on others is masked by their abstraction. When you use Microsoft Word, for example, you enter a tiny mental space created by thousands of Microsoft programmers. In the case of software that controls the physical world, rather than merely a symbolic world, this path is less trivial. The programmers decided the steps everyone on board *Hyperion* would need to take to do everything from dimming the lights to raising the sails. In a thousand subtle and unsubtle ways they were reinventing the experience of living on board a boat.

This late afternoon in December 1998 was one of the last the three young programmers had before *Hyperion* left its dock and headed out across the Atlantic. None of the young men spoke. Presumably each was absorbed in his own little chain of logic, though you could never be sure. Then all hell broke loose.

It began with a problem, posed by Lance's computer. Somewhere on the boat an alarm went off, and the words "Error Message" appeared on Lance's screen. Lance shook his dark mane, sipped his cappuccino, and pretended not to notice. The boat was equipped with more than three thousand alarms. All were capable, in theory, of shouting insults at the captain, but normally they just made an annoying, high-pitched beep-beep-beep sound. At this stage of the work alarms rang constantly; you could hardly grab a beer from the fridge without triggering a red alert. Lance pointed to the message on his screen and said, "The computer has no sense of proportion. It doesn't know whether what happened is serious or trivial. You get used to ignoring these alarm messages."

*"Hey! Hey! Hey! Hey! Hey! Hey! Hey!"*

This time the alarm came from a human being. Screams. They came from the galley.

*"Hey! Hey! Hey! Hey! Hey! . . ."* It was a high-pitched protest. And it was followed immediately by the sound of dishes crashing onto the floor.

The computer programmers swiveled in their chairs. Before them unfolded a puzzling scene. A thick slice out of the middle of the table that separated the galley from the lower salon rose up into the air, as if by magic. A partition had been built into the table between the galley and the rest of the boat; like everything else on the boat, it was automated. Tina, *Hyperion*'s chef, was throwing her slight frame across the rising slice of wood, in a futile bid to hold it in place. The dishes stacked on the table flew in eight directions. The whole thing was as inevitable as an execution. Steve and Lance and Tim watched as the partition rose and the dishes crashed and the cook in the galley slowly vanished. As she disappeared behind the partition, Tina's screams become muffled, then silent.

"What the hell caused that?" asked Steve.

"I didn't do anything," said Tim.

"Who hit what?" asked Steve.

"I was working on the DVD player just before it happened," says Lance. "Maybe that did it."

The three young men in T-shirts and blue jeans shared a chuckle. The DVD player was *Hyperion*'s movie system. Like everything else on board, it was controlled through the computers. In suggesting that the computer code for the movies caused Tina's table to rise up into the ceiling and send dishes flying, Lance had made a joke. Computer humor.

They quickly forgot the incident. They became lost once again in their sea blue screens. Now, as they typed, they also spoke. "The great thing about this project," said Tim, "is that it's software that talks to physical things rather than software that just talks to other software. You can *see* the effect of what you are doing." Lance disagreed. He thought Tim's need to *see* his work manifested in the physical world outside the computer betrayed a weakness of spirit. "Real nerds," Lance said, "get just as excited when they're talking to other software."

"Jim doesn't," said Steve.

"Jim is juiced about other things," said Lance. "He can now be master of his own domain by virtue of his expertise in computers. He can kick back and enjoy his Burgundy while the computer controls the wind and the sails."

"You'd like it too," said Steve.

"I'm embarrassed to admit it," said Lance "It juices me too. But— here's the thing—Jim doesn't give a shit about the technology."

Steve looked up, dubious.

"No really," said Lance, "in the beginning I remember I asked Jim about doing all the screens in 3-D. He said, 'Fuck 3-D.' I said, 'Jim, you *invented* 3-D.'"

"*Hey! Hey! Hey! Hey! Hey! . . .*"

This time Tina's screams came more shrilly. Down in the galley Tina's table was now falling as mysteriously as it had risen. As it did this, it created something like a B-movie earthquake effect, sucking anything that wasn't nailed down into its new fissure. Tina fought to rescue a towel from vanishing into the inner earth.

The three programmers watched her struggle, a bit more contemplatively, then returned to their screens. They were thinking. Computer thoughts. Finally Steve rose, very casually, and walked down three steps into the lower salon and down another three steps into the galley. He lingered beside the light switch that Jim Clark often used to illustrate the main point about the marvelous flexibility of computers. At the end of a long day of programming, with a glass of fine Burgundy in his hand, Clark would flick the light switch on and off and say, "This switch sends a signal to the computer to turn the lights on and off. But I could just as easily program this switch to turn the engine on, or to raise the sails. If I wanted to control the boat from right here, I could."

Steve now stood facing one of the boat's twenty-five computer screens. The ubiquitous flat-panel displays gave the yacht the feel of the ATM wing of a shiny new bank. Everywhere you turned, another ATM machine! Steve poked at the kitchen screen delicately, like a new account holder making his first withdrawal, and then, apparently satisfied, returned to the main salon and his seat in front of his computer. He punched a few more keys. Then he shouted, almost triumphantly, "Lance that was you who caused that problem!"

Lance looked up; Tim trotted around to their side of the cafeteria table. On Steve's sea blue computer screen a single line of code flashed. It would have been perfectly meaningless to everyone else on the boat, but to these three young men it was an important message. It said,

HYP 24 Request PLC Write P24-Control S430303-10 1:(0): null

HYP 24 referred to the twenty-fourth computer in the long row of Silicon Graphics machines down below. HYP 24 also happened to be the machine on which Lance was working.

The rest of the line consisted of a command issued by computer number 24 to another, lower-level computer, called a PLC, that controlled the sensor that caused Tina's table to rise and fall. That was one way to understand *Hyperion*: as a network of sensors that spoke to each other. Someone had pressed a button that sent an electrical signal along the wires to the twenty-fourth computer, which had generated an electrical signal that ran back up to Tina's table. Whatever Lance had been doing to the movie system appeared to be the culprit. While obviously not critical in itself—the boat could sail without movies—the message suggested a deeper and more troubling problem. The problem was: Why had Lance's computer issued this command? And if Lance could hit a button and send Tina's table into the ceiling, what else might Lance be able to do to the boat simply by hitting a button?

No one dared say this, however. All operated on the assumption that the computers inevitably would come through in the clutch.

"What's going on with the partition?" Tina asked. A sign on the wall of her galley hinted at her exasperation with the Home of the Future. It read "Smart People Spend Hours Learning to Use New Technology. Smarter People Find Ways to Weasel Out of It."

The three young men remained lost in their computer thoughts. They were all nice young men. They did not wish Tina harm. But the only way they knew to help was through their machines. They failed to respond to the cry from below.

"I don't know," said Tina. "Maybe I'm just along for the ride here."

The three young men dithered over a single computer until a rude, new clumping sound interrupted their meditations. Allan Prior was making his way down the stairs to see what on earth the shouting was about. The captain knew just enough to be worried. He said, "I heard 'Lance' and 'problem' in the same sentence."

God Mode

Allan Prior was a sailor's sailor, if such a thing can be said to exist on a 157-foot yacht decorated with thirty million dollars worth of French Impressionist paintings and run by a computer. He had finished the Whitbread around-the-world sailboat race three times, and had won it once. The Whitbread race is one of those rites of passage, like swimming the English Channel or eating one hundred and twenty cream donuts at a sitting, that indicate a man's willingness to suffer for his art. Back in New Zealand, where Allan grew up, the Whitbread race is a national obsession. In the late 1970s a psychiatrist at the University of Auckland made a study of the strange desire of young New Zealand men to leap into small boats with seven friends, a few sacks of powdered food, and a commitment not to bathe or shave or wipe or sleep for six weeks at a stretch. The psychiatrist evidently decided that the thing had to be seen to be believed, and so made a documentary film of his study. He called his film *No Use Calling Home to Mum*.

When *No Use Calling Home to Mum* made its debut on New Zealand television, the station's switchboard received so many protests that they never again aired the film. To this day, if you want to watch it, you have to purchase a samizdat copy for five hundred dollars. *No Use Calling Home to Mum* was distinguished from other disturbing television programs by its absolute lack of the usual offensive material. The film contained no sex, no nudity, no blasphemy. It advanced no political or religious heresy. It was perhaps the only film ever made to give offense solely through its main characters' grotesque violations of ordinary standards of personal cleanliness. For thirty days at a stretch the only swipes the young New Zealand sailors made at personal hygiene were from a box of Handi Wipes. When those thirty days were distilled down to an hour and a half of television, the brave young sailors of New Zealand turned their nation's stomach.

Allan Prior had been one of those brave young sailors. The idea of it still pleased him. He was now in his midforties but an odd smile still played across his face whenever he recalled the nauseating details of his youth. He was, in many ways, still living the life of a Whitbread around-the-world sailor. He rarely bathed. He never changed. He attacked his food with an artless violence that impressed his ship mates so deeply that they would relive their last meal with him in the way people do who have just witnessed a traffic accident together. Once, during dinner, the crew members had watched their new captain reach up into his wiry salt-and-pepper hair, pluck loose some strange particle, and eat it. He had made a deep impression on them. However damning *No Use Calling Home to Mum* might have been, it clearly did not begin to explore their captain's ability to do things that, if captured on film and broadcast on television, might inspire large numbers of people to call in to complain.

Still, Allan enjoyed a serious reputation in sailing circles. He was, in fact, a gifted sailor. He had instincts and experience no computer could match—at least not yet. He was Kasparov in the early days of fighting Deep Blue. At least one of the crew members of *Hyperion* referred to him without irony as the Legend.

Allan had been slow to assimilate the computer. In his mind's eye, when Allan envisioned a sailboat, he still saw a shell outfitted with a sail and eight Kiwis with skin like leather and no real conviction about personal hygiene. A computer had no place in this picture. In the beginning he'd treated the new technology as a stowaway. "I think he hated us," Steve says. But over time the programmers, with the owner behind them, came to terms with the captain, or felt they had. "Allan has in a sense been broken," Lance says. "He's seen what a disastrous state the software was in. And can be in. And so when it does work, even a little, he's happy!"

That was debatable. Over the past year and a half, as the boat was being built, Allan had developed a hard crust of cynicism about the boys from Silicon Valley. When Jim Clark was around, he did a fair job of disguising his true feelings. But when Clark was nowhere in sight Allan did not deny himself his bit of fun at the expense of the technogeeks hired by Clark to turn his boat into a computer. He'd creep up behind them as they hunched over their terminals and whisper little menacing thoughts into their delicate ears. "During the America's Cup trials," he'd say, "we had a separate boat for the computer room—twelve computer nerds throwing up on their keyboards. They were supposed to tell us how we could go faster." He'd pause for effect. "But it's a bit of a problem doing anything on a computer when you get the diced carrot stuck behind the 'e' key."

It didn't take a psychiatrist to see that Allan would have been just as happy setting off in one of those wooden boats built by Wolter's grandfather. Happier, probably. Then, at least, he would not have to pretend to be interested in the endless series of malfunctions brought on board his ship by Clark's twenty-four computers.

This raised the obvious question: Why take the job at all? Allan Prior took the job as captain of Jim Clark's boat for the same reason pretty much everyone else took the jobs Clark offered them. He thought Clark would make him rich. Clark offered 12,500 stock options in Healthscape, the company born from the Magic Diamond, with the promise of more to come. If Healthscape panned out the way Clark had said it would, Allan would make a million dollars. Maybe more. Allan had cut the deal cut by every captain of one of Clark's new enterprises: endure the humiliation of not fully understanding your job, and you might never need to work again.

By the time Allan arrived beside the computer programmers' table, a small crowd had gathered around to see what caused the commotion in the galley. No one was sure exactly what had happened, other than that Tina's table kept vanishing into the ceiling, and that it had been told to vanish by the computer. This sort of confusion was considered normal by a computer programmer, especially by a programmer of Clark's new sailboat. First you told the machine what to do, then the machine invariably failed to do exactly what you told it to do, and then you spent days trying to figure out why it had refused. This last stage was known as debugging, a word that entered the language back in the early 1960s when some programmers who were having trouble with their computer found that a large moth had landed inside it and died. In the past several months whenever Allan had asked Steve Hague how much longer it would take before he, Allan, didn't need to worry about the computer, Steve would say, "We're seeing improvement, but the boat still has bugs." Allan did not find this sort of talk reassuring.

At length Steve told Allan that he had an idea. He hadn't found the bug. But at least he knew where to look for it. Somehow the computer had been given the signal that someone wanted to watch a movie. It had responded by sealing the kitchen off from the rest of the boat. The instruction "I want to watch a movie" was therefore obviously tied to the instruction "close all the doors and windows." Lance reminded Steve that at the moment Tina's table vanished into the ceiling he was working on the boat's  movie system.

Allan hovered behind the programmers' table. His boat was about to cross the Atlantic Ocean, and the DVD player was throwing the boat's new lords and masters into a tizzy. The captain was meant to be up on the deck bossing people around, not down below being mystified. He leaned in and posed an obvious question. "It couldn't happen that you'd press the button for the hot water, and the mainsail would go up?" he asked.

"Oh, no, no, no," said Lance. "It's just that this part of the code hasn't been tested."

"Yes," said Allan, "well, we need to make sure that everything is tested."

Allan was inching up to the question that he really wanted to ask. "So in the guest cabin," he finally said, "you can show the passengers the screen, but they can't do anything on it, right?"

It took a moment for Steve to realize what Allan had asked. He had asked: Do I alone control this boat? It was not a bad question. Everything on the boat could be controlled, at least in theory, from any

of the twenty-five flat-panel displays. Allan quite reasonably had wondered: What was to prevent a guest from punching a few buttons and,
say, running the boat onto a reef? He was picturing some Silicon Valley
nerd genius who'd never been on a boat reeling into his bedroom after
putting away a couple of bottles of Jim Clark's fine wine and taking
charge.

"No," said Steve, "we've built in different levels of access." Actually,
the programmers had created four levels of access to the computer system. The lowliest deckhand was permitted what they called level-one
access. Level-one access allowed the holder to turn off the deck lights,
for instance. The highest level was formally called level-four access, and
informally known by the programmers as "God Mode." God Mode
enabled the user to control the entire boat from any one computer
screen. The good news, for Allan, was that only a few people had been
given passwords for God Mode: Allan, Simon, the programmers, and
Clark. The bad news was that the secret passwords had leaked not only
to the entire crew but also to the Dutch boatyard workers. Allan did-
n't want to hear any more about God Mode.

"We shut down three-quarters of the features in the guest cabin," said
Steve. "The rationale is you don't want some guests waking up in the
middle of the night, seeing some alarm going off, and thinking that the
ship is sinking, when all it is is a refrigerator stopped running."

Allan grunted what sounded like his approval.

Steve returned to the task at hand, and pulled up on his screen the
code that controlled the movies. Lance had written it—the audiovisu-
al system was really the last piece of code written by Lance that had
not been rewritten by someone else, usually Clark. Sure enough, the
code took a typically unorthodox, Lance-like approach. When you
punched the button for "Movies" on the touch screen, the computer
instructed *Hyperion* to reconfigure itself for your viewing pleasure. The
boat came alive with hums and whirs. The big screen in the main salon
rose, the lights in the neighboring rooms dimmed, the shutters over the
portholes shut, and the various openings leading out of the main salon
into the galley below and the bridge above closed. When the boat's
computers were finished, it was just you, your movie, silence, and darkness.

"That's cool," someone said. "It's like a James Bond movie."

Lance smiled. It was.

"Maybe if you're James Bond it's cool," said Steve.

A bright line ran through the programmers' world, and it divided the air between Lance and Steve. On one side of the line were the aesthetes who took pleasure in the computer's complexity, and spent a great deal of time writing deliciously elaborate programs that caused others to exclaim "cool!" when they saw it but often had no economic purpose. On the other side of the line were the utilitarians. They were interested only in the computer's crude and brutish ability to impose its will on the world around it. Lance was in love with the computer's beauty, Steve with its power.

Allan did not recognize this distinction. He simply thought of the young men from Silicon Valley as geeks who didn't belong on his boat. His strategy was to preserve at least the illusion, if not the fact, of command. "You tell us when we can watch a movie," he said, sternly. "And we'll keep an eye out for anything that moves." For good measure he tossed a bit of technical criticism on top of the disdain. "I've been here a long time," he said, "and I still don't know where everything is. The dimmers for the lights—where the hell are they? Are they a computer application? Or are they on a wall?"

Then he left. And for some inexplicable reason everyone else decided the problem was more or less solved, which it wasn't. Tina glared at the programmers and said, "If I am at the mercy of this computer, I'll be a paranoid cook." She returned to the galley.

A fog rolled in. Tim glanced up and marveled at its thickness.

Lance said, "Yeah, it looks like the inside of my brain."

Steve shot him a look. "We haven't figured this out yet," he said.

The truth was, they were more confused than ever. The code suggested that a lot more should happen after Lance told the computer to play a movie than Tina's table vanishing into the ceiling. Lights should have dimmed, doors should have closed, shutters should have shut, and the giant movie screen should have emerged from its hiding place inside the woodwork.

"The question is why the computer is doing this in the first place," said Lance, philosophically. Lance was blessed with a peace-loving nature. No matter how massive the weight of public opinion against him, he refused to feel as if he was being attacked, or even criticized.

"It's doing it because someone saw it on *Star Trek* and wanted one just like it," said Steve, pointedly.

Lance ignored him.

Next came the standard debugging ritual. When a computer does something unexpected, its programmers often try to provoke it into repeating the behavior. That way they can be sure they have found the source of the problem. At Steve's insistence Lance retyped the code he had typed one hour before, when Tina's table first vanished into the ceiling. Nothing happened. The table did not budge.

For the next seven minutes the three men stared in silence into the sea blue screens. Many computer thoughts.

Finally Steve offered a new hypothesis: it wasn't Lance's fault at all. Lance might have programmed the movie system to behave like a James Bond movie, but Lance's program *did not work*. All the cool stuff that Lance told the computer to do—dim the lights, raise the movie screen, close the doors and shutters, send tables into the ceilings, light a fire, and pour a glass of Burgundy—had failed to occur. Ergo, Tina's table should not have moved either.

Lance accepted Steve's new hypothesis with the same indifference he had extended to the one before it. He knew that Steve was still guessing. So did Tim, who returned to his own terminal and asked the computer to run a complete history of itself. A computer, unlike the people who program it, can remember the experiences it has had in life. All of these experiences are electrical, of course, but the electricity is used to store information. The information contains clues to many mysteries. Some of these mysteries are even interesting.

While they waited for the computer to search itself, the three young men reasoned aloud. All agreed that what Steve had just said made sense: if Lance had told the computer to play a movie on the big screen in the main salon, a lot more than Tina's table should have moved. But if someone had told the computer that he wanted to watch a movie in *the galley*, the computer quite possibly would have responded by merely sealing off the galley. There was no reason this could *not* have happened. After all, it was possible to watch a movie on any of the boat's twenty-five flat-panel display screens. Tim and Lance and Steve followed this train of thought to what seemed to be its obvious conclusions: if someone had demanded a movie in the galley, then the problem was not caused by Lance or Steve or Tim. At the moment the computer crime was committed, all three programmers had been sitting together in the long cafeteria table in the main salon. They were each other's alibi.

Steve raised his chin like a coyote preparing to howl at the moon. *"Yonboxum!"* he shouted.

Jan Bocksum was the beleaguered Dutch fellow at the Huisman Shipyard assigned by Wolter Huisman to help the sailing novices from Silicon Valley gain sufficient understanding of the boat that they could control it. He'd quit, or threatened to, several times over the past two and a half years. He kept saying that he knew how software should be written because he knew how Microsoft wrote software. Microsoft deployed thousands of programmers in human waves whenever it sought to create something new. Jim Clark had deployed three young men on top of a Jenny Craig weight loss center in Menlo Park, California. But Jan Bocksum was given no choice. By edict from Wolter Huisman, he and four or five other stout and sturdy Dutch workers had acquired a working knowledge of Clark's new computer system. None of them actually knew how to program the boat, but all of them knew how to use the computer. More to the point, they knew the password to gain entry to the system. Any one might have ordered a movie in the galley.

Soon enough the Dutch workers stood uneasily beside the long cafeteria table like children called before the principal.

"In the past hour and a half," Steve asked, "did any of you play with the touch screen in the galley?"

They shook their heads in unison. Steve looked at them for a moment as if they were political prisoners—which, in a sense, they were. None of the Dutchmen broke down and confessed, however, so Steve dismissed them. "The trouble is," said Tim after the Dutch workers had left, "they all use the same password. Anyone could have done it, and no one wants to admit it."

The young men returned to their keyboards, and for maybe ten minutes the only sound was of fingers typing. A few minutes later Tim's computer spewed out the historical record. It, too, was silent on the matter of Tina's table. So far as the computer was concerned, Tina's table had levitated all by itself. "What about a wiring problem?" asked Tim.

"Well," said Lance, "Simon has been fastidious about the cable making." Having ceased to be the prime suspect, Lance had become more animated. He was now leaping to the defense of others. Simon was the crew member responsible for the computer hardware at sea. He'd just returned from his training course in Silicon Valley. He now worshiped the programmers, and the programmers appreciated it.

"Nah," said Steve, "Hyperion 24 received an instruction. It's just unclear where the instruction came from."

More silence.

More tap-tap-tapping on keyboards. Clark turned up to see how they were coming along. Steve explained the problem with Tina's table. Clark shrugged. His attitude seemed to be that there were so many big things wrong with the software that no one should be overly concerned with small matter such as furniture vanishing into the ceiling. His unconcern acted as a narcotic on the programmers. Steve actually giggled. "I'm not sure I'm cut out to be a manager," he said.

"It's an affliction that goes with enjoying actual work," said Clark, and returned to his computer in his cabin.

Fifteen minutes later Tim looked up from his keyboard and admitted the obvious. "Well, that's unsatisfying. We have no idea why it happened. It would be nice to have closure." Nice . . . but not necessary. Tim was leading them to a popular solution to an intractable computer bug. Give up! Forget about it! Hope it doesn't happen again! The boat still had dozens of bugs. What was so special about this one?

The three young men breathed easier. The bug that sent Tina's table into the ceiling underwent a subtle change in status. No longer was it a problem bug. A critical bug. A meaningful bug. It was a bug that could be ignored. It could be hunted down tomorrow, or the next day, or even the next. Or maybe never. Steve snickered, conspiratorially. "It's going to be difficult to concentrate with Tina shrieking all the time," he said. "Tina did not quite shriek," reflected Lance. "It was more of a warble." The three young men in T-shirts and blue jeans shared a final chuckle and returned to their computers.

## How Chickens Become Pork

It seemed at least worth asking why anyone would hand his life over to a computer program that made its own programmer uneasy. Each crew member of *Hyperion* had his reasons. Robert the British engineer hoped to be the first engineer with total command of both computers and boats. Simon the Canadian deckhand had fallen in love with the idea, if not the fact, of computers. Jaime the Australian first mate left a great job with the Japanese America's Cup challenge for the chance to sail the boat of the future. "This boat has an aura," he'd say. "Everyone in yachting knows about it, or wants to know about it." Tina the American chef simply liked Jim Clark more than anyone she'd ever worked for. She was a brilliant cook, and she knew it, and she knew Clark knew it. Clark's praise counted for a lot with her.

But the larger reason *Hyperion*'s crew members agreed to cross the Atlantic Ocean on a boat run by a computer that did not seem to work very well is that already they were in so deep that they really could not turn around. Clark liked to say that human beings, when they took risks, fell into one of two types, pigs or chickens. "The difference between these two kinds of people," he'd say, "is the difference between the pig and the chicken in the ham-and-eggs breakfast. The chicken is interested, the pig is committed. If you are going to do anything worth doing, you need a lot of pigs." The members of *Hyperion*'s crew were now pigs, for a very simple reason: they all had a stake in Clark's Internet businesses. Clark couldn't stand the idea of anyone's working for him without having the chance to accumulate a bit of wealth. He'd given *Hyperion*'s crew members that chance by handing them stock options in Healtheon.

If the crew members couldn't exactly explain the Magic Diamond that put Jim Clark at the center of 15 percent of the U.S. economy, they had heard Clark and others say that the new enterprise might one day be as big as Microsoft. And they knew that they would also get shares in the new new thing, whatever that turned out to be, and that the new new thing would likely be even bigger. Like a lot of people who entered ClarkWorld, the crew members of *Hyperion* suspected that Jim Clark would make their dreams come true. They needed only to keep his boat floating long enough for that to happen.

The funny thing was that the engineers at Healtheon felt much the same way. They, too, were chickens who had been transformed into pigs. And they, too, soon found that pigs paid a surprisingly high price to play a role at Clark's breakfast table.

The first bad sign came for Healtheon about six months after the engineers built their software for Blue Cross/Blue Shield of Massachusetts. The software created by Pavan's group was something of a triumph. It was secure, reliable, and worked as well for ten million people as for ten. They had done the work of several years in six months. And Blue Cross/Blue Shield did not want it. After saying how pleased it was with the work, Blue Cross/Blue Shield of Massachusetts then announced that it could not really afford to focus on new technology. Blue Cross/Blue Shield had run into financial trouble; and, as always happened in bad times, its investment in the future needed to be reduced. It fired its new-technology group.

For most of 1996 the engineers did what they were told by their sales force. The sales force was in turn put together by a Kleiner Perkins venture capitalist, David Schnell, who, against his better judgment, had agreed to captain Clark's new ship. The sales force told them that the key to the Magic Diamond was to write the software to enable corporate employees to interact with their health plans over the Internet. They wrote this software . . . and no one wanted it! The sales people hired by David Schnell had led them down a blind alley. "They had hired a bunch of perfectly nice people to sell who might as well have been selling insurance," says Stuart Liroff. "A bunch of insurance salesmen—and they didn't have a clue. Good old boys." The good old boys were wrong! Worse than wrong. One day in late 1996 the engineers looked up and realized that they were no longer even thinking about the Magic Diamond. They were doing nothing but talking to big companies about making it possible for their employees to handle all their health care problems over the Internet, rather than with the usual blizzard of paperwork. A worthy goal perhaps, but nothing so grand as the original ambition of taking over the $1.5 trillion health care industry. In short, they realized that the business was misguided. And when they realized this, they were angry. "At that point," says Pavan. "We engineers took over the business."

The engineers, who had always been content to act on instructions from the marketing department, did what they had never before done. They kicked the salesmen to one side—eventually they were all fired—and went out on the road to sell their software themselves. They were looking for the keys to the Magic Diamond. If they found one large and important customer, they figured, others would follow. Briefly, they believed they might be hired to sort out Fidelity's health care plan, but that came to nothing. Fidelity would pay them $20 million to do this. Clark reappeared and told them that Netscape's first contract, with MCI, had been for only $6 million: they were three times better than Netscape!

And then in March 1997 Fidelity announced it had decided not to fiddle around with new technology after all, and the engineers found themselves without anyone who wanted to buy what they had done. "We'd just given up our lives for six months," says Stuart. "My wife was pissed at me. My daughter was crying because I never came home. We worked twenty-hour days. And then finally we deliver the product and it was like: What did we just do? We gave up so much . . . for *this*? It was a total look-inward kind of thing. We were all pretty pissed. Pavan,

Kittu and myself . . . we'd sit around having these nighttime meetings to discuss what to do, and we were all essentially yelling at one another. We'd all gotten into this fucking thing. We put our life into this fucking thing. We'd been led down a path. The period in 1996 was the most awful time in any of our lives. We knew we had created something very significant. It was just that we couldn't sell it to anybody. And what did we know? Pavan and Kittu and I, we didn't know shit. We just built what they told us to build. It was ITV all over again."

Their main fear was the main fear of every new Silicon Valley company, mass exodus. These companies could not withstand pessimism, and now there was a lot of it at Healtheon. It got so bad that Pavan went to his white board and drew what he called a "loyalty matrix." The first ten engineers he'd hired, he figured, were loyal to him. He called each and told them to find the people who were loyal to them, and persuade them not to quit. It only took a few people trickling out the door for the flood to begin.

It was the second time in a few years that a highly talented group of engineers had raced down a path Clark had put them on, and yet, oddly enough, they didn't blame Clark. It did not even occur to them to blame Clark. Through it all they viewed Clark as their patron. Whenever the Healtheon board of directors convened, the venture capitalists streamed past the engineers without saying a word. Clark stopped and spent half the day talking to them about the software. Whenever the Healtheon board spoke of watering down the equity stakes that had been given to the engineers, Clark fought it. The engineers assumed that Clark was the only one in the place who stuck up for them.

Instead, they blamed David Schnell, the venture capitalist who had been installed by Kleiner Perkins as temporary CEO. They told Clark, as Clark later said, that "David occasionally left customers with the impression that the train was leaving the station, and if they didn't get on now, they would be left behind." (This can be useful for a customer to feel but it should never be explicitly said.) But, of course, Schnell was the problem! Schnell was a venture capitalist, and venture capitalists normally did not need to be polite to anyone, as people usually came to them on hands and knees to plead for money. And as a venture capitalist Schnell had the tendency, suddenly unfortunate, to make a few quick bucks rather than reshape the world in his image. He had pushed the engineers away from the Magic Diamond and toward this mundane little backwater called benefits administrations, where he thought they might make money immediately. And he didn't even do this well.

What Clark and his engineers realized was that they needed a charismatic leader who could make the Magic Diamond real. What they needed was one of those guys with gray hair and soothing manners who could speak to the CEOs of large health care companies in their own language. One of those guys from mainstream corporate America who instantly, by his mere presence on the scene, made the implausible plausible. What they needed, in other words, was something Jim Clark alone could never provide. A Serious American Executive.

Until that moment of high despair in early 1997, it was never entirely clear why Clark had gone to the venture capitalists on Sand Hill Road in the first place. He didn't need their money. He had more money than all of them combined. But he did, after all, need them: he needed them to translate his extraordinary ambition into the ordinary language understood by corporate America. The man who groped for the new new thing was in many ways ill suited for mainstream business. Clark knew that the time would come to put a smiley corporate face on his ferocious ambition. He knew, also, that he did not know how to do this. As one longtime Clark watcher put it, "Jim is smart enough to know when he shouldn't trust himself." In particular, Clark sensed that alone he was unlikely to entice a Serious American Executive into running his insanely ambitious company. The Serious American Executive would get one long whiff of ClarkWorld and run the other way. Premised as they were not on profits but on perceptions, these new Internet businesses were still all but unrecognizable to the Serious American Executive. A simple background check would reveal that, translated into business-speak, "Jim Clark" meant "Big Trouble."

The venture capitalists, on the other hand, talked the talk and walked the walk. In tone and spirit they were not all that different from Serious American Executives. The VCs had been to business school, they spoke the jargon, they wore the suits, or at least owned them. The VCs kept their neckties on hooks on the back of their office doors, so they could go either way. They were pleasantly free of the odor of a man on a suicide mission. One VC in particular had a gift for persuading mainstream CEOs that the only place to be was a Silicon Valley start-up: John

Doerr. Doerr was the only VC whom Clark favored with something akin to respect. He asked Doerr to join Healtheon's board and to help him recruit a CEO. Doerr, who had told a lot of people that Healtheon might one day be the biggest company Kleiner Perkins ever backed, then set out to find the Serious American Executive who could make the Magic Diamond plausible to the wider world. He found him at a conference in Phoenix, Arizona. His name was Mike Long.

Long had graduated from the University of North Carolina at Chapel Hill in 1974 with a degree in history and spent the next twenty years building a nice little computer services business in Austin, Texas, called Continuum. In 1996 Continuum sold itself for 1.7 billion dollars to another equally obscure computer services company called Computer Sciences. It was a big deal at the time—the seventh largest deal ever done in the computer industry. Everything about Mike Long was reassuring to Jim Clark: his gentle manner, his prematurely gray hair, his ability to appear to be in complete control. When Mike Long entered a room, everyone in it felt somehow better. He attracted followers as a magnet attracts filings. In other words, he was exactly the right man to take an inherently implausible idea and lead others to believe in it.

It did not occur to Mike Long that he wanted to work in Silicon Valley until John Doerr put it to him. Over six months Doerr called Long "more than a hundred times" and talked him into leaving his stable, successful company, called Computer Sciences, and joining the Internet revolution. Long flew out to California to meet Jim Clark. When asked his first impressions of Clark, he'd say, "Jim's a visionary." He'd also say, "Jim's an eccentric."

It took Long six months to extract himself from his old company. When he arrived at Healtheon in July 1997, the place was in high despair. The entire company, now more than one hundred people, assembled in a room. They switched off the fake waterfall so that no one missed a word. Long rose and explained how he intended to restore the company to the heart of the Magic Diamond. "It was clear what had happened," he later said. "This company started out with great ambitions, and then the ambition got smaller and smaller. I just took it back to Jim's original vision." This was exactly what the engineers wanted to hear. They did not know exactly what it was that Mike Long did, but they sensed he did it well. "He uses all these incredible words and way of speaking," says Stuart, though he can't remember any of them. It was the engineer's way of saying that at last Healtheon had found its Serious American Executive.

The Serious American Executive, for his part, found chaos. At the board meeting in September 1997 Mike Long announced he was running out of money. Before the meeting Dick Kramlich and his partners at New Enterprise Associates had valued their portfolio of investments. They ran down a list and guess how much each company was now worth. When it came to Healtheon, they wrote "0." Healtheon was as good as finished, they assumed. Along with Clark they had already put six million dollars into the company, and they had no desire to put in more. And so when Long said he needed money the venture capitalists looked hard at the shiny conference table. Finally, they came up with a plan to raise twenty million dollars from outside investors. Of course, if they had thought Healtheon had a future, they would have kept it to themselves. Since they did not, they went looking elsewhere for capital.

The exception was Clark. Clark called Long a few days after the board meeting and told him that he had thought about it and had decided that Healtheon was simply too good an opportunity to let others in on. He said he would personally provide Long with as much money as he needed. If Long needed twenty million dollars, Clark would cut him a check for twenty million the next day.

Of course, this meant that Clark would acquire an even larger stake in the company. But since the venture capitalists had valued the company at zero, he did not imagine they would object. Long called the venture capitalists with Clark's proposal. Their sense that Healtheon was worth very little warred with their fear that Jim Clark knew something they did not. Somewhere deep down they realized how bad they would look if Healtheon by some miracle became an enormous success, and Clark made off with it all. Almost before they knew what they had done, they threw their money on the table—eight million dollars. Clark supplied the other twelve million himself.

That moment was a small, but important, turning point in Silicon Valley capitalism. Actually, that's not quite accurate. The phrase "turning point" suggests that there would be no backtracking, when backtracking was inevitable. Still, Clark's behavior was significant. He was, for that brief, curious moment, the orchestra's conductor. He set the tempo. In the past, the venture capitalists had always done that. The Silicon Valley venture capitalists had always been the first to put money into any new technology business. The Internet boom had turned venture capitalism into a license to print money; half of the investment bankers on Wall Street longed to work for NEA or Kleiner Perkins, because working as a VC put you closer to the source of wealth. To the recipes. It was as if everyone on Wall Street at once realized that if you wanted the finest cut of meat you had to muscle your way into the kitchen. Partners at Wall Street firms begged to be let in. Once you were let into the Great Society of Sand Hill Road, you were given first crack at these miraculous enterprises at a small fraction of the cost to Wall Street investment bankers—never mind the general investing public. But there were only a handful of people so privileged, and Kramlich and Doerr were two of the most important. Capitalism's machinery favored these capitalists as it had never favored anyone else in its history.

Clark jammed a wrench into this machine. He needed the venture capitalists to help him put a serious face on his precious concepts. He needed John Doerr to talk Mike Long into running the business. Other than that, so far as Clark was concerned, the finance department of the American economy was expendable. He didn't need the VC's blessing. And he certainly didn't need their money. He now sat on a billion dollars of Netscape shares and could do whatever the hell he pleased with them. And what pleased him was to put it at great risk. The VCs did not care to make these sort of colossal bets on the future. They sprinkled their money around a lot of different companies and counted on the law of averages to take care of the rest. Clark took a different approach. He said with some conviction: I *know* how to make a lot of money in the future. And since I know how to make a lot of money in the future, I am going to put all my money on it.

It was a difference of temperament as much as anything else. Clark had walked up to a roulette wheel surrounded by more or less reasonable men, and laid all *his* chips on 00.

And it scared the hell out of the others at the table. The VCs could tolerate companies' going bust—they had so many of them—but they could not tolerate missing out on the new new thing. And so they poured their money in. They threw good money after bad into an enter-prise they suspected would fail. They had wanted to be chickens; Clark forced them to be pigs. "I think Jim knew exactly what he was doing when he called Mike Long and said he would give him all the money he needed," says Dick Kramlich. "Jim has come a long way since Silicon Graphics."

One summer afternoon, after a meeting with the venture capitalists about Healtheon's future, Clark hopped into one of his sports cars and launched himself in the direction of San Francisco. With the top down and the speedometer's needle nudging past 100 he had to holler to make himself heard. "I'm starting to feel poor!" he shouted.

He intended it as both a joke and a complaint. He felt poor, and he realized that it was funny, or at least odd, that he felt poor. After all, his Netscape holdings were still worth nearly $600 million. Even if Microsoft succeeded in driving Netscape out of business (which Clark believed it would do), he thought he would soon be much richer than he now was. Despite all appearances he felt certain Healtheon would be an embarrassingly big success. Indeed, one of his purposes at the meeting that morning was to increase his stake in the company. No, he was less concerned about Healtheon than about the new new thing— whatever *that* might be. Whatever it was, it had to be even bigger and more dramatic than Healtheon. That was Clark's one rule about his new new things: each one bigger than the last. "The idea so far is that I've put all my wood behind a single arrow," he explained. "The risk now is

that the next time the arrow gets so huge that the whole world is looking at it. And it's not an arrow anymore, it's an ICBM. 'Well, Jim Clark
failed.' That'll be the story. And it'll be a *big* story.'"

The thought made him happy. He was saying that he could live with
his inevitable failure, because it would, inevitably, be spectacular. Just
twenty minutes before, when we'd climbed into his car, he'd been in a
dark mood. He'd cursed Silicon Valley venture capitalists as "parasites,"
and complained about the fees charged by Wall Street investment
bankers when they took Silicon Valley companies public. Yet now, suddenly, he was happy in the world. The adventure story telling itself to
his imagination had soothed him. Or maybe it was just the speed of his
car. All he had to do is gun some machine into its highest gear to redis-
cover the sunny side of life.

The trip from Healtheon's main office on the northern fringes of San
Jose to downtown San Francisco took an hour. We rolled up in front of
a skyscraper, parked illegally, strolled into the elevator, and pressed a
button. Up, up, up we rose, and as we did I became aware of his incon-
gruity. Downtown San Francisco was one of those old-fashioned places
where businessmen went to work in suits and measured their status by
their views of the Bay. Clark wore a yellow polo shirt, khaki slacks held
up by a soiled sailor's belt, and his rat-gnawed pair of sneakers with their
grimy MEPHISTO label. The bike messengers were better dressed.

He had come to San Francisco to open a Swiss bank account. Why
he wanted a Swiss bank account was complicated. It had to do with
Europe.

Clark's arrival in the Dutch boatyard had caused a financial mating
signal to be broadcast across the European landmass. Princes, dukes,
counts, barons, and every species of European lounge lizard came running to embrace the future. Clark's tendency to trust people when he
first met them had landed him in a mess. He'd lent one of the more
egregious lizards a couple of hundred thousand dollars so that the lizard
might buy shares in @Home. The lizard had made a bundle for himself and then, perhaps out of some fuzzy Jamesian notion that rich
Americans were sufficiently awed by European lounge lizards that they
would rather forgive them their debts than make a social stink, failed
to repay the loan. At that point Clark's tendency to destroy people who
betrayed his trust kicked in. (It may have taken him a hundred years,

but Henry James's American had learned a lot.) He found the name of the man's Swiss banker, Bank Julius Baer, and flew in to see the head of the place to inform him of his client's debts. Now, to complete the humiliation, he was opening an account at Julius Baer's San Francisco branch, so that, if the lizard reneged on his debts, he would do so in full view of his hoity-toity bankers. Clark figured that the man would either pay up or suffer shame and humiliation in Switzerland.

The head of Bank Julius Baer's San Francisco branch met us as we stepped off the elevator. He was clearly delighted that the rich American was opening an account, even if he meant to deposit only the required minimum. His round face suggested his eagerness to please, his paunch a willingness to do lunch. But it was less his appearance than his manners, an unfortunate mixture of deference and command, that set him apart.

"I won't waste your time with our promotional materials," he said, wasting Clark's time with the promotional material, before tossing the glossy brochures to one side. He clasped to his chest a serious-looking document with no gloss at all, and led Clark into a room with a lot of dark wood. Clark sat on one side of the table, the Swiss banker on the other. From the document in his hand, the banker said, he would read a series of questions that all Swiss bankers asked new customers.

"Occupation?" he asked.

Clark paused. His face betrayed a perfect lack of understanding. The first question! Already he was stumped!

"Executive," he said, at length. Then he glanced over at me, apologetically. "They usually don't have a category for what I do. So when they ask I just say executive." The Swiss banker laughed nervously. "We never asked such things until very recently . . . ten years ago," he said. "Until then we asked *nothing*. But now . . ." He shrugged, and in that tiny gesture was the silent scream of a man standing on top of a collapsing tradition. Some combination of direct pressure from the American government and indirect pressure from the public conscience had forced Swiss bankers to become indiscreet.

The Swiss banking tradition, however, was wasted on Clark. The trouble with the new American rich, from the Swiss-banking point of view, was that they had nothing financial to hide. Clark's wealth was as public as great wealth has ever been. People who cared to know how much he was worth needed only to check a few documents at the Securities and Exchange Commission. Or if they didn't want to take the trouble, they could pick up a copy of the *Forbes* annual list of the four hundred richest Americans, on which Clark's name and a fair estimate of his fortune now appeared. Or if they weren't big on reading, they could just ask Clark. He didn't see much point in pretending his money was some kind of secret.

"Investment objective?" asked the Swiss banker.

Clark said, "To get my money back."

"Risk profile?" asked the banker.

Clark just stared at him. "What do you mean?" he asked. The banker didn't quite know how to put it, so he paused and made a bit of small talk. You could see him trying to find the string of phrases, or perhaps the mood, that would cause an American searcher for the new new thing to hand over his financial affairs to the Bank Julius Baer. He was like a man working his way through a ring of old keys in a futile attempt to open a shiny new lock. The lock politely declined to open.

Finally, the banker just skidded his questionnaire across the mahogany table and asked Clark to fill it out himself.

Clark gazed intently at the document. "INVESTMENT PROFILE," was written in bold letters across the top. The questionnaire might be new to Swiss banking, but it nevertheless reflected hoary Swiss assumptions about money. It assumed, in particular, that any money deposited with Bank Julius Baer was (a) not earned by anyone still living and (b) terrified of being lost.

As Clark studied the document, his face acquired the pained expression of a well-meaning child who is trying his best to answer a difficult question. He was often this way when faced with new situations, or with people he did not know. He wanted badly to do what was expected of him. It was only after he determined that this was somehow impossible that he went ahead and did whatever he wanted.

Now he was doing his best to please Bank Julius Baer. Yet he could not fathom how the bank's questions applied to him. He arrived at the first category, marked "Risk/Reward." A simple-minded graph with an arrow pointing up and to the right illustrated the principle that the more risk you take with your money, the more you stand to gain or lose. In the past ten months Clark had "lost" $600 million simply by holding on to his shares in Netscape. "If they only knew," he said. The Swiss banker chuckled unhappily. Clark remained straight-faced. His eyes drifted farther down the page, to a category marked "Return Objectives and Risk Tolerance." This was a summary of the typical Swiss banker's idea of the range of possible attitudes toward financial risk. It read,

Conservative: I seek to . . . minimize investment volatility.

Moderate Growth: I want to take some risk while also preserving capital.

High Capital Growth: I have a minimum time horizon of five years with which to pursue my objectives.

Next to each risk profile was a little square box. Clark passed quickly over the first two and paused for a moment at the third, wondering, probably, where they put the box for people who sought to turn ten million dollars into one billion in a few months. Finally he looked up with the most perplexed expression.

"I think this is for a different . . . person," he said.

And then, at that moment, something inside him gave. There he was, the maker of the fastest money ever made legally. He was the spiritual leader of a new financial movement that believed in putting all of its chips on 00. He had not the faintest desire to "manage" that money, or to "diversify his holdings," or to employ any of those gentle verbs that emanate from bankers and inspire people who are not bankers to hand their money over to them. At that moment Clark's investment portfolio, such as it was, looked like this:

Healtheon: 9,500,000 shares. Estimated Market Value: 0.
Netscape: 15,500,000 shares. Estimated Market Value: $550,000,000.

Microsoft was gobbling up Netscape's market share, and thus Netscape's share price, and thus Clark's wealth. And yet Clark hadn't a thought in the world of "preserving" that wealth. He had no interest in preservation of any sort. His life was dedicated to the fine art of tearing down and building anew. He didn't buy U.S. Treasury bonds, or stock in companies outside of Silicon Valley, or for that matter stock in anything outside the outrageously volatile Internet sector. A year or so before he had bought and sold a million shares in @Home, and made a quick $45 million. Other than that he sank his wealth in his newest company, and left it all there until the new new thing came into view.

This gorgeous financial myopia was common in the Valley, and one of the chief sources of its success. The technologist's tendency to commit all his resources to new technology, by financing ever more new technology, had generated one of the great economic miracles in human history. Now this paunchy Swiss banker in his humid gray suit was offering up his Swiss recipe for handling money. In Clark's mind it was a recipe only for mediocrity and stability, which came to the same thing. All the attitudes designed to keep people locked in one place were right there, in the questionnaire. Presenting it to Clark, and asking him to fill it out, was not merely poor commercial judgment. It was a social gaffe, on the order of inviting the fastest gun in the West to court at Versailles.

"No one I know would know what any of this means," Clark said, finally.

By now he was actually giggling. The Swiss banker laughed too, but less sincerely. The customer was laughing! At the Bank Julius Baer questionnaire! At the Bank Julius Baer! Clark skipped over one of Julius Baer's questions, then another, then a third. Finally, he paused at a section near the bottom of the questionnaire entitled "The Larger Picture." It read,

> The assets invested with Julius Baer Group will be:
>    Most of my financial assets
>    Only part of my financial assets
>    _____of my financial assets.

As the Swiss banker attempted to divide a couple of hundred thousand into $550,000,000, Clark hunched down low over the third line on the form and entered ".00035."

"Wonder what their computer will do with that," he said. Then he thanked the banker politely and left.

Never was a man's love of risk so beautifully amplified by his environment as Clark's was in Silicon Valley. In late 1997 Healtheon was worth nothing, at least as far as the venture capitalists were concerned. By the summer of 1998 it was deemed worthy by Wall Street investment bankers of a public share offering. It still wasn't a viable company; it was losing money at a rate of fifty million dollars a year. But it was suddenly plausible. That is, it could be held out to investors as a company that might one day make vast sums of money. Investors would believe this. Or so said the investment bankers.

A bit more than a month after Clark visited the Swiss bank, the Wall Street investment bankers visited Healtheon. In 1986 when Clark had wanted Wall Street bankers to sell Silicon Graphics to the public, he flew to New York City, hat in hand. Many of the bankers treated him poorly. The CEO of Salomon Brothers, John Gutfreund, stood him up—left him sitting like some hick in the lobby of Salomon Brothers. These days the investment bankers came to Silicon Valley. This was only one of many recent changes along the capitalist food chain. Wall Street had gone from being the celebrities of the money culture to being its lackeys.

It was in June 1998 that six bankers from Goldman Sachs visited Healtheon; directly on their heels came five more bankers from Morgan Stanley. Together with Long, Pavan Nigam, Jim Clark, and a dozen Healtheon employees, they crammed their lightly starched selves into a small conference room. What ensued was a wonderfully elaborate money ballet.

It took an hour or so for the dance to begin: when billions of dollars are on the line, you can't simply talk about money. It's too important. Mike Long took the seat at the head of the conference table. The investment bankers took seats along the table. The Healtheon employees sat in chairs back against the wall. Clark took a chair by the door, which, to the consternation of the bankers, he opened a crack. They didn't understand that nothing of true importance happened behind closed doors. The room stayed too stuffy for his tastes anyway, and all through the meeting he kept getting up and wandering around outside in the halls. Long introduced the Healtheon employees and then turned to the one man in the room who needed no introduction. "Jim Clark," he said, "why don't you tell us about your original vision here."

Jim Clark obliged. "Just after Netscape I was interested in a vertical market," he began, deploying the usual Internet lingo. A vertical market was a market for a single good or service, like books or travel. A horizontal market was a market that cut across many different goods and services, like a Web browser. Netscape was in a horizontal market; Healtheon was in a vertical market. "I always thought that the biggest opportunity on the Internet was the vertical markets," Clark continued. "I didn't know anything about health care, but I was looking for something worth doing and . . ."

He went on for a few minutes about why turning the $1.5 trillion health care market on its head was "worth doing." Then he leaned his chair back on two legs against the wall and as much as handed the floor back to Mike Long. "The Internet changes everything," said Long. "Everyone can get connected on the Internet. And thank you, Jim, for that."

The bankers chuckled appreciatively. By their tone and their manner they conveyed the general idea that everyone who mattered in this new world was in this one little room. They felt safe here. The playing field was now Silicon Valley. Of course, an investment banker in Silicon Valley wasn't exactly a player. He was more of a waterboy. But at least he was *in* Silicon Valley. His colleagues back in New York were relegated to the bleacher seats of capitalism—and it nearly killed them. After all, what possibly could be the point of being an investment banker if you didn't make more money than everyone else?

Still, Wall Street bankers were higher up on the capitalist food chain than Swiss bankers. They participated directly in the miracle of Jim Clark, or thought they did. True, they'd been shoved a rung or two down the chain by entrepreneurs like Clark and venture capitalists like John Doerr. True, when Morgan Stanley and Goldman Sachs called Mike Long and said in their puffed-up way that they would take Healtheon public only if they were given sole possession of the deal, Long had only to say in a stern voice "put that in writing" before they caved and said they would do whatever he said, when he said it. But they'd made hundreds of millions of dollars off the Internet boom. They could plausibly claim, at least at that moment, to be the perpetrators rather than the victims of change. To take a company like Healtheon public they charged 7 percent of all monies raised, plus expenses. If a company raised $50 million, the investment bank would net $3.5 million for a few weeks of work. That fee was usually just a kind of down payment. Once the stock price of one of these Internet companies took off, it could be used to acquire other companies with lower stock prices. The Wall Street bankers acted as agents for these acquisitions. Their fees did not make them as rich as Clark or the people who worked for Clark or the people who worked for the people who worked for Clark or even the people who worked for the people who worked for the people who worked for Clark. But they were richer than Swiss bankers.

The meeting with the Wall Street bankers lasted four hours, from two until six, with one long break for coffee and phone calls. Long introduced the company with the new Healtheon diagram. The new diagram was even more impressive than the Magic Diamond, which it had replaced. It looked like this:

Informally known as the Chart of Many Bubbles, eleven to be exact, it still showed Healtheon in the center. But now the little company, which still had fewer than two hundred employees, sat in the middle of many obviously complicated things. The Chart of Many Bubbles proved that Mike Long, before he took over the health care industry, had at least bothered to learn the names of its component parts. The Morgan Stanley people took only a polite interest in the Chart of Many

Bubbles, however. The opening of the meeting was pure ritual, a sprin-
kling of holy water over the sheep before it was slaughtered. You could
tell how serious they were about it from their attitude toward the black
box on the conference table. One of their colleagues, a woman who
had stayed home sick, listened by speaker phone. From time to time a
squeak or a gurgle emanated from the box at the center of the conference table. A baby! The woman from Morgan Stanley was holding a
baby, and the baby was refusing to keep quiet. Each time it mewled,
the room used it as an excuse to depart from the Chart of Many Bubbles
and share a hearty laugh.

"If you're going to play the health care game," Mike Long said, "you've
got to have a large percentage of your staff that can talk the talk."

"Gibagibagibagiba" went the baby.

"Ho, ho, ho," went all the people in the room.

But the Chart of Many Bubbles suggested one obvious question, and
the investment bankers raised it: How would all the companies in the
little bubbles feel about a Silicon Valley upstart organizing them into a
Chart of Many Bubbles and moving into the middle? Long had a long
and happy answer: Healtheon could slide in and eliminate $250 billion
in waste without causing the people who made their living wastefully
to raise hell, and it would do this by forming partnerships with the
stronger companies. The stronger companies in each sector would use
Healtheon services to kill the weaker ones. By the time the stronger
companies figured out that Healtheon didn't need them either, it would
be too late. The way Long said all this was perfectly soothing. He was
not describing a ferocious upheaval in which hundreds of billions of
capital would be redirected and hundreds of thousands of people would
need to find new jobs. He was describing a friendly bake-off.

This was the Easy Listening version of Clark's original intention.
Clark had seen the health care system as he saw much of the world, in
black and white. To his way of thinking there were health care profes-
sionals who clearly served a purpose. They were called doctors. And
there were people who clearly needed health care. They were called
patients. Everyone else in between—the hundreds of billions in paperwork and bullshit—could go. All Mike Long's soothing talk about "part-
nering" and "win-win relationships with other health care firms" was a
smoke screen for what Clark was up to when he created Healtheon.

"We want to empower the doctors and the patients and get all the other assholes out of the way," Clark had once told me, then laughed. "Except for us. One asshole in the middle."

Long didn't mention the part about the one asshole in the middle. Instead, he handed the Chart of Many Bubbles to the doctors and other health care authorities in the room, mercenaries in a new civil war. Each man in turn explained how he planned to worm his way into his particular bubble and make it his own. First the drug companies (the drug company SmithKline had a seat on the Healtheon board), then the insurers (the insurance company United Heath Care also had a board seat), PPOs, HMOs, hospitals, doctors, patients, and so on. Each bubble represented a gargantuan market all its own. Over the past nine months Mike Long had talked one large entity in each bubble into becoming a guinea pig for Healtheon's software. In essence, the Healtheon employees were explaining to the Wall Street bankers how they planned to build, simultaneously, eleven separate multibillion-dollar businesses.

"So what have you been doing for the last year?" asked one of the bankers, when they'd finished. Everyone laughed. The baby cried. Everyone laughed some more.

"Pavan Nigam will now explain why all of this is going to work," said Mike Long.

Pavan had been sitting quietly to one side pretending to be interested. Now he rose and stood in front of a giant screen, and I wondered if this is what he imagined when he put down the copy of *USA Today* in the Delhi hotel and decided to become an Internet entrepreneur. "Three years ago this would have been impossible to pull off," he began and then launched into a perfectly baffling presentation on the inner workings of Healtheon's software. Abstraction followed abstraction in the manner of contemporary art criticism. The Morgan Stanley people did not have much to say to this. How could they? They didn't understand it any better than you or I could. If they could write software, they wouldn't be schlepping companies for a living. But at the end of it one of them, perhaps hoping to dispel the impression that the reason investment bankers are investment bankers is that they don't have the brains to be software engineers, asked, "Is there any major piece of the platform that has not been built?" *Platform.*

"Not really," said Pavan.

The investment bankers just nodded knowingly. No one dared dig further. The baby squalled. Everyone laughed.

Through it all Clark had remained silent. At one point, when the bankers were asking about Healtheon's possibilities, he said, "This could be as big as Microsoft, and quicker too." Otherwise he sat back and watched the proceedings with the detachment of a small boy who has rolled a rock down a hill and watched it become an avalanche. His chief contribution to the meeting was to be there. He was attached to the business in the same way that Jack Nicholson was attached to a film script—thus increasing the likelihood that the script will become a movie. Simply by floating around and taking an interest, he makes all involved feel as if they are engaged in something very special.

"What about competitors?" asked one of the bankers. "IBM has something called Health Data Networks."

Clark came alive, briefly. "They've got nothing on us," he said. "As soon as we hire a PR person, we're going to flatten them."

All talk of competition ended right there. The conversation turned to finances. The bankers asked several perfunctory questions: How much money did Mike Long think the company required? ($40 million) How fast could it grow? (How fast did they want it to grow?) How much was at stake? (The future of the single biggest market.) "The benefits of first-mover advantage in this space are so huge," said Long. "That's why we have this land-grab strategy." The bankers agreed mightily with this statement. One of them said, "That's true in every Internet space. Amazon.com is doing $87 million a quarter. Barnes and Noble is only doing $9 million. And Barnes and Noble has been as good as it gets in responding to the Internet threat."

"That's why we are in a mad panic to go out and *get lives on the system,*" said Long, calmly. "Lives" was what health care business people called their customers. Mike Long was the sort of man who could claim to be in "a mad panic," while giving the impression of being in such complete control that there was no point in further discussion.

"The investor base is becoming a lot more creative in evaluating these deals," said the woman in the box on the table. The investment bankers had all these wonderfully soothing phrases that implied the world outside the room was climate controlled. The investor base! What she was referring to was a teeming peristaltic mass of junkies high on the giddiest boom the U.S. stock market had ever seen.

"No traditional Graham and Dodd investor invested in AOL," said a banker at the table. "They shorted it. And got fucked. They're learning the new model."

Mike Long said, "The main point is that *nobody* has driven a growth strategy in health care."

"That's why this is such an exciting opportunity," said one of the bankers. "It's like AOL in the beginning. Or Yahoo."

The baby in the box made the most perfectly delightful noises. This time no one paid it any mind.

They'd arrived at the true purpose of their meeting. The true purpose of the meeting was *not* to determine whether Healtheon was worthy of Wall Street's attention. It was to determine just how enthusiastic the bankers were prepared to sound about Healtheon. Their money was cheap: there was so much money pouring into the Valley that Mike Long had about twelve different ways he could get his hands on what he needed. The Valley was a little experiment of capitalism with too much capital. For a brief but shining moment capital lost its purchase on its own process. The process took on a momentum all its own, and the old-fashioned capitalist just came along for the ride. All he could offer was his ability to influence the minds of investors who had not figured out what had happened. The investment bankers were no longer selling money; they were selling talk.

The people from Wall Street now fell over each other praising the future of Healtheon. One said, "The opportunity really is huge." Another said, "The only problem is finding a way to explain it." A third said, "It's like AOL all over again." For the first time Clark became truly interested. "The market opportunity here is bigger then all of those guys put together—bigger than Netscape, than Amazon, than AOL, than Yahoo, than *all* of them," he said. "That's why when I look at your revenue projections they seem laughably small."

What *was* Healtheon worth? How did a sane person value a company that had never made a profit? The old formulas of old Graham and Dodd investors like Warren Buffett no longer applied. By those formulas Healtheon was worth zero. The company's balance sheet was filled with negative numbers. It showed losses running out as far as the eye could see. Like other Internet companies, it said to the stock market: our future will look nothing like our present; ergo, you cannot determine our value by looking at the present. You must close your eyes and imagine a new world. Look to the future! The future is bright! The belief was partly self-fulfilling: belief often is. Once the stock price took off, the company was halfway home. The competition would fall away or, more likely, offer itself for sale to Healtheon. Mike Long spoke of "an M&A strategy for growth." What he meant by that was that as soon as he was able to buy potential competitors with Healtheon stock he would do so.

The Internet formula for success turned traditional capitalism on its head. Traditionally a company persuaded people to invest in it by making profits. Now it persuaded people to invest in it first, and hoped the profits would follow.

Clark had understood the ass-backward nature of the enterprise from the start. The ass-backward nature of the enterprise is what gave him his tactical advantage. The trick was for Healtheon to get itself designated by the financial markets the Official Health Care Sponsor of the Miracle Economy. That in turn depended on Healtheon's being viewed not as a health care company but as an Internet company. And that, in turn, depended on shrewd public relations. And public relations was driven in part by what the bankers said about the company. But since the bankers desperately wanted the fees that came from running the deal, they would say whatever they had to say to please Jim Clark and Mike Long, within reason. They did this with clear consciences. If they succeeded in persuading the capital markets that Healtheon belonged at the heart of the Chart of Many Bubbles, Healtheon might very well wind up at the heart of the Chart of Many Bubbles. In this new world skepticism was not a sign of intelligence. It was a sin.

When you sat back and looked at it, you saw that a single assumption underpinned the entire boom: the future would be better than the past. Healtheon existed in a state of pure possibility. It was the golden boy in his senior year headed toward some undefinable great height. The stock market would be asked to imagine the most breathtaking possibilities for it. It would be asked to devalue the past, to cease its usual talk about "track records," and to invest everything in an idea of how the future might turn out.

In other words, the stock market was being asked to adopt Jim Clark's value system. And the amazing thing is, it did.

The meeting lasted two hours more, and in those hours the baby found its way right up into the speaker phone. It cooed, it giggled, it spoke these adorable baby words. No one flinched or even smiled. I doubt anyone even heard it this time. From the moment the conversation had turned to the dollar value that might be placed on Healtheon, the baby had been priced out of the meeting.


A few days later Healtheon selected Morgan Stanley to lead its public offering. A few days after that the stock markets crashed. The bad news that ostensibly caused the collapse had nothing to do with the U.S. stock market. On Friday, July 22, 1998, a rumor passed along trading desks that Russia intended to default on its foreign debt. The rumor caused a panic, and the panic forced Russia to default. One large foreign country reneging on its debts caused investors to suspect that others would follow. This in turn led to the fear of all kinds of financial risk. Investors pulled their money out of corporate stocks and bonds and put it into cash or U.S. government bonds. Between July 1 and October 1 the Dow Jones industrial average fell 2000 points, or 25 percent. The riskier Nasdaq composite—the best measure of Silicon Valley's fortunes—fell from 2900 to 1450, or 50 percent. Netscape fell from 41 to 16. Clark went from being worth $640 million to being worth $248 million, give or take $50 million.

This period tested Clark's resolve. Some part of him feared that the game was over. The truth was, *he* thought most Internet stocks were ridiculously overpriced. He thought that Microsoft would wind up controlling the lion's share of Internet profits, and that most of the golden children of the miracle economy were doomed. "Fucking Yahoo is not worth thirty billion dollars," he'd say. "Once Microsoft controls the browser market, they'll take over Yahoo's market too." The trouble was, he could not say publicly what he thought about Microsoft without hurting Healtheon. He thought that one day soon Microsoft would begin to take over the vertical markets on the Internet. "They're already into travel," he said. "They'll get into everything else."

Still, Clark did not sell his Netscape stock and buy U.S. Treasury bonds or, more logically, Microsoft stock. It was as if he had decided that the first in must also be the last out. I think he almost would prefer to be poor again than buy shares in Microsoft. Almost.

The stock market crash screwed up Clark's immediate plans for Healtheon. It caused Morgan Stanley—and every other Wall Street banker—to become cautious. Wall Street had taken 370 companies public in the year up to August; between August and October they had taken only one public. The IPOs of five new Internet companies (Earthweb, Theglobe.com, Interworld, Multex, Netgrocer) were postponed until further notice. Morgan Stanley canceled all but two of its IPOs scheduled for the fall. One of the two it did not cancel was Healtheon.

In retrospect it's odd that they went ahead. On the first of October 1998, in what was widely viewed as the worst market for IPOs since the early 1970s, they set out to sell a company, and restore the vigor to Jim Clark's bank account. At four in the morning, in an airport in rural New Jersey, five men piled onto Clark's plane: Clark, Mike Long, Healtheon's CFO Jay Westerman, an investment banker, and I.

## 13

## Cheese Sandwiches for Breakfast

N ew companies are sold to the public in much the same spirit as new books, new music, and new politicians. The sellers leap onto airplanes and fly to many cities, where they put on a show for the perfect strangers who they hope will buy their product. In the case of a new company, the strangers are money managers and the show is called "the road show."

The Healtheon road show had the same two stages as most road shows for Silicon Valley companies. The first stage was in Europe. Europe was a useful place to open not because it had a lot of money managers dying to invest in new technology companies but because it didn't. Europeans were famously clueless about new things, not to mention new new things. When the Netscape road show had passed through London, and after Jim Barksdale had spent an hour explaining to a group of Englishmen what, exactly, the Netscape browser did, one of the investors raised his hands and asked, "Do you need a *modem* to use your product?" The way he said it you could tell he was pleased he'd heard of a modem.

Europe was the place to polish the act before taking it onto the stage that really mattered, the United States. You could flop in Europe, and Europeans would never know. "What we'll tell Americans when we come back is far more complicated," said the Morgan Stanley man simply, as Clark's plane leveled off at 37,000 feet.

Once over the Atlantic, Mike Long and his CFO, Jay Westerman, reviewed their slide show. The road show was, in fact, a traveling slide show. The slide show was the preferred technique for rendering essentially abstract concepts—"the future," "software," "the U.S. health care industry"—concrete. Unless they have seen a slide show, investors do not truly believe they have been shown a business, especially when the business is an abstract promise to make a lot of money rather than a concrete, profit-making enterprise. And so, together with the man from Morgan Stanley, the Healtheon executives sat in the big swivel chairs in the back of Clark's jet and examined the first slide in the show. It was the Chart of Many Bubbles.

I should say that from the start it was clear this was not Clark's show but Mike Long's. Clark was along only because Long had asked him to come, on the theory that Clark's reputation for inventing the future couldn't hurt and might help. After all, Jim Clark had made a lot of money for investors over the years. Clark for his part would have preferred to be working on his boat. He listened politely to Long's presentation. Occasionally he walked to the back of the plane and sat himself in front of the blue Silicon Graphics work station he carried with him wherever he went. There were still many kinks in his own software, and the boat was due to cross the Atlantic a few weeks hence. He was determined that, if something went wrong, it was not going to be *his* code that caused the problem.

Clark's priorities were not lost on Long. Before he set the dates for the Healtheon road show, he made sure it didn't interfere with the launching of the boat.

The trouble with Mike Long's slide show was that he couldn't just tell investors what he really thought: that he intended to build the world's biggest company. They wouldn't believe him; they'd laugh him off the stage. To translate Jim Clark's ambition into the language of the global investor, Long had to tease them with charts and numbers and hope they arrived at their own rosy conclusions. But here, outside of Silicon Valley, the Chart of Many Bubbles looked perfectly baffling. No

ignorant person could conclude anything from it. Long seemed to realize that he could never truly explain Healtheon's software, or the U.S.
health care industry, to foreigners. He groped for a simpler way to show
Europeans exactly how Healtheon intended to seize the world's largest
market.

"I sort of like the physician metric," he said. He sounded hopeful but
looked weary. He hadn't slept properly in several days.

The physician metric was a complicated-sounding phrase for a simple idea: the number of doctors who used Healtheon's service. Investors
needed some way to evaluate how well Healtheon was doing. Investors
liked to be able to count progress in dollars. Long wanted them to count
progress in doctors.

"I like the physician metric too," said the Morgan Stanley man.

"You think there are too many things on that slide?" Long asked,
holding up one of the charts that followed the Chart of Many Bubbles.
The slide was a war zone of arrows and swooshes.

"The simpler the better," said the Morgan Stanley man. "Think AOL.
One of the great things about AOL was that they hammered into the
heads of investors the idea that all that mattered was the number of sub-
scribers."

Clark said, "That's exactly right."

The Morgan Stanley man became more enthusiastic about the physician metric. He wanted to call Mary Meeker, the Morgan Stanley analyst who was fast making a name for herself as the leading authority on
Internet businesses, and "bake" into her mind the idea that investors
should focus only on the number of physicians hooked up to
Healtheon's service. Long leaned over to Clark and said, "Hell, we could
get 150,000 more physicians with just two deals."

"Really?" said Clark. He was interested again.

The two men danced together around the next heuristic problem:
how to explain to investors how much money Healtheon intended to
make, without sounding absurd. "I don't think I have to say it," said
Long. "I think all I have to do is say that there are 700,000 physicians
in the United States and that we feel we have a legitimate shot in sign-
ing up 500,000 of those. Each doctor represents $20,000 a year in rev-
enues. I'll just say, 'You do the math.'"

Clark thought this was a great idea, as did the man from Morgan

Stanley. *You do the math*. The Healtheon men and their banker were not just creating a presentation. They were inventing the manner in which their business would be judged, at least for the next few years, while they lost great sums of money. *You do the math* became one of Mike Long's favorite phrases. *You do the math* gave the investors something to do with their hands while he spoke. And if they actually did the math, they arrived at the most fantastic calculations. Multiply 500,000 doctors by $20,000 a year and you wound up with $10 billion a year in revenues. Ten billion a year that did not even include foreign health care markets, which Healtheon now also had vague ambitions to conquer. Microsoft, America's most highly valued corporation, had only $8 billion annually in revenues.

Everyone was happy with the physician metric. The man from Morgan Stanley was so happy that he presumed a familiarity with Clark. Clark had settled himself in behind his computer work station. The Morgan Stanley man leaned over to chat about the sailboat. The sailboat had people back in the Valley talking—it was yet more evidence that Clark was just a little . . . different. "I was wondering, Jim," the Morgan Stanley man asked, "what happens if the computers go down? Is there a mechanical override or backup or something?"

"The computers won't go down," said Clark, so gruffly that the investment bankers flinched. Clearly, there'd be no questions about the boat from investment bankers on this trip. Clark let the Wall Street people sell his companies to the public and make him billions of dollars, but only because he hadn't yet figured out a way to get rid of them. But he'd never let them into his sacred world of machines.


The first two days in London nothing much happened. The British were hard to sell to, but the British were always hard to sell to. In these situations they tended not to even cross that invisible mental line that separates spectators from customers. Dapper British men in expensive suits came to see Mike Long's slide show with the air of people watching a tennis match. They asked questions that suggested, if not keen interest, at least mild curiosity. Long made his pitch in Britain seven times inside of thirty-six hours. He was moving too fast to notice that something was terribly wrong. It wasn't until the third morning in Amsterdam when it dawned on him, as it dawned on everyone else, how unlikely he was to sell anything to anyone, much less sell the new new thing to Europeans. The vision of a technology company rising up out of the miasma of the U.S. health care industry and changing the world was suddenly, horribly implausible. Change required optimism, and optimism was suddenly scarce.

The first morning on the European continent we gathered in the conference room of a fancy Amsterdam hotel. Long had not slept in forty-eight hours. The U.S. stock market had finished 200 points lower the day before, having fallen 250 points the day before that. The German stock market had just opened down 8 percent, the equivalent of a 600-point drop in the Dow. Banks around the world were announcing massive losses from loans they'd made to Long-Term Capital, an American hedge fund gone sour. Holland's biggest brokerage firm, ING Barings, announced that morning its new plans to cut 1,200 jobs. The Bloomberg news service had an article quoting IPO experts saying that the business of companies with huge losses and no foreseeable profits trading for many multiples of their revenues had been stopped in its tracks by the new skepticism of financial markets.

Clark arrived at the breakfast with a stack of faxes from Healtheon's publicist. They turned out to be Healtheon's first reviews. There was a front-page article in the *Wall Street Journal*, a big spread in *Business Week*, a smaller spread in *U.S. News & World Report*, and a long article from *Bloomberg News*. Before his slide show Long declined to read any of them. Still, he could see from Clark's face that the reviews were not good. *Business Week* quoted Jim Barksdale, the Mike Long of Netscape, describing Clark as "a maniac who has his mania only partly under control." The *Wall Street Journal's* front-page story suggested that Healtheon's software was not finished.

Long looked around for the slide projector. It didn't exist. Normally, the slide projector had something wrong with it but at least it existed. Normally, Clark just fixed it.

He looked out over the breakfast table. Along it sat half a dozen surprisingly young Dutchmen with their pallid Dutch skin and lank Dutch hair. They dug into droopy cheese sandwiches. Cheese sandwiches! At seven in the morning! The thought did not obviously interfere with their pleasure in the free meal. Each one of them ate for three. The gusto with which they attacked the cheese sandwiches caused Long to wonder if they had come, perhaps, for the food. Were these people really the power brokers of the northern European financial markets? Of course not! The power brokers were all back in their offices trying to figure out how to sell their Internet stocks.

Wearily, Long produced the paper version of his slide show. He held it up before him, like a second-grade teacher with an alphabet chart. The first slide was no longer the Chart of Many Bubbles. The Chart of Many Bubbles had baffled one too many Englishmen. The first slide was a list of the people who sat on Healtheon's board of directors: Jim Clark, John Doerr, Dick Kramlich, a virtual who's who of Silicon Valley. "Everyone at our company who is not on this chart," Long said, "is under twenty-six years old and works twenty-four hours a day seven days a week and sleeps in his cubicle."

No one at the conference table laughed. No one even broke a smile. From their expressions of incomprehension it was unclear whether they understood English. They looked to be about twelve years old. Their suits were the off-the-rack polyester sacks that every European male bought before his first day at the bank. Their socks drooped.

Still, Long worked his way steadily through the slide show. The phrases rolled off his tongue: *We think doctors want to pay for our services by the drink. . . . The Internet changes everything. . . . There is constant media scrutiny of this company. . . . A one-point-five-trillion-dollar market is ours to win or lose. . . . You do the math.*

Their faces remained uninspired. There was not the slightest sign of comprehension in them. If there was a sound in that room, it was the sound of air being let out of a tire. The Internet and all it stood for felt woefully out of place. What could it mean to a dozen Dutchmen who were still getting their minds around the idea of electric power?

A lesser man would have caved in and walked out of the place. After all, why did Mike Long need to be going without sleep for forty-eight hours for the privilege of explaining the U.S. health care system to a handful of Dutch adolescents? He was plenty rich enough that he didn't need to work. He was, at least on the surface, a modest man; certainly he had no further material needs. More to the point, he was not like Jim Clark, who was forever doomed to grope for the new new thing. He could have given up, then and there. Yet he didn't. The Serious American Executive had signed on for his tour of duty in the Internet wars. Having signed on, he was going to finish.

After the Dutch paper slide show we drove in silence back to Clark's plane. There, while detained on the runway, Long asked for and received the front-page article from the *Wall Street Journal*. He sat in one of the big swivel chairs and placed the piece on his lap, unread. He could have been a director preparing to read the reviews of his latest film, or a politician checking the papers to see how his latest policy speech went down.

But before he started, Long lowered his expectations. That was one of the little psychological tricks he played on himself. As the Serious American Executive, he was not allowed to show great emotion. He could not permit himself to be visibly upset or disappointed. Thrilled as Mike Long had been by the physician metric, he never let himself hope that he could sell Europeans on the idea. For instance, as we drove in from the airport to central London, he brought up a trip to Europe he had made recently with his father. His father had been an infantry-man in World War II. Long gathered up twenty or so snapshots his father had brought back from the war, grabbed his father by the hand, and set out to revisit the sites and retake the photos. They tracked down ten of the twenty places. "And the thing was," said Long, on his return to Europe, "they were all the same. We retook this one picture in Pisa, beside the statue of Garibaldi. In the old picture there was a shutter hanging off one of the houses by a single hinge. That had been fixed. Other than that the two photos were identical."

This had been Long's way of saying: if Healtheon failed to sell in Europe, he could blame the failure on the European resistance to change. Now, before he read the article on the front page of the *Wall Street Journal*, Mike Long said, "George is a cynical guy." He was refer-ring to George Anders, the *Journal* reporter who had written the arti-cle. If George Anders panned Healtheon in the *Wall Street Journal*, it was because George was a cynical guy.

And then Mike Long began to read. For the next hour he read and reread the article many times. He read it front to back, then back to front. He skipped to the middle to reexamine a particularly noxious pas-sage. He put it down, then picked it up again, as if starting in on it fresh might somehow alter its meaning. In that hour Long did not speak or change expression. He was a man in a trance.

The article about Healtheon that appeared on the front page of the

*Wall Street Journal* on October 2, 1998, was a rocket from pre-Internet America. It quoted industry experts saying things like "a lot of the challenges we face in health care have very little to do with the Internet." It pointed out that Pavan and his team of engineers were late delivering Healtheon's software to doctors, and left it to the reader to surmise that this just might be because the software did not work. It went on to say,

> Much of Healtheon's allure comes from its two main backers. The company's Chairman, James Clark, is a co-founder of Silicon Graphics Inc. and Netscape Communications Corp., whose Web browsers have helped Internet mania sweep the world. Healtheon's main venture capitalist is Kleiner Perkins Caufield & Byers, which has shown a Midas touch on its Internet investments. . . . But Healtheon has struggled to live up to its pedigree. . . . For much of this year, Mr. Clark, the company's chairman, was away from the U.S. for about a week each month, including visits to a Dutch boat yard building a yacht for him.

The implication was clear: no man who spent a week a month in Holland building a boat could plausibly claim to reform the U.S. health care system. Never mind that only a man who spent most of his time programming a boat to sail itself would persist in his quixotic ambition to reform the U.S. health care system. Just a few months earlier no journalist would have dared to cast such a skeptical eye upon any enterprise associated with Jim Clark. The climate of the Internet had changed. Clark was suddenly like one of those big hairy mastodons at the dawn of a new Ice Age. ClarkWorld was now treacherous. Stocks were falling fast, and Internet stocks were falling fastest.

Mike Long, like everyone else on board the jet, up to and including Clark's pilots, who held shares in the Healtheon, knew instantly that the road show was over. Oh, they would travel from city to city in the United States with the slide show. They would explain the Chart of Many Bubbles fifty times more. But wherever they went in America the article in the *Wall Street Journal* would follow them.

That article marked the final rite of passage for Mike Long, the Serious American Executive. He had spent twenty years building a robust computer business in Austin, Texas, without reading a word about himself, except perhaps in the local paper. Certainly no one dared to criticize him publicly. No reporter would ever dare analyze him and dissect his business. Now, as Long read the *Wall Street Journal*, he found that he had opened himself up to a new set of forces. The Serious American Executive read the piece over and over again. He'd just become a citizen of ClarkWorld.

"Pavan doesn't fidget," Long finally said. His voice was cold with anger.

"What?" asked Clark, who through it all had been sitting next to Long and paying him no attention.

"It says here that 'Pavan Nigam "fidgeted" when asked for a firm delivery date for the software.' Pavan does not fidget." Then Long tossed the article onto the seat and wandered back to a sofa to take a nap. Clark just watched him leave. "Mike's going to have to get used to the press" was all that Clark said.


The final leg of the European road show was a triumph of habit over reason. Mike Long went on selling even after it was clear that selling was a waste of time. The Europeans probably would not have been able to *do the math* in any case. But at least, as he stared out at teenage European investors devouring their bizarre breakfast foods, Long could remain hopeful for his prospects in America. Now he knew that he was doomed in America, too. Selling Healtheon required him to manage the perceptions of investors. No investors would be able to evaluate Healtheon's software; they relied on the reputations of the people involved. Now those reputations had been called into question. Until now investors would have wanted to believe that the software worked; now they would want to believe it would not. For that reason Pavan Nigam was called out of his cube at Healtheon and onto the road show.

Of course, in a rising stock market the *Wall Street Journal* might not have had such effect. Indeed, the people at the *Journal* might not have had the nerve to run such an article, as they faced the likelihood of being made to look like fools the moment Healtheon's stock took off. But with the market collapsing the article was as definitive as a stake in the heart. After his final European presentation Mike Long returned to the plane, flew back to the United States, and finished the job. As he traveled the country he wrote e-mails to Kittu and Stuart and the three hundred or so other employees back in the Valley, who he knew were simply waiting to find out how rich they had become. They convey the spirit of a man disguising from his loved ones his knowledge that he will be executed in the morning.

From New York he wrote:

The first thing you notice about presenting in New York City versus Europe and the West Coast is that courtesy and benefit of the doubt go out the window. This is in your face territory. The demeanor of many of the investors is outright hostility. This is partly by design to test your knowledge and conviction and partly just the way people are that live here. We responded with equal aggression.

From Philadelphia:

One benefit that the bankers provide in each city is one of those long black limos that high school kids take their dates to the prom in. This car proved to be a big asset in Philly where we were reminded that when objects collide mass matters. Three cars crashed into us on a rain slick freeway on the way back to the airport. Next thing you know we're helping drivers from two crashed cars into the back of the limo to lie down and wait for the ambulances to arrive.

Mass matters.

The one thing that is very obvious about money managers is that their self esteem and attitude is heavily dependent on how their performance chart looks each day.

From Dallas:

There is always a lot of anxiety with our bankers about the length of our presentations. The goal is to tell the entire story in twenty minutes or less, a worthy goal that Pavan, Jay and I are still striving for.

From Chicago:

There is no one else out here but us. Can a successful IPO be done in this market?

From San Francisco:

For a dinner presentation which turned out to be in an open restaurant that was full of interesting but perplexed people who didn't realize they were going to get an investor presentation during dinner. One thing you notice right away is that you're presenting at a lot of breakfasts, lunch and dinner forums and everyone gets to eat except us because we're talking. Answering difficult questions from potential investors with your mouth full of food is bad form. There are always sandwiches of some age and variety in the car between meetings.

The road show came to a screeching halt in New York in late October 1998. A couple of hundred institutional investors who had spent the morning selling any stock or bond not fully guaranteed by the U.S. government gathered over lunch in a hotel ballroom to hear the riskiest idea they'd heard in a while. Before Mike Long's slide show Clark offered a few encouraging remarks. A male investor raised his hand and asked Clark to comment on the article in the *Journal*, and the quotation from the health care executive who said the Internet is irrelevant to his industry. "It's quite typical of larger companies that are threatened by smaller companies," Clark said. "They say, 'It's not important.' And that's what keeps them from responding."

Mike Long then rose and delivered the slide show. The phrases rolled off his tongue: *The Internet changes everything. . . . There is constant media scrutiny of this company. . . . A one-point-five-trillion-dollar market is ours to win or lose. . . . You do the math.*

He made all the right noises. But at the end of the show the investors had only one question.

"If you guys are successful," a New York investor asked, "how long will it take before Microsoft is in the business?"

Mike Long got this world-weary look on his face, and repeated the question for anyone who hadn't heard it. "The question is Microsoft. Are they going to blow us away? . . . Well, their strategy is that they are going to dominate all vertical industries. And their hubris is unlimited. So, yes, we have to assume that they are coming, sooner or later."

The man from Morgan Stanley rose and said, "Thank you very much. And we're looking for an early-next-week pricing."

It never came. A few days later the man from Morgan Stanley drove from his office on Sand Hill Road down to Healtheon and told Mike Long that they hadn't found enough interested investors to justify taking Healtheon public. Oh, they probably could sell a small stake in the company to a handful of believers—at the same price that Clark and the venture capitalists had paid for it. But what was the point in that? A few hours later, after a conversation with Clark, Mike Long canceled the deal. The deal had been, of course, central to all of Mike Long's plans. Without a highly valued share price, he would be unable to buy all the little companies he wanted to buy, and seize control of the entire U.S. health care industry. Nevertheless, he called all the employees together in a conference room and persuaded them that one day soon they would triumph.

But even as he spoke he knew he had one very immediate problem: he needed another forty million dollars just to keep the company running. He called the Wall Street bankers and the venture capitalists and Jim Clark, and told them.

At that moment, I think, it dawned on Clark that the food chain of capitalism was missing a link and that, if he summoned the nerve to hoist himself up, he could be that link. And that if he didn't have the nerve to do so he would make a mockery of his entire remarkable climb. He once told me, "I can't be a venture capitalist, because I'm not that kind of person, and I can't be a manager, because I'm not that kind of person. The only thing I can do is start 'em." His role in the Valley was suddenly clear: he was the author of the story. He was the man with the nerve to invent the tale in which all the characters—the engineers, the VCs, the managers, the bankers—agreed to play the role he assigned to them. And if he was going to retain his privilege of telling the stories, he had to make sure that the stories had happy endings. If that meant supplying forty million dollars more to Healtheon, so be it.

In that decision, taken during a financial panic described by Alan

Greenspan, the chairman of the Federal Reserve, as "the worst" he'd ever seen, you could, if you looked closely enough, see the first glimpse of the new new thing. Clark's willingness to take risks others shunned was the source of his financial power. He was the guy who always won the game of chicken because his opponents suspected he might actually enjoy a head-on collision. With the markets falling fast, and the financiers hemming and hawing, he called first Mike Long and then the investment bankers, and told them all he'd like to supply the entire forty million dollars to Healtheon. Forty million dollars suddenly looked like real money. Forty million dollars was the annual budget for a medium-sized city. More to the point, forty million dollars was at that moment nearly 20 percent of the after-tax value of Clark's Netscape stock, itself falling rapidly.

Clark's faith in his new enterprise was actually faith in his own imagination, as the new enterprise was merely an extension of that imagination. The power of that faith, once again, was transforming. One moment the financiers were wondering aloud where the forty million dollars was going to come from. The next moment they were trying to prevent Clark from supplying the full amount, and acquiring for himself an even larger stake in the troubled company. In the end the bankers and the venture capitalists agreed to let Clark give Mike Long twenty of the forty million dollars he needed. They supplied the rest. And so Clark bought half the canceled IPO, at six dollars a share.

I spoke to him a few hours after he did this. Technology stocks were collapsing, and a new pessimism had found its way into the heart of the miracle economy. All Clark said was, "I'll be a billionaire again soon." And then he returned to the serious business of programming his boat, and to the search for the new new thing.

## 14

## Could Go Either Way

Clark said that Netscape "made anarchy respectable." Late at night, when no one else was around, he must have wondered how long the odd sentiment could survive in corporate America. Institutions loathe disorder. They seek to socialize forces of anarchy. It's one of the many internal contradictions that have failed to collapse capitalism: wealth generation is suppressed by those who are supposedly most interested in wealth. Rapid technological change threatens people who already have power, even when those people are technologists. This simple fact creates a certain internal tension in putatively high-technology corporations. While promoting change, big established companies also wish for change to occur slowly enough that it does not overwhelm them. Netscape was so threatening to the established order because it suggested change could happen outside of that order, as fast as people like Jim Clark could make it happen, without regard to the establishment.

Any number of events could conspire with the high-technology establishment to nudge the anarchic spirit off center stage and back to its usual, less reputable place in the wings. The stock market could collapse, for instance. Back in August 1995, when Netscape went public, the stock market had more or less said, "Okay, we know it is insane to encourage a company that has no profits, no clear idea of how it will make profits, and is, in fact, sort of making up its business as it goes along, but so long as we all agree to pretend that this is reasonable commercial behavior, we may create a miracle." When the Healtheon public offering failed in October 1998, the stock market was saying, "Wait a minute. Maybe this was all a big mistake."

But the market was not quite the threat to ClarkWorld that Microsoft was. About a year after Clark created Netscape, on June 21, 1995, the company's marketing director and Clark's old buddy from Silicon Graphics, Mike Homer, called Clark and told him that seven Microsoft executives, led by a man named Dan Rosen and acting on instructions from Bill Gates, had flown down to Silicon Valley and told Netscape that, unless Netscape gave Microsoft a seat on its board and sold Microsoft a piece of the business, Microsoft would put Netscape out of business.

This was more of a promise than a threat. To run on the world's five hundred million or so personal computers, Netscape's browser needed to be compatible with the latest release of Microsoft Windows—at that time Windows 95. Anyone who wished to write software for the personal computer obviously had to make sure that it was compatible with Windows. Netscape, like every other software company, needed Microsoft to release early versions of something called "the APIs" for Windows. API stood for application programming interface, a typically incomprehensible piece of geekspeak. An API was a kind of keyhole into Windows. To create keys that fit, Netscape needed to know the shapes of the holes. Microsoft's programmers routinely provided these to programmers who created software that didn't threaten Microsoft. They had been slower than usual to provide them to Netscape. On June 21, 1995, they told Netscape that unless Netscape caved in to its demands, they would not provide them at all. As the Microsoft executive Dan Rosen put it, according to notes kept during the meeting by Netscape's Marc Andreessen, "If we had a special relationship, you wouldn't be in this position."

Later Clark recalled what he thought the moment he put down the phone: "Fuck these assholes." A simple thought, easily acted upon. He immediately called Gary Reback, an attorney with the Silicon Valley law firm of Wilson Sonsini Goodrich & Rosati, told him what Homer had just said, and asked Reback to inform the U.S. Department of Justice (DOJ). Two days later Reback did just this—though he arranged for it to appear as if the DOJ had requested the information. Clark later told me that he'd taken this initiative because he "didn't think Barksdale [Jim Barksdale, Netscape's new CEO] was going to do anything about it." In any case, after Reback mailed his letter, the DOJ invited him in for an informal chat. At the time the DOJ was toying with the idea of revisiting a settlement it had reached with Microsoft a few months before, in which Microsoft had agreed not to "bundle" new products with the operating system. Clark and Reback, together with several Netscape executives, flew to Washington.

At his one and only meeting in Washington, D.C., with U.S. government lawyers, Clark first tried to explain what was about to happen in the computer business. The Justice Department had been concerned with Microsoft Network—an ill-conceived early attempt by Microsoft to "contain" the Internet in a single, Microsoft-controlled space. Microsoft Network was a threat to no one, Clark argued, since it missed the whole point of the Internet, which was that it was uncontainable. The threat, he said, was Microsoft's inevitable entry into the new market for Internet browsers.

Back in 1990 Clark had described his telecomputer as "a kind of underbelly thing with Microsoft." If the digital revolution occurred on the television rather than the personal computer, he figured, there was at least a chance Microsoft would not control it. Netscape also was "a kind of underbelly thing," but it lived much closer to the belly. To get onto the Internet, at least for the moment, you had to go through a personal computer. And the personal computer had a single point of entry—the first window that popped up on the computer screen after a user had logged on. To get to any software inside the computer the user had to pass through that window. Since Microsoft controlled that window, it controlled everything on the other side of it, too. This sort of power was not unique to the computer industry—the railroad industry had some of the same monopolistic tendencies. But in the computer industry the power was much harder for outsiders to discern, and thus to fight.

The Internet challenged Microsoft's monopoly power, in a round-about way. The Internet did not have an "operating system" as such. Instead, it had several points of leverage from which the dominant company could nudge consumers this way or that. The first and seemingly most important was the browser—the software that enabled you to travel on the Internet. Computer users tended to follow the path of least technical resistance. Netscape's browser, which made it easy for people to travel around the Internet, was the first real window out of Windows. Windows became merely a starting point for a longer and more interesting trip. In the long run the Internet would make it possible for users to reach out and collect all the software needed to run their computers. In the extreme case, it could render Microsoft's operating system superfluous.

Of course, Microsoft held itself out as a friend of change and progress. Its founder, Bill Gates, the world's richest man, was forever publishing books and articles under his name the sole purpose of which was to convey the idea that he was some kind of visionary. Gates's first book, published in November 1995, was called *The Road Ahead. The Road Ahead* came out a year and a half after Clark had said, "The Internet is the future of all data communication, and all communications are data communications," and yet the author barely mentioned the Internet. The books and the magazine interviews and the advertising campaigns were a smoke screen. All Bill Gates wanted from the future was for it to look exactly like the present. To survive, Microsoft didn't need to discover the new new thing but to tame it.

That is why Clark knew, from the moment he created Netscape, that sooner or later, and probably sooner, Microsoft would seek to destroy him. Clark told the DOJ lawyers that Microsoft would use its monopoly to control the market for Internet browsers. For instance, Microsoft would be able to go to computer manufacturers such as Dell and Compaq and say, in effect, "If you include on your machine Netscape's browser, or exclude Microsoft's Internet Explorer, we'll put you out of business." And the DOJ's lawyers did not think that mattered! At least they didn't at first. "Jim had sort of seen the future," says Gary Reback, "and he kept saying to the Justice people *that's not it.* He'd seen the future before Bill Gates, and he was trying to explain it to the Justice Department. But the Justice Department insisted on fighting the previous battle."

It was almost instantly clear to Clark that any legal action would come too late to make any financial difference to him. An hour into the meeting he began to fidget; an hour after that he walked out, and left the others behind to finish what he had started. "It was just clear to me that it was a waste of time," he said. "At that point I sort of gave up on the American legal system." "When I caught up to him," recalls Gary Reback, "Jim said, 'Sorry, I just couldn't take it any more. But you keep it up.'"

It was a full two years after Clark, through Reback, alerted the DOJ before the DOJ formally announced it had come around to his way of thinking. One reason it came around was that Reback had indeed kept it up. He peppered the government with news from the front lines of the browser war between Netscape and Microsoft. In March 1997 President Clinton appointed, and the Senate confirmed, Joel Klein as the department's new chief of antitrust enforcement. The truth was, no one expected Klein to enforce anything; the senators who voted against his confirmation were Democrats who feared he'd lie down on the job. Klein later explained how he came to his surprising October 1997 decision to sue Microsoft:

We got a white paper from Netscape and Gary Reback right around the time I took over in the fall of 1996. I decided to put the investigators into Section 1 and Section 2 of the antitrust law, and to see if there were any violations of the consent decree [in which Microsoft had agreed not to "bundle" new products with new versions of Windows]. We started to put resources behind the San Francisco office, and they started the process of collecting data.

That data in turn led Klein and his chief economist, Dan Rubinfeld, to reconsider their former view of Microsoft as a benign force. In the summer of 1998, while Clark was arguing with the investment bankers about what Healtheon was worth and hunting down bugs in his boat's software, the lawyers from Washington and New York passed through Silicon Valley to collect testimony. The lawyers for Microsoft questioned Clark; they were followed a few weeks later by the lawyers for the DOJ; both groups videotaped Clark's testimony. Several times that summer Clark turned up in the Seascape office wearing a suit. Whenever he put on a suit, he had the air of a man who had been invited to a costume party he did not wish to attend. On those days he looked like every other American businessman. It was an odd sight, a man with hundreds of millions of dollars and an inclination to do whatever he wanted to do, up to and including turning entire industries on their heads, agreeing to live by someone else's dress code. Very deep inside him Clark harbored the desire to be *a good boy*. The real rebels never exactly play the assigned role.

To Clark the upcoming Microsoft antitrust trial was moot. In the three years since he phoned Gary Reback, Netscape's share of the Internet browser market had fallen from 85 percent to 45 percent. Microsoft's share had risen from zero to 50 percent. When people logged onto the Internet, their first impression was, increasingly, Microsoft's Internet Explorer. More important, the market expected Microsoft to win; ergo, Microsoft would win. That simple fact gave Microsoft fantastic power over the Internet's future. Its software was regaining its purchase on the consumer. Once that happened the goods and services Microsoft sold over the Internet would have a critical edge on the goods and services of others. "I can *guarantee* you what will happen next," Clark said, often and loudly, usually apropos of nothing. "First Microsoft will put us out of the browser business. The moment they have control of the browser business, they will cut out the links to other portals [Yahoo, Excite, Lycos, etc.]. You'll have to go through Microsoft's portal. And once they've got control of the portal business, they'll get all the vertical markets. You don't think that's what they want to do? They're already doing travel. I guarantee you that Microsoft has the market power to take over every vertical market. Sooner or later they'll get to health care."

Three months later, and a few days after Healtheon, seeking to control the largest vertical market, canceled its IPO, the greatest antitrust trial of the era opened. The American legal system, in effect, would decide how well a man should be rewarded who gropes for the new new thing. By then pretty much everyone, including Clark, had forgotten the phone call to Gary Reback that set the trial in motion. Certainly no one saw the Microsoft antitrust trial for what it was: yet another rock Clark had pushed off the side of a cliff, and watched with godlike detachment, as it became an avalanche.

An American court of law is in many ways un-American. In our every-day lives we Americans celebrate the subversion of the social order; everywhere a visitor to our country looks he will find a poor American boy trying to make good, usually with the encouragement of his soci-ety. An American courtroom is designed first and foremost to preserve the social order, to keep the poor boy down. The judge sits on a raised dais from which he can condescend to the lawyers, the lawyers stand up so that they may condescend to the seated witness, and the witness, though he may have no one to whom he can plausibly condescend other than perhaps the curiosity seekers on the hard benches at the back of the room, at least has the comfort of his upholstered chair. If any-one dares to step the slightest bit out of line, a large man emerges from the back to shout, "Order in the court!" If the judge decides he needs to relieve himself, the large man appears again to shout, "All rise!" And everyone in the room stands and waits stupidly until the judge has ambled off to pee. There is not a "please" or a "thank you" or a "by your leave" in any of this. Our democracy's system of justice is a feudal soci-ety in miniature.

The U.S. District Court in Washington, D.C., had the charm and efficiency of a Soviet customs office. The ceiling of grime-streaked white tiles was lit by horrible fluorescent lights. The seal of the United States over the full-moon face of Judge Thomas Penfield Jackson appeared to be made of the same hard plastic as a Halloween mask. For a number of reasons not worth going into, the main one being that the DOJ was not seeking monetary damages, there was no jury. The judge would render a verdict. Although it was one of the great antitrust trials since the antitrust laws were created back in 1890, the judge elected to hold it in the small courtroom. Most of the 450 reporters who turned up on the first day were left to rot in halls.

The judge permitted each side to call just twelve witnesses. The DOJ's case now included companies other than Netscape, but Netscape was still the centerpiece. Microsoft stood accused by its government not merely of being a monopoly—in itself, not illegal—but of abusing its monopoly powers to put Netscape (and others) out of business. Netscape offered the best documented example of Microsoft's abuse of power, thanks in large part to the early heads-up from Clark. As a result, the government wanted one strong witness from Netscape. "We thought about calling Jim Clark," one of the Justice Department lawyers told me during a recess, "and in many ways he might have been great because he was so knowledgeable about the technology. But the guy is a kind of maniac. He's not someone who you can discipline enough so you can say, 'Jim here is what we want you to do.'"

And so in the end the DOJ settled on Jim Barksdale, who, after all, had been hired by Clark and Doerr because he knew how to play his role. He put the same acceptably conventional face on Netscape's legal affairs as he did on its business affairs.

The trial's opening arguments lasted just two days. The DOJ introduced endless e-mails and memos showing how Microsoft bribed and blackmailed companies into harming Netscape. ("How much do we have to pay you to screw Netscape?" Gates asked executives of America Online in early 1996.) On the third day Microsoft called Barksdale to the stand. His job—from the point of view of the DOJ—was (a) to lend further credence to the notes supplied from the June 21, 1995, meeting between Microsoft and Netscape; (b) to explain how Microsoft had abused its monopoly to undermine Netscape; and (c) to come across as a reasonable, trustworthy guy. This last assignment was maybe the most critical because the judge, who hadn't the first clue about software, was forced to chose between conflicting accounts of the same events. It was made difficult by Microsoft's lead lawyer.

This lawyer was a natural heavy, a great Hogarthian ball of pink flesh with jowls that rippled over his white starched shirt. The potted biography said that his name was John Warden and that he had grown up in Evansville, Indiana, graduated from the Harvard Law School, and been for twelve years a partner at a fancy New York City corporate law firm, Sullivan & Cromwell. Through it all he'd somehow preserved an accent that would have made a hillbilly blush. He was proud of it, too. He'd lean into his microphone in the well of the U.S. district courtroom and boom out his questions in the Voice of God, causing the fifty spectators in the back of the room to jolt upright on their hard wooden pews. He was a hick, or pretending to be a hick, probably out of some old-fashioned belief that hicks, even make-believe hicks, are more appealing to juries than $1,000-an-hour New York lawyers, which is what he actually was.

In any case, his voice had the dull rolling groan of thunder from a bolt of lightning that has struck nothing, far away. And it hadn't taken him long to prove that high technology sounded far less impressive when discussed by a fat hick. He went on about "Web sahts" and "Netscayup" and "the Innernet" and "mode-ums," and with every sylla- ble he made the whole of the modern condition sound a little bit ridicu- lous. When he mentioned AOL, it sounded like a yodel. *AOOOLLLLL!* The witness he addressed as *Mis-ter Barksday-ulll.*

Before he ever heard of Jim Clark, or of Netscape, or of this mess of a trial into which Clark, with a flick of his left wrist, had thrust him, Jim Barksdale had made a reputation for himself as a manager at Federal Express and McCaw Cellular. He'd grown up in Mississippi and retained just enough of the piney woods patter to offer a passing imitation of a good ol' boy. All that was left of his linguistic origins was the just-below-upper crust southerner's habit of transforming soft consonants into hard ones. (He said "ma-toor" instead of "machoor.") Clearly he'd arrived at a point where he himself did not comprehend hickspeak. When Warden thrust a document into his hand and asked him to "read the first sayn- tance" of one of Gary Reback's memos aloud to the courtroom, Barksdale replied, "The first *sentence?*" "Just read the sayntance, Mister Barksdayul," the lawyer boomed back at him, rudely. Everyone with the possible exception of Barksdale viewed the fat hick's rudeness as a ploy to get under Barksdale's skin.

For nearly five full days the two men argued violently about subjects neither fully understood. Neither had a software engineers's grasp of Internet browser technology. But Barksdale was nothing if not shrewd. He soon figured out that he knew more than Warden, or for that mat- ter any of the lawyers, and used his superior understanding to embar- rass his tormentors—subtly, of course. For instance, Warden asked Barksdale whether before the critical meeting between Netscape and Microsoft on June 21, 1995, he knew that Microsoft intended to include "all the functions of a browser" in its operating system—thus implying that the meeting could hardly have been the shock Barksdale now claimed it was. "A browser or the functions of a browser?" asked Barksdale, cleverly. This threw Warden, who stammered a bit. For five days he wore the expression of a C student who has been asked to explain to the whole class the difference between an algorithm and a logarithm. He was a triple agent in his own soul: a big-city lawyer who thought he had adopted strategically the surface mannerisms of a stupid hick but who was, for the purposes of this trial, a stupid hick.

"A browser is a separate, stand-alone product," said Barksdale, pressing his advantage. "It's a *thing*. It walks like a duck, quacks like a duck, it's a duck!"

"It is?" hollered Warden, recovering. "Show me one! *Whey's the duck?*" "One" was two syllables. Wuh-uhn.

"Right here!" shouted Barksdale, pointing over the sleek dark wooden bar of the witness box to one of the U.S. District Court's computers, which looked nothing like a duck.

End of discussion. Having proved nothing, Warden then proceeded to establish, beyond a shadow of a doubt, that the people who worked for Netscape ("Netscayup") had funny names. He proved his point by pronouncing them. A Netscape salesman named Ram Shriram (pronounced "Rom Shree-Rom") he called *Ram Sha-ram* (rhymes with Sha-ZAM!). He referred to Mitchell Baker, a Netscape lawyer, as *Mister* Mitchell Baker. "That's *Missus* Mitchell Baker," said Barksdale. "Some of these nayums," said Warden, "you just can't tell. Could go either way." By the time he was confronted with a Netscape employee named Alan Louie, the Microsoft lawyer knew better than to assume anything about these people from Northern California. "It is *Mister* Alan Loueeee?" he boomed. Barksdale nodded. "And I assume it is *Lou-eeeee?*" His tone said, "These Netscayup people got the girls with the boys names and the boys with the girls names. What the hayl kind a ennaprise you runnin' anyway?"

Soon came the time for the Microsoft lawyer to question the letter Jim Clark had told Gary Reback to write to the Justice Department, immediately after the critical meeting between Microsoft and Netscape on June 21, 1995. Brandishing the letter, Warden asked Barksdale to concede that it omitted any mention of Microsoft's alleged offer to divide the market for browsers. (The idea was that if Microsoft had indeed made such a blatantly illegal suggestion, Netscape's lawyer would have at least mentioned it in his complaint to the DOJ.)

"Mr. Barksday-ul," said Warden, "does the letter say anything about a proposal to divide markets?"

Barksdale replied that he hadn't read Reback's letter, which was now before him. Warden asked him to look it over. "You want me to read this?" asked Barksdale, incredulously, holding up the letter like a turd.

"Yes," said Warden.

Once earlier Barksdale had waved his hand over some documents placed before him and declared, "These things are totally useless." Now he snorted, "A *four*-page single-spaced letter?"

"I was able to read through it fairly quickly," said Warden, plaintively.

"Well, you're a much smarter man than I am," said Barksdale, his voice dripping with condescension. The journalists in the bleacher seats exploded in laughter. Rich businessmen were honestly incapable of treating lawyers with anything but disdain.

"No," boomed Warden, in a desperate bid to recover whatever advantage there was in being the only fat hick in the room. "You're a much smarter man, Mr. Barksday-ul. That's why you're worth wu-uhn hunnerd million dollars, and the bank owns my howwwwwse."

At this point the judge peered down from the bench and said, sharply, "Are you through, Mr. Warden?"

He was. Barksdale wasn't. He'd been asked to recall the late stages of negotiations between Microsoft and Netscape, after Netscape had concluded that Microsoft never would divulge the critical code Netscape needed to make its browser compatible with Windows 95. He'd be damned if he wasn't going to recall it. He gazed out over the courtroom. It was, of course, filled with lawyers. "By now it had gotten down to the lawyers," Barksdale sighed, "and when that happens, you might as well forget about it."

Again, the journalists exploded in laughter. There it was again, plain as day. Oh, the disdain! Oh, the contempt! And if the disdain could be expressed just like that to some of the most highly paid lawyers in the land, what did it say about all those other lawyers rowed up along the conference tables in the well of the courtroom, who spent all their day tapping keyboards and whispering secrets. What about all those bright young things who had sacrificed the best years of their lives to the Harvard Law School and who now lived for the merest word of approval from the fat hick? Who did Jim Barksdale, Serious American Executive, think these whisperers of secrets and tappers of laptops were? Serfs!

As the disorder in the court subsided, Barksdale smiled and leaned over to the judge, like a man about to tell a joke in a duck blind. "I mean that in an appropriate way, Your Honor." His Honor blushed. What could he say? He was a lawyer. And this man was worth $100 million.

The only man who could peer down upon Barksdale with the same Olympian disdain as Barksdale peered down upon lawyers wasn't present to do so. But he made a dramatic appearance. Clark didn't come in person; he spent the early days of the Microsoft trial rushing to ready his boat to cross the Atlantic Ocean. But his image appeared on the giant screen in the courtroom, and he answered a few questions in a tone that suggested that people who worked as lawyers for Microsoft could not begin to understand the new new thing. "You obviously aren't a businessman," he said sarcastically at one point. *Bidnessman.* The law changes everything it touches, however, and it now did so in a way for which Clark was ill prepared, by probing his past. The American legal system opened up the cardboard boxes beside the old tuba in Clark's guest bedroom and went digging for damning evidence.

Up until then Microsoft's defense was not much more than a gloriously indiscriminate, flailing attack on Netscape. It consisted of four arguments. (1) Microsoft never bullied Netscape, especially not in the critical June 21, 1995, meeting between the two companies that had inspired Jim Clark to call the Department of Justice in the first place. (2) Even if Microsoft did bully Netscape in that meeting, the meeting was "a setup" to frame Microsoft for an antitrust suit. (3) Microsoft could not possibly be held responsible for Netscape's failure, because Netscape hadn't failed; it was still a market leader and a powerful innovator in Internet browser technology. (4) Netscape had failed badly, but through its own ineptitude. As evidence of this last point Microsoft's lawyer introduced a new book by two Harvard Business School professors, called *Competing on Internet Time.* The professors argued that Netscape courted disaster from the start, by taunting Microsoft. "Mooning the Giant" was what the business school professors had called this tactic. Clark had mooned the giant, first by referring to Microsoft in public as "the Death Star" and then by permitting his twenty-two-year-old associate, Marc Andreessen, to brag to journalists that Netscape would put Microsoft out of business.

Barksdale adopted a self-deprecating tone. Whenever the Microsoft lawyers set out to argue how successful Netscape remained, Jim Barksdale tried to maintain pretty much the opposite. And so the spectators witnessed the odd spectacle of two companies, both keenly aware that they were in a line of work where the perception of success led to success and the perception of failure to failure, bad-mouthing themselves. The rhetoric of the courtroom was very nearly the opposite of the rhetoric of the business world. The trick for Microsoft was to persuade the judge that it didn't have a monopoly without also persuading the stock market. The trick for Netscape was to avoid seeming pathetic.

And then Jim Clark entered the courtroom. A man who cared more about his past would have covered his tracks. Some part of his mind would have been devoted to viewing his actions as they would be viewed by history. But that wasn't the way he was built. Clark was inventing his life as he went along. Pushing forward in this manner, he left a mess behind him for others to clean up. The mess was often inspired, but it was still a mess. And out of the mess the lawyers for Microsoft plucked a single e-mail. It had been sent by Clark to the Microsoft executives Dan Rosen and Brad Silverberg on December 29, 1994, at three in the morning. "I'd like to convince you to reconsider," it began. It ran on for a full page, but the gist of it could be boiled down to a single passage:

> We want to make this company a success, but not at Microsoft's expense. We'd like to work with you. Working together could be in your self-interest as well as ours. Depending on your interest level, you might take an equity position in Netscape, with the ability to expand that position later. . . . Given the worry that exists regarding Microsoft's dominance of practically everything, we might be a good indirect way to get into the Internet business.

He concluded, "No one in my organization knows about this message."

Projected onto the big screen, Clark's e-mail had different effects on different people. Judge Thomas Penfield Jackson wore what was becoming his usual expression of profound bemusement. An e-mail sent at three in the morning was just further evidence that these technology billionaires were a bit . . . touched. The judge had his own idea of work, which was that it ended punctually at five in the afternoon. You wouldn't be catching *him* hunched over any little rectangular screen at three in the morning, trying to figure out how to make a billion dollars. His court was in session for two hours and fifteen minutes each morning and the same each afternoon. Four and a half hours a day, four days a week. Fridays were holidays. So were lots of other days, chosen seemingly at random by the judge. The very idea of someone's writing an e-mail at three in the morning on December 29, which was, after all, still part of Christmas vacation, struck him as preposterous.

The lawyers for the Department of Justice were glum. They were doing their best to persuade the judge that Microsoft had muscled Netscape around. If Clark had invited Microsoft into his business back in December 1994, how could the DOJ now claim that Microsoft had forced its charms upon Netscape in June 1995? The DOJ's lawyers were still angry at Clark. He hadn't told them about his overture to Microsoft; the department's lawyers had learned about it only when the e-mail was produced by Microsoft in pretrial evidence.

Finally, there was Barksdale's reaction to Clark's astonishing e-mail, which amounted to an offer to serve as a kind of Trojan horse for Microsoft's invasion of the Internet. Clark had talked Barksdale into leaving his job with AT&T. Barksdale had agreed to run Netscape on the condition that he have complete control. Clark and John Doerr had both agreed not to meddle. And now this! Clark's e-mail inviting Microsoft to sit in on his business was written *five days* before Barksdale reported for work. And the only reason Barksdale knew about it now was that the Department of Justice lawyers had warned him it was coming before he took the stand.

Forewarned, Barksdale sought to maintain that Clark's e-mail had been written in "a moment of weakness." The Microsoft lawyer, of course, hoped to persuade the judge that the e-mail was not the act of a man fighting his demons at three in the morning but a deliberate corporate policy. He wanted to force Barksdale to concede that he and Clark were part of a unified team and that, therefore, Barksdale must have known of the e-mail. Once he had Barksdale under oath, he offered him a terrible choice. Barksdale could agree that he, like Jim Clark, had been happy to invite Microsoft into Netscape's business, and thus torpedo the government's entire case. Or he could seem like a fool who was not privy to the intimate affairs of his own company.

"Mr. Barksdale," the Microsoft lawyer boomed. *Barksday-ul.* Barksdale looked up.

"Is Mr. Clark a highly secretive man?" asked the lawyer.

"He can be very secretive, yes sir," replied Barksdale.

"Mr. Clark has had a very successful business career, has he not?" asked the lawyer.

"Yes, he has," replied Barksdale.

"And does he enjoy a public reputation for veracity?" asked the lawyer.

"I couldn't comment on that," replied Barksdale. "I don't know."

"Do you regard him as a truthful man?" It took him so long to ask the question that a swarm of mosquitos could have hatched in his mouth. "Truthful" emerged from his fat throat as *tru-u-u-uth . . . fullll.* "Man" became *mayan.* Even "Clark" became two syllables. *Clar-ark.*

Nevertheless, Barksdale needed time to think. Had it been a movie instead of real life, he would have flashed back to the preceding three years. Right from the moment he left the secure womb of Serious American Business and entered ClarkWorld, Barksdale's life had become a constant struggle to preserve his dignity. At dinner parties Barksdale told a funny story about his first trip down to Silicon Valley, when he and his wife met up with a realtor Clark had put him on to, with the assurance that she was the best in the business.

Clark's real estate agent turned out to be one of those loud, garrulous people who, as they drive, insist on making eye contact with the passengers in the back seat. "You want to see Scott Cook's house?" she hollered over her shoulder to a terrified Mr. and Mrs. Jim Barksdale. Scott Cook was the chairman of Intuit, the financial software company. "Is it for sale?" asked Barksdale. "No," said the woman. "Then I don't want to see it," said Barksdale. Clark's realtor ignored him and squealed through this enormous bronze gate and into Scott Cook's driveway. Out of the house shot Mrs. Scott Cook to investigate this intrusion. Clark's realtor had panicked, backed up and tried to make a quick getaway but ended up rolling back into Mrs. Cook's newly planted garden. There she became stuck in the mud. Wheels spun, plants flew. Mrs. Cook was livid. She looked at Barksdale as if he were some kind of criminal. They had to call a fire truck and a tow truck to extract him, his wife, and Clark's realtor from the garden. The episode lasted an hour.

At the time it appeared to be a freak incident. In retrospect, it was the keynote for Barksdale's career in ClarkWorld. Clark had treated him as gently as Clark was capable of treating any captain, but that was still more roughly than Barksdale had ever been treated. The IPO had been an excellent case in point. Barksdale had wanted Netscape to remain a private company. He liked the old-fashioned method of waiting until a company was profitable before taking on public shareholders. But just a few months after Barksdale joined the company Clark showed up for a board meeting with Frank Quattrone and Larry Sonsini in tow. Quattrone and Sonsini were, respectively, the leading investment banker and the leading lawyer in Silicon Valley. During the meeting Clark, who was of course eager to get the money to pay for his boat, turned to them and asked what they thought about taking Netscape public. Lawyers and investment bankers make their fortunes when companies go public. Both men joined Clark in pushing Barksdale to do the deed. All so that Jim Clark could pay for his boat!

You might have thought Clark would have been well satisfied to get his money. You might have thought he'd move on. Not a bit! Clark was forever hounding Barksdale to follow Yahoo and Excite into the portal business. "Portal," like "browser," was another coinage of the Internet. On the heels of Netscape several people at once had the bright idea of creating a sort of doorway, or portal, into the new virtual world. The browser enabled the user to travel around the Internet, but how would he know where to go? The information on the Internet cried out to be organized, and the portal companies responded to the cry. Clark kept telling Barksdale that the future was not in selling browser but in attracting the masses to Netscape's own rather lackluster portal. Worse, he was right! On technical matters Barksdale was at the mercy of Marc Andreessen, the young man who had first shown Clark an Internet browser and helped him create Netscape. Andreessen had stayed on as Netscape's technical authority, but he had threatened to quit half a dozen times, and threatened to sell all his Netscape shares more often than that. Imagine what the financial press would have done with that! As it was, Andreessen had unloaded a quarter of his stake near the low, at sixteen dollars a share. Jim Barksdale, Serious American Executive, was no longer a leader of men. He was a baby-sitter.

On top of it all there was this trial. It might as well have been Clark's doing. Once it became inevitable that Netscape would be the center-piece of the DOJ's complaint against Microsoft, Barksdale took charge of the matter, of course. That was his job—to lend order and reason to other people's anarchies. But the whole reason Clark had called Gary Reback, and had him write the letter to the Justice Department, was his fear that Barksdale would never have done anything. And he was probably right.

As Barksdale sat unhappily in the witness box he considered the question. Did he regard Jim Clark as a truthful man? Already he had sworn that he had never seen Clark's e-mail. This might be strictly true—after all, Barksdale hadn't figured out how to read his own e-mail—but his profession of ignorance did not begin to capture the spirit of that moment. The DOJ had shown Netscape's counsel Roberta Katz a copy of Clark's e-mail, and Katz had helped Barksdale prepare for his cross-examination. They both knew that he would be shown Clark's e-mail, and asked to explain it. Barksdale's show of ignorance was for effect: if he didn't know about it, then it must not be terribly important. But the truth was he was shocked. He'd been hired to confer a certain dignity on Clark's new enterprise, and the e-mail stripped him of that. The e-mail made him seem like the hired help, who had been told only as much as he needed to know.

"Do you regard Jim Clark as a truthful man?" the lawyer had asked.

"I regard him as a salesman," replied Barksdale.

"I'm not going to touch that, Mr. Barksdale," said the Microsoft lawyer, and moved on to less interesting matters.

# 15

## At Sea in the Home of the Future

To spend any time at all with Clark you had to foreswear the usual conveniences that come with planning ahead: advance-purchase airline tickets, hotel reservations, clean underwear. Clark's friends learned to take it in stride when the call came from Jim—always from a cell phone, usually a thousand miles or so from where they expected him to be at that moment—that began, "Hey, um, I just wanted to let you know that, um, there's been a change of plans. I won't be meeting you in Nairobi this afternoon." Clark's wife Nancy Rutter had long ago figured out that any plans he made were not plans at all. A plan was merely a theory of how he might spend his day; at all times it clashed in his mind with half a dozen other theories.

It came as no surprise to anyone who knew Clark—and it certainly did not surprise his new crew—that before he crossed the Atlantic Ocean on his new computerized yacht he first had to change his mind seven or eight times about whether to do it. First he said that he would not miss the crossing for the world. Then he said that he might have to miss it to give a speech to some students at Stanford University. Then he saw that he could cancel the speech to make the crossing, and became more excited than ever about sailing across the ocean. Once he set the date of departure, he said the boat could not leave, because on that day the curtains in the boat's living room were not exactly the way he wanted them to be. On and on he went. He was a man with a daisy, playing "She loves me, she loves me not," except that he was doing it with his entire life.

Finally, at four o' clock one morning in January 1999, or three months after Healtheon canceled its IPO, we boarded Clark's plane in Palm Beach, Florida, and flew to the Canary Islands: I, Clark, and *Hyperion's* chef, Tina Braddock, whom Clark had decided to take with him wherever he went. The rest of its crew and the software engineer Steve Hague were already on board. (Lance and Tim had been sent back to the room on top of the Jenny Craig weight loss center in Menlo Park, California.) *Hyperion* had just passed Spain on its way to a dock in Grand Canary, where it planned to collect us the next day. Clark's jet was fired up and ready to go. His luggage compartment was crammed with food and wine for the crossing. After seven years of writing software that could sail a boat, Clark, at last, had the chance to watch his program guide his boat across an ocean. Even so, no one on his jet could predict what would happen next. When Clark went off to fiddle with something in the back of his plane, Tina leaned across the aisle and said, nervously, "I wonder if we're really going to go."

She knew! Somewhere was a reason for not sailing across the Atlantic Ocean on *Hyperion's* maiden voyage. She also knew that she would have to wait to find out what that might be.

By the time we arrived on Grand Canary, the crowd of islanders had already gathered. It was an ugly dock, in an industrial area, half a mile from any place to which a sane human being would voluntarily venture. Yet all that night the people came and gawked. At midnight islanders streamed down the dock on foot, or puttered out in shambolic old cars, stopped, and peered into the boat. By midnight there was not much to see: a few people milling around; Steve and Jim down below plinking commands into their computers; and Allan Prior perched in his captain's chair, wearing the same outfit he'd worn the past three days, staring, for reasons that would soon become clear, into the computer screen.

A few hours after we arrived, Allan took his position at the helm, behind the row of computer screens, punched a few buttons, and sailed *Hyperion* into the Atlantic Ocean.

As we pushed away from the Canary Island dock and headed out to sea, the crew and the passengers gathered around the captain and took one long, last look. From the guest cabins came Steve and Clark and Louie Psihoyos, the photographer Clark had hired to document the crossing. From the kitchen came Tina and her steward, Peter, and his assistant, Kristi; from the deck came the first mate, Jaime, and the two deckhands, Simon Hutchins and the curiously named Celcelia. The sun beamed and the sea stretched out calmly as if the Atlantic were inviting us to cross. Just when it seemed that everyone was present and basking in the pride of departure, the kitchen floor opened up and a man climbed out of a hole. He looked as if he had not seen sunlight for a century. He was the engineer, Robert.

That is how eleven of the twelve people on board began crossing the Atlantic Ocean—with a sense of adventure. For most people who do it there is some romance in sailing across the Atlantic Ocean. Columbus, no less, had left from the Canary Islands and sailed for three months to the Caribbean. We would follow Columbus's route, though we'd need only ten days to make the same trip. Imagine! The rest of us did; only Clark didn't, or wouldn't, or couldn't imagine. He was not one of those people who can be sustained for long by other people's fictions. He required his own. He saw the romance in the journey, or at any rate he saw that there *should* be romance in it. Certainly, the idea of it appealed to him. If it hadn't, he wouldn't have hired a photographer to come along to document it. But it soon became clear why he'd been so reluctant to come. The reality of the thing would nearly kill him.

The reality of crossing the Atlantic on a sailboat is that it is tedious. Very, very tedious. At least when it goes well it is tedious. When it goes badly it is treacherous. Not long after we departed, Robert, the engineer, gave me and Louie, who, it was clear to all, had to be watched like a couple of morons, a tour of the stuff that was used only when things went wrong: the life rafts, the fancy life jackets with special whistles and flares, the man-overboard system, the fire alarms. Robert tapped the side of the canister of gas hanging from a wall and used, apparently, to put out fires. ("The chances that you'll be firing the gases are very remote," he said. "But if everyone else on board is dead, you know, have a go.") So far as I could tell there were several ways to die while crossing an ocean on a sailboat; if there weren't, it wouldn't be an adventure. One was to be run over by a tanker so large that it didn't even realize it had hit you. The second was to be swept up in a storm that caused the mast to snap or the boat to capsize. A third was to fall overboard. The fourth, and most likely, was to die of boredom.

Clark was concerned only with the fourth. For him the crossing was a study in absences: no change, no diversion, no stimulation, no new place to go. He seemed to know at the outset that there are only so many times you can find Orion's belt, or scan the horizon for whales and porpoises that fail to materialize, or remind yourself that an ocean crossing is meant to be the thrill of a lifetime before you begin to doubt the whole enterprise. The average man would require perhaps three days to discover his inner mutineer. It took Clark a bit under three hours. Exactly two hours and forty minutes into the ten-day trip, he turned to me and said, "I don't know why the fuck I came on this. It's going to be boring as hell." He then walked over to Allan, who struck the pose of the captain at the helm, and gave an order to relay to the computers, which amounted to: "Get across this ocean in a straight line, as fast as you possibly can."

Then he went down below into the living room and moped. On a boat the living room is for some reason called the "salon." Clark sank into one of the deep upholstered chairs in his salon and surveyed his creation. A Monet landscape hung on the wall over his head, and a Picasso portrait from his Blue Period hung on the wall eight feet across from him—when he set out to make enough money to build his boat, he'd overshot a bit. Here was the moment in the Hollywood movie where the script would direct him to wave his hand over his brand-new, $37 million boat decorated with another $30 million in paintings and say what an amazing thing it was that a poor boy from Plainview, Texas, could sail off into the sunset in such a machine, bought and paid for with money he'd made inside of eighteen months. Instead, his mouth squinched up into its terrifying pucker of irritation. You could see that his mind had got hold of some object it disapproved of and was working itself into a tizzy. Finally, he said, "They should have extended the woodwork around the portholes."

The crew looked up to see what was wrong with the portholes. They were rimmed by white painted aluminum rather than the dark teak and mahogany of the rest of the interior. They seemed fine to me, more than fine, and obviously they had seemed fine to the fifty or so Dutch master woodworkers who had created the interior. But here we were, at sea at last, and all Clark could think about was how they might have been better. The man chose his own path to madness, and it was the path not of the pessimist but of the utopian. He was on an endless search for some unattainable solution. The perfect world. The moment he suspected that he had created that perfect world, however, he found something in it that needed to be changed.

For the other eleven people on board the trip began calmly enough. Those who had business went about it. Celcelia and Jaime and Simon swabbed the decks and tested the sails.  Steve hunched over his computer for hours on end until his posture called to mind Ichabod Crane with a backache. Clark, once he became tired of finding things that were wrong with his new boat, vanished into his cabin to find things that were wrong with his computer code. For the first few days he appeared only to eat, to drink, or to consult with Steve about some intractable bug. The seas were neither calm nor rough. There were no tankers or, for that matter, ships of any sort on the horizon. The only voice on the radio was static, punctuated by the occasional squawking from Filipino deckhands on the supertankers we could not see. "Filipino monkey! Filipino monkey!" they'd holler hysterically at each other for some reason no one could explain. Then they burst into mad howls. They sounded like people who rammed sailboats for kicks.

For the first few days we lived in a changeless world. Our biggest challenge, at least at the outset, was to avoid getting on each other's nerves. The challenge was heightened by a strangely powerful form of sleep deprivation, known as the "watch." Other than Clark everyone on board was required to sit two four-hour watches to ensure that we were not plowed under by the Filipino monkeys. Allan Prior posted the watch schedule just before we left. It looked like this:

12:00–4:00: Jaime, Celcelia, Peter
4:00–8:00: Robert, Simon, Louie, Michael
8:00–12:00: Allan, Kristi, Steve

The person listed first on each shift was officially designated "captain of the watch." Our watch had four people on it because it included the two people—me and Louie, the photographer—who had no business on the boat. The captain had assumed that two idiots added up to one useful person. Actually, they didn't even add up to that, as we discovered one evening when Robert was below inspecting the engine room. Struck by an intensely painful bowel movement, Simon hopped around the deck on one foot for twenty minutes straight rather than entrust Louie and me with the job of spotting supertankers before they crushed us.

The watch schedule repeated itself each twelve hours. In the grand scheme of human suffering a four-hour watch does not sound like much. Until you have gazed into perfect, unchanging blankness for four hours straight, you might even think it soothing. Coupled with the churning of the sea and the creaking of the boat, it was deadly. The sea transformed the boat's beds into souped-up, turbo-charged versions of the coin-operated vibrating beds in a 1970 Holiday Inn. The new Dutch woodwork crackled like strings of miniature firecrackers. All in all, bedtime on *Hyperion* was more an idea than a fact. This was true not merely for the landlubbers but for everyone on board. Before long, eyes were rheumy, nerves frayed, and the feelings that are normally well sealed inside people's hearts began to leak—then gush—out.

For the first few days Captain Allan Prior either sat at the wheel or hovered covetously over the computer with an intensity that surprised me, given how often he disavowed any interest in the thing. Once every half hour or so something minor went wrong, or the computer believed it went wrong, and an alarm sounded. "Beep-beep-beep," it went, as Clark had not yet had time to write the code that enabled the computer to shout at the crew. Whenever the alarm made its irritating noise, another crew member shouted out "Robert! Alarm!" and Robert, the stout young engineer, would pop out through some hatch in the floor, wander over, punch a button or two on the computer, and the annoying beep-beep-beep ceased. On the surface, at least, all seemed well.

All was not well—though, apart from Clark's obvious discontent, the signs of this were subtle. On the first night Louie's cabin overheated, all by itself. Louie emerged for our 4:00 A.M. watch with trickles of sweat running down the sides of his face. He asked, quite reasonably, "Why's it so fucking hot in my cabin?" It turned out that it was hot because the computer decided it should be hot. It took about two hours of punching buttons on the computers to persuade it to lower the temperature, only to have the computer decide, seemingly by edict, to raise it again. On the second night, as Steve slept in the cabin he and I shared, someone mistakenly activated the flat-panel display screen tucked inside the ceiling. Our cabin, for some reason I never understood, had one computer screen in a drawer by the bed and another hidden up in the ceiling. At two in the morning the ceiling over Steve's head opened with an eerie hum, and a green glowing screen dropped down from a new hole, like a UFO. It had scared the hell out of him, as it would have out of anyone.

Obviously, these were mere ripples in the pond. Changes in technology are not simple matters. Often they change the way people interact with their surroundings, and with each other. Invent the automobile, and people will travel more often; invent air-conditioning, and they'll travel south. *Hyperion* offered a neat little illustration of the early stages of technically inspired social chaos. There is, or was, until Jim Clark got ahold of it, probably no space in the Western world outside of a church more highly ritualized than a sailboat. It has its own peculiar vocabulary designed to mystify outsiders. Lee, jib, splice tang, furl, gimbal—not one in ten intelligent landlubbers could define half of them. There are customs and traditions on a sailboat. There is a carefully observed pecking order. The captain lords it over the first mate, the first mate lords it over the deckhands, the deckhands lord it over the stewards. Into this neat little feudal environment Clark had thrust his anarchic temperament and his twenty-five Silicon Graphics computers—more computing power than you'd find in a big, fully automated factory. The crew members who did not understand computers suddenly discovered they were at the mercy of those who did. This posed some obvious threats to the peace.

As I say, the early signs that the technologist's utopia was anything but a utopia were subtle. On our watch, for instance, Simon and Robert preferred not to sit together. When Robert entered a conversation,

Simon left it. Either I sat with Simon on the deck and Louie sat with Robert on the bridge, or, more often, I sat with Robert on the bridge and Louie sat with Simon on the deck. The two crew members were clearly avoiding each other, without making that big a deal of it. On the third evening Robert and I sat together in the tall swivel chairs on the bridge, facing the bank of five glowing flat-panel display screens. Outside, the sea washed gently against the hull and the stars twinkled. Robert began to talk about what it meant to be an engineer. When he used the word "engineer," he clearly meant "old-fashioned engineer" and not "computer geek." He held the view that there were two kinds of people in the world, those who did the work and those who got the credit. Real engineers belonged in the former category. Among other things, he felt that engineers had been generally neglected by history.

"Who invented the gas turbine engine?" he asked, a bit sharply.

I had no idea.

"Frank Whittle," he said. "Who was the chief engineer on the Apollo project?"

I said I didn't know the answer to that one either.

"Exactly," said Robert, and rested his case. In the darkness I could hear him smiling. "But if you want to get your picture in the paper now," he said, "All you have to do is sit in front of a computer screen." He whistled a bit to himself, then said, "When something goes wrong with this boat, everyone assumes the engineer broke it. When the computer program goes wrong, everyone assumes the geeks *fix* it. *Why* do you think that is?"

The room was dark except for the glowing orange screens. The waves rocked the boat back and forth. Robert was no more than a thick shadow. "The problem here," that voice now said, "is that Jim has built the most technologically sophisticated boat ever built and staffed it with nontechnical people."

This statement made no immediate sense whatsoever to me. After all, Simon had been hired by Clark to present the computers to the crew with a human face. Simon could not program a computer, but he had learned, from a three-week stint at Silicon Graphics, how to perform some rudimentary technical tasks. If your laptop crashed, Simon was distinctly more likely than you were to solve the problem. He belonged to the growing tribe of semitechnical people whose main function is to respond to mankind's complaints about its computers. Undoubtedly, he was the first deckhand in history who, to become a deckhand, needed to know some computer science. I said as much to Robert.

"If something goes really wrong, Simon can't fix it," said Robert. "That's one of the reasons there's friction between me and Simon. I told Allan that I thought the person on board who was to be the computer interface should have fifteen years training in the area. Allan doesn't have any idea how it all works. And neither does Simon. *Simon cannot program the computer.* These aren't technical people. And you want things to work when you press the button on the computer."

Apparently, Robert had already become slightly fed up by things not working when he pressed a button on the computer. He was, after all, a technical man. There were times, he said, when he couldn't figure out how to turn out the lights. And it bothered him.

Late on the fourth day at sea we turned south and switched on the engine. South was the wrong direction for anyone making a beeline for the New World. Just a few hours earlier Clark had said he was in a hurry to get back home, as he really needed to give this speech to two thousand doctors who might become customers of Healtheon. But now he'd changed his mind about the urgency of arriving on time; he said he wanted to get out of the cold.

As a weak wind blew from the wrong direction, the computer reeled the mainsail back into the boom and revved the engine to a brisk twelve knots. For the moment we would forget the joy of sailing and rely on the engine to get us across. Clark retired to his cabin at ten o' clock, and I went to the guest cabin soon afterward. At midnight Steve's watch ended, and he came into the cabin and fell into the other bed. He reflected briefly on his curious role: the man who wrote the code that controlled the sailboat. The boat was not meant to be carrying a programmer, but now a programmer was indispensable. "Back at the boatyard we really didn't have a chance to test the system, because we never had the full system up and running," he said. "I needed to be around just to understand the computers because no one else does—except Jim, and Jim doesn't want to fuck with explaining it all to Simon. I still wonder how this boat will function without either me or Lance or Tim or Jim on board. If there's a serious failure, I guess they'll just reboot the computers and hope for the best."

I asked the obvious question how *Hyperion* had come to pass. "I'm not sure how much Jim knew about sailing, to be honest," he said. "He just had this idea he wanted to sail a boat by remote control."

"He sailed a *lot* before he left Silicon Graphics," I said, because he had.

"Maybe," said Steve. "But this thing kind of started as a lab experiment." Then he said again what he had said once before, so disconcertingly. "I don't think Jim understood that people's lives depended on this stuff working properly."

Then he fell into a deep sleep. The boat whirred and clicked and rose and fell. The new wood creaking into place sounded like a tall tree just before it snaps. Other than that, I realized, every noise on board was the result of the computer doing something. I stared at the ceiling and envied Steve his snore.

Half an hour later, just before one in the morning, the engine stopped. The whirring and clicking stopped with it. The boat went quiet.

When the engine quit for the first time, I was rolling around in bed, attempting to calculate the size of the waves from the violence with which I was thrown back against the wall and forth into the safety board that had been installed to prevent me from being hurled out of the bed altogether. Even I could tell that something had gone wrong. One moment there was the low whir and the feel of a machine cutting purposefully through the waters. The next moment the boat was adrift. The waves rocked the bed more violently than before, and in new directions. Up top I went.

The watch from midnight to four in the morning was manned by Jaime, the Australian first mate, Peter, the American steward, and Celcelia, the Swedish deckhand. Normally, they'd be wandering about checking up on things. When I arrived, all three were in the control room, pushing buttons on the computer screens. They were clearly perplexed. A small red light marked "Alarm" flashed on the computer, which emitted its annoying high-pitched beep. Luckily, the next person to arrive was Robert.

"I couldn't sleep," he said, popping his head through the hatch. "What's happened?"

"The engine just stopped," said Jaime.

"Well, that's unfortunate," said Robert, and moved to the screen and switched off the alarms. The beeping sound ceased. In its place appeared the man who invented the idea of the beeping sound. "What's going on?" said Clark, climbing up the stairs from the main salon to the control room. "It sounded like the engine stopped." He moved into a position immediately in front of the bank of display screens. He punched in the password that enabled him to enter God Mode. The darkness was relieved only by the light orange glow of the computer screens.

It was just past one in the morning. To fully appreciate what happened next, you have to remember that it had been at least four days since anyone had slept properly. Now, six of the twelve people on board were in the control room. Robert and Jim, their faces lit a pale orange, poked woozily at the computer screens while the first mate, Jaime, hovered behind them and waited to hear the news. The screens offered no end of information: the sea beneath us was 5,732 meters deep, the wind behind us blew at sixteen knots, the boat we were on drifted at a little more than a knot, in the direction of Antarctica, the wine cellar was cooled to perfection, the door to the captain's cabin was closed, the captain's lights were out . . . on and on the computer went, explaining everything but what we wanted to know: *Why had the engine stopped?* The engine was our salvation. The engine would propel us out of the path of cackling Filipino monkeys. The engine was what would take us home instead of to Antarctica.

Robert vanished into the bowels of the boat. Four minutes later the engine restarted, and everyone breathed easier. Robert reappeared with the look of a man trying to disguise, even to himself, how pleased he was with his work. Thirty seconds later he had some help: the engine quit again. Again Robert vanished, again the engine restarted, again everyone breathed easier. And again Robert reappeared, but this time without a trace of self-satisfaction. The engine rewarded his humility. This time it did not quit.

Louie now stumbled up the stairs from his cabin. Like all good photographers, Louie clearly had a talent for turning up where he wasn't wanted, and remaining inconspicuous. Soon he was snapping away.

"Now you know," drolled Robert, just loud enough for Clark to hear but not so loud that he clearly *intended* Clark to hear; "if you want to get your picture in the newspaper, all you have to do is go to a screen, open up about five windows, and look like you know what you're doing."

Clark said nothing. Robert fixed things. Robert was *useful*. There was nothing wrong with Robert. Ergo, Robert was permitted his careful bit of insolence in this tense moment. Clark and Robert then stood together at the computer screens. Clark naturally wanted to know what Robert had done. Robert explained to Clark that the problem was in something called the "sea chest." The sea chest took in salt water from the ocean to cool the engine. The salt water did not actually circulate through the engine, of course. It merely drew away heat from the outside surface of the engine. If the sea chest contained air, rather than water, the engine lost some of its ability to cool itself. The computer understood that it was dangerous for the engine to overheat. When the engine overheated, the computer shut the engine down.

"When I went down the first time, I saw air in the sea chest," Robert said. "I must not have got it all the first time I blew it out."

On that lovely mahogany bridge at one in the morning there were three responses to our condition. The five nontechnical people—me, Louie, Jaime, Peter, Celcelia—were pleased as punch. The sea chest—whatever the hell that was—had been fixed! The engine worked! We would not drift into Antarctica! The mechanical man—Robert—was satisfied but hardly pleased. Anytime the engine failed, his world became slightly less certain. The third response came from Clark. Clark always insisted on his own response to any technical problem, and it gave him a kind of control over the opinion surrounding the problem. He was distinctly concerned. After listening to Robert's explanation, he said, "That doesn't make sense." Robert asked him why not. "The seas are too calm," said Clark. "I can see how the sea chest might take in air when the boat was really being tossed around, but it shouldn't take in air in these conditions."

At that point the engine was running fine, and so this sounded like the idle carping of an intellectual. Clark pressed his point anyway. "If the engine was overheating," he said, "we should have had an alarm *before* it shut down." He motioned to the computer screen. "The alarms that went off were all in response to the engine shutting down. They came *after*."

It wasn't that Robert failed to see the reason in Clark's thinking. He saw it clearly enough. Robert had worked for a lot of rich yacht owners; Clark was the first who presumed accurately to know a great deal about his machine. Robert was forever saying things like "The difference between talking to Jim and talking to Allan is the difference between talking to someone who understands what you are trying to tell him *instantly* and someone who you know will never understand." But Robert was equipped with a disposition slightly different from Clark's: when the machines were working, he was not inclined to suspect that something was wrong. And the engine worked! Robert said as much. Clark appeared to agree: if the engine was running, Robert must have fixed it. Wearily, Robert returned to bed. Clark kept fiddling with the computer.

Fifteen minutes later the engine quit again.

This time, as the ocean hurled us crazily, Jaime and Peter and Celcelia spoke nervously among themselves, though when they saw me coming they shut up. When the crew begins to hide the situation from the passengers, the passengers should begin to worry. "This is crazy," Clark said, more to himself than to the five people who watched him with incomprehension. "I can't figure it out."

He pointed to what he was unable to figure out. Attached to the engine were dozens of sensors. The sensors measured pretty much everything that can be measured inside an engine. The computer ordered and monitored this data. But one piece of data—the pressure on the engine—made no sense. The number on the pressure gauge should always be positive, there being no such thing as negative pressure. The number should also be fairly small—typically it read between 1 and 2. Now the computer screen read -38883354.6669. It was a crazy number. The computer clearly had a screw loose.

Clark said, "Steve." He turned around as if he expected to find Steve over his shoulder. "Steve is . . . where?" he asked.

"Steve's asleep," said Jaime. It was now well past two in the morning. Steve was more than asleep, I said. Steve was in a coma.

"Wake him up," said Clark.

Steve was awakened. He struggled out of bed and up onto the bridge. He did not look well. The truth was that Steve's brain, unlike Clark's, had a limited appetite for technical malfunction. Steve long ago had banned computers from his home back in Silicon Valley to prevent the blasted machines from following him everywhere he went. Here on the high seas he could not escape them; here home was a computer.

In that falsely bright tone peculiar to people hoping to persuade others that they are fully conscious when they are not, Steve said, "So, what's up?"

"Something is fucking up these computers," said Clark.

"That's new," said Steve.

Steve and Clark now stared at the screens together. Clark pressed buttons with more energy than before, like a man who needed to get his money out of the ATM in a hurry. Apparently, a lot of the data was strange. According to the computer, for instance, the wind direction was exactly the opposite of what it had been a few minutes earlier. "The wind has really come around," said Clark. He turned to Jaime. "Has the wind changed?"

Jaime said that the wind had not changed. Sailors know these things.

"But this screen shows the wind coming out of the north," said Clark. "It was coming out of the south."

"This computer is definitely a bit funky," said Steve. "The wind direction is wrong on it."

"What the hell is going on?" Clark said. It wasn't really a question. He wasn't exactly angry at Steve, more at the situation in which Steve, unfortunately, happened to be central.

"The computers have some strange problems," said Steve.

The only two people on board equipped even to discuss the computer for more than a minute or two stared uncomprehendingly at the funky screens. This was not obviously dramatic. One hundred years from now, I thought, if they dredged us up perfectly preserved from the bottom of the ocean, the salvage team would conclude we had gone down without a struggle, staring blithely into a row of computer screens. On the other hand, one hundred years from now salvage crews might understand that staring at the computer screen on Jim Clark's boat was the fiercest form of struggle. With computer people, the appearance of inaction masks the drama of their thoughts. They were maybe the first tyrants to attempt to conquer the world logically. The screen was the fodder for their endless series of "if . . . then" statements. If the computer triggered alarms before the engine overheated, then the engine must not have overheated. If the engine did not overheat, then the trouble might lie outside the engine. If the problem was outside the engine, then it could be inside the computer.

Since all of the important problems on the boat, with the exception of who had sex with whom and how well we ate, were routed through the computer, this thought was not terribly reassuring. At length Clark decided he could not get what he wanted out of the computers on the bridge. "Let's go downstairs," he said. We did.

Once they were seated in front of the Silicon Graphics work station built into the wall of his cabin, Clark's conversation with Steve vanished into a black hole of arcana.

"This negative number is very strange," said Clark.

"The MSB is in units of 10," said Steve. God knows what it meant, but that's what he said.

"But you see here—it keeps flipping back to a large negative number," said Clark, punching a button. "Which causes me to be suspicious that it's not in our code."

None of this made any sense to anyone who had not programmed the computer. But the general drift was now at least clear to me: the problem might be not in the engine but in the software that controlled the engine. Clark thought that the crude computers attached to the engine—known as PLCs, for programmable logic controllers—could be transmitting bad data to the fancy Silicon Graphics machines in the computer room. He thought that the computers had wrongly perceived something wrong with the engine, and so switched the engine off. A problem in the software implicated Steve, but only in a general way. The PLCs had been programmed by some Dutch guys back in the boatyard. The programming of PLCs was meant to be trivial, which was why the job had been left to the Dutch guys in the first place.

Steve and Jim were well on their way to a long, baffling conversation about the boat's software, but before they could get there the engine *started up*. The boat stopped pitching madly. It cut with renewed purpose through the sea. The engine, it seemed, had a mind of its own. Then Robert appeared with a sneaky smile on his face. All by himself, without telling anyone, he'd woken up, clambered down to the engine room, blown out the sea chest, and started up the engine. Now, however, he conceded that he could not swear he had fixed the deeper problem, since he was not sure what the deeper problem was. But at least the boat was running again. Clark and Steve returned to the bridge; this time Robert followed.

Up top, in front of the four big computer screens, Clark complained about the state of his art. "Steve, something is *really* fucking these computers up," he said. Steve muttered something about there being a lot more work to do. Clark then hit the button that pulled up the map of the world, with *Hyperion* on it. Its accuracy had actually slipped since the trials in the North Sea. The boat appeared on the map as a blue scaphoid. At that moment, according to the computer, we were cruising just north of Yemen. Clark just stared at the screen as his yacht crept across the Saudi Arabian desert. "Fuck it" was all he said.

Even he was too tired to think about what it might mean. In any case, he was soon distracted by other problems. On each side of the bridge were the radar screens that let us know if we were about to be plowed under by Filipino monkeys. The radar screen on the left began to blink, like a faulty light bulb. All the other pieces of equipment, along with the data they generated, had been stuffed away in cabinets, where they played the bit part of sending data directly to the computers. Clark's software acted as a kind of operating system through which every other instrument must connect; he had played the same sort of trick on the manufacturers of sailboat equipment as Microsoft played on the entire software industry. The radar was the lone exception. The radar was the only instrument Clark had neglected to subsume; he just never quite got around to doing it. When he saw the blinking radar, Clark's shoulders sagged. The radar had been his responsibility. "I guess I created that problem," he said.

It was now well past three in the morning. No one wanted to bother with yet another computer problem. The engine was running fine. Robert was obviously exhausted. Still, he could not hide how pleased he was by his response to a potential crisis. "Had we been in the Straits of Gibraltar with an oil tanker coming towards us," he said, "we'd have been all right. I had that engine running in five minutes." He headed off to rescue sleep from the two hours before our watch. Steve wandered out on the aft deck and gazed up at the world's tallest mast. He noticed how much it resembled an endless chain of crucifixes that reached up, and finally vanished, into the starry night sky. "You could hang huge statues of Jesus from each spreader, and it would look like a Mexican pickup truck," he said. With that he stumbled over to one of the computer screens on deck—the one Allan sat in front of but ignored—and stuck a yellow Post-it sticker on its surface. It read, "Allan: I fucked up the longitude program. We are not in the Arabian desert. Steve."

Then he, too, went back to bed. Clark soon followed. It was nearly four in the morning. After three hours of struggle *Hyperion* was once again pointed south. The two men who fully understood the computer, and the one man who fully understood the engine, had exhausted themselves. At no point did it occur to any of these technical people to wake Allan Prior. Through it all he had slept soundly. In a technological crisis, the captain was plainly of no use. And all crises on board *Hyperion* were now technological.

## 16

**Chasing Ghosts**

The morning after the engine failed, the seas were unusually calm. For the first time since we'd left the Canaries, the sun shone bright and hot. Normally, there weren't more than two people on the bridge. Everyone who wasn't on watch either ate or slept, or tried to. That afternoon was an exception. Simon and Jaime and Celcelia swabbed the decks. Steve hunted for the bug that might have disturbed the engine. Robert nosed around in the kitchen cupboards, and then disappeared down into the bowels of the ship. It was as if each person on board had offered himself a fresh start. Someone spotted a school of porpoises gamboling in the bow wake. Even Clark, in a brief but failed stab at genuine enthusiasm, came up top to see.

"Hyp 4 is talking to Hyp 19," said Steve, hunched over a computer and trying to find the bug that generated the numbers that made no sense. Each of the twenty-five computers on board had been assigned a number. According to Steve they had already acquired their own personalities—a trait that did not bode well for the Home of the Future. Now two of the more troublesome were speaking to each other.

"What?" said Allan, disinterestedly two seats away. He wasn't listening. He was reading intently from another computer screen.

"There is something funky going on here," said Steve.

Allan continued staring into his own screen. Finally, after Steve had ascertained he was being ignored, and gone back to the mystery at hand, Allan looked up. He said, with the satisfaction of a man at the end of a long day's work, "@Home just bought Excite." Long pause. "That's all right."

"Really?" said Simon, the computer deckhand, who was passing through. "What did the stock do?" He was interested.

"That's all right!" exclaimed Allan, again, more to himself than to Simon or Steve. He hit a few buttons on the keyboard he had hooked up to the computer. He was recalculating the value of his portfolio of highly volatile technology stocks.

This turned out to be why Allan occasionally could be found, rapt, in front of a computer screen. Twice a day, once at noon and again at seven in the evening, he logged onto the Internet through the satellite phone. The satellite phone on board *Hyperion* had the mysterious authority of the conch in *Lord of the Flies*. It cost either twelve or twenty dollars a minute, depending on which crew member quoted you the price. Its time was precious, except, of course, when Clark used it. Even in mid-Atlantic, Clark spent hours on end on the phone, talking to journalists about Healtheon, to friends who wanted him to invest in their new Internet start-up, to anyone he thought might divert his mind from the tedium of the ocean crossing. For everyone else but Allan the satellite phone was off-limits. The captain's control over it gave him his one real source of power, the power to determine what news came on board, and when it came. When Allan logged on, he pulled down three clumps of digital data precious to the crew: e-mail, the weather forecasts for the middle of the Atlantic Ocean, and the news from Wall Street.

All in all, this took him about four minutes. In those four minutes Allan sat rapt before one of the five flat-panel display screens on the bridge. It was the only time you ever saw him volunteer his attention to a computer screen, and the event clearly meant something to him. His shoulders tensed; then he swiveled in his high captain's chair and punched several buttons. One button sent the e-mails to their various recipients, another sent the closing prices of stocks in his portfolio to a separate screen, a third sent financial analyses and the weather forecasts to the printer. He then turned fully around in his chair, opened the mahogany drawer with the printer inside of it, and grabbed the financial analyses. The weather forecasts presumably could wait.

That day @Home, the company that sought to deliver the Internet into American homes through the pipes owned by cable television companies, had announced it would be acquiring Excite, the Internet portal company. Excite's stock price had jumped forty-two points; @Home's had leaped six points. Clark had helped create @Home and talked Tom Jermoluk, his old friend from Silicon Graphics, into running the company. By shrewdly following Clark's interest, Allan had purchased shares in @Home; by shrewdly following Allan's movements, Simon had done the same. Clark had sold his shares, and made forty million dollars. Not Allan and Simon. They had held on. That was their strategy.

Broadly, there are two types of stock market investors. The first might be called "value" investors. Probably the most famous set of rules for value investing were those laid down in the 1950s by Benjamin Graham and David Dodd. Graham and Dodd investors subject companies to careful analysis. They derive their sense of the fair value of a company's stock price from its profits. A company with no profits holds no appeal for a Graham and Dodd investor. As a result, no committed Graham and Dodd investor ever bought an Internet stock. Graham and Dodd investors are people who place a very high value on having the last laugh. In exchange for the privilege they have missed out on a lot of laughs in between.

*Hyperion* was no place for any Graham and Dodd investor. Graham and Dodd's classic text sat unread on the galley shelf, a tribute to some aborted attempt at serious financial analysis. The investors on board during our crossing fell into the second broad category, kamikaze investors. Kamikaze investors treat the market as more of a guessing game. They follow hunches, charts, rumors, and tips in an endless pursuit of the hot stock. Their view of the stock market is essentially mystical or, at any rate, impervious to analysis. To the kamikaze investor no price is too high to pay for a stock, because it can always go higher. They rely heavily on the giddiness of others.

Allan was a species of kamikaze investor. Until he met Clark two years earlier, and Clark gave him options in Netscape, Allan had never invested in the stock market. But Netscape got him interested, more than interested. Soon he had bought shares in Cisco, @Home, Intel, Lucent—the list was as long as his arm, and most of what was on it had soared on a wing and a prayer. But Allan proved to have a wonderful touch: everything he bought went up, all the time. The exception had been the few months in the late summer and early fall of 1998, when the stock market collapsed. But from about the time the Microsoft trial opened, the market had soared. Deals were once again being done; IPOs were once again roaring. The combination of @Home with Excite, which valued the loss-making Excite at nearly $7 billion, was just another case in point. What Allan saw when he gazed into the computer screen were the rewards that came to a man who waited for his moment. They were the fruits that fell into the hands of the fellow who refused to budge from beneath the tree.

For Captain Allan Prior, the effect of the brief market collapse, which had doomed Healtheon's IPO, was probably not very different from its effect on the millions of other Internet investors. It convinced him of the wisdom of his ways. Like most small Internet investors, Allan had clung to his portfolio of Netscapes and @Homes and Excites and Ciscos right through the crash. That portfolio, accumulated over the past eighteen months in a Dutch boatyard, was now worth three times what it had been just a couple of months ago. This proved to Allan that he should never sell the stocks he'd bought. No matter what the market did next, Allan maintained, he intended to hold on to his portfolio. Allan confined himself to one investment decision: whether to buy shares in a new company when it went public. Oddly enough, he never intended to act on information he dug up about his investments. This did nothing to allay his interest in the information. In the middle of the Atlantic Ocean he pored over downloaded documents like a man perpetually on a hair trigger.

Many of the crew of *Hyperion*, in the spirit of their captain, had also become kamikaze investors. All of them owned shares in Netscape and Healtheon; a few of them owned shares in other Silicon Valley companies; Allan Prior owned them all. The frustration of selling too early was as alien to them as it was to their captain. They, like millions others like them, believed the future would be better than the past. This happy mood was what egged Clark on in his quest to invent that future.

Today they saw for the umpteenth time the brilliance of the strategy. Cisco, another of their favorites, was up more than three points. AOL was up, too. Lucent was up again; it had quadrupled in the eighteen months since Allan first discovered it. Indeed, every single stock into which Allan had plunged was up big.

"The problem with investing in the U.S.," said Allan, still talking mainly to himself, "is the capital gains tax."

"They get you even if you aren't a U.S. citizen," said Simon, knowledgeably.

I asked Simon how he made his investment decisions. "I just take Allan's advice," said Simon, causing Graham and Dodd to perform a pas de deux in their graves. "He's been right most of the time."

"Most of the time," said Allan, somewhat modestly. He'd told Simon to buy @Home when @Home was at 25. Today the stock had reached 57.

"Except on eBay," said Simon.

"eBay!" exclaimed Allan. "Should have done that one." eBay had gone public a few months earlier. Since then it had gone from 10 to 215.

"But imagine the capital gains tax if we had!" said Simon.

"It is unfair," agreed Allan, "but . . . still." He looked at his printout. His newly recalculated wealth appeared to diminish his sense of being done wrong by the U.S. government. The truth was, since Allan never sold, the U.S. capital gains tax was to him more a theoretical than a practical problem.

"I don't really see the point of selling," he said.

The remark caught Steve's attention. Steve was a day trader. "Day trader" was one of those phrases popularized by the Internet, which made it cheaper and easier and less embarrassing (since, like masturbation, it typically was a purely private act) for people to buy and sell the same stock in the same day. As a confirmed day trader, Steve enjoyed looking for patterns in stock prices and thought the market often offered these up to anyone willing to watch. "Netscape used to go through a regular cycle," Steve explained, without looking up from his screen. "You'd buy it at 20 and sell it at 28. There was nothing to it, really."

"Netscape used to be the dog of my portfolio," said Allan. "Now . . ." He gazed down the long page listing his portfolio . . . he'd bought Netscape at 44 . . . it had plunged to 17 . . . but now . . .

"It's all right!" he said. Not as all right as the portfolio, but then the portfolio is up 300 percent.

For the next half hour or so, until Robert wandered up from the engine room, the computer programmer and the deckhand and the skipper of *Hyperion* dwelled on the miracle of Internet investing. Then Robert appeared, and Allan found something else to do. "I think they are all mad," said Robert, after Allan had left. "Allan just sits there all day thinking about his money. But if you ask him what any of these companies *do*, he has no idea. He wants to be rich. But he's not logical about his money."

That night the engine quit again.

It happened at nearly the same time as before, around two in the morning. Once again Jaime, Peter, and Celcelia were on watch; once again Clark, Steve, and Robert came out of their berths to cope with the problem; once again the captain was left to sleep. The only difference this time was the level of frustration on Robert's face. He'd spent the better part of the day searching for whatever had caused the engine to fail the night before. At some point he decided that he must have fixed it. "Every engineer will tell you," he said, "that it is much harder to find what's wrong with a machine when it seems to be working. It's called chasing ghosts. I spent all day chasing ghosts."

This time Robert did not tarry on the bridge with Clark, who, once again in God Mode, sat punching buttons on the computer screen. Instead, he went immediately down two sets of stairs to the engine room. The engine room was the only place on board to which no thought had been given about the comfort of the people inside it. It was hot. It was loud enough that Robert needed ear mufflers. But it was as tidy as any place on the boat, maybe tidier. Robert's tools hung neatly in their racks, and his dirty cloths were piled primly in a can outside. "A good engineer has to be orderly," Robert shouted over the roar of the machines. "If I died tomorrow, someone else could come into my world and pick up where I left off—because there is a logical way of doing it. A structure." He paused. "If you want to be a good engineer you have to be willing to be replaceable. This whole 'I'm irreplaceable' thing drives me bloody nuts."

Once inside the engine room Robert's face was transformed. His movements, usually lethargic, quickened. In a few square feet he performed a kind of dance with his machines. Clearly, he could have done it blindfolded. A few years ago, when Robert had sought to have himself certified to work on power boats, he'd done pretty much just that. He'd gone for the test, back home in England, and his interviewer had asked him detailed questions about the engine room of a supertanker. The test was designed for people who had worked on container ships. Robert, who had never seen the inside of a container ship, failed badly. He spent the next two weeks in a library; from books he built a three-dimensional model of a supertanker's engine room. He committed the entire complex space to memory, and returned to the test center. The same interviewer fired questions at him—asking him to walk through the little steps of repairing various machines on board a supertanker—expecting him of course to fail. Robert recorded a perfect score. The man assumed Robert had spent the preceding two weeks on board a ship. He said, "It's like a different bloke has walked in here." At the end of the test he wanted to shake Robert's hand.

Now Robert moved around a space he knew from hard experience. On board he had 1,400 spare parts—$300 *thousand* of spare parts—and he understood where each of them went. Again he flushed out the sea chest and restarted the engine. The engine was busted in a way that permitted him to switch it back on easily enough. Once the engine started, he did not wait around to see if it would keep on chugging. Certain now that the problem was more fundamental than air in the sea chest, he went hunting for it. He pulled himself beneath the giant BMW engine and fiddled a bit. Then he popped up and removed a cap from the top of it, and fiddled a bit more. As he fiddled, Steve wandered in. From the discomfort on his face it was clear Steve hadn't spent much time here. "It's *bloody* hot in here," he said. Although Steve's title was "engineer," he had about as much experience of low technology as I did. He was the new new engineer.

"We don't have an air-conditioned office," said Robert, from under the engine.

"No air-conditioned office with cappuccinos and dirty pictures on the Web twenty-four hours a day," said Steve, looking around. Here they were, a pair of British engineers employed by the same American billionaire, ostensibly working on the same project, and their idea of "work" could hardly have been more different. Steve watched Robert tinker with the machinery with the same impotent expression computer illiterates wore when they watched someone like Steve write software. It was the expression of a man who has nothing whatsoever to offer to the problem at hand. Finally, Robert climbed up and out from under the engine and said, "I don't think it's the engine."

Which meant that the problem was the sensor, or the network linking it to the rest of the boat. A chain of information ran through *Hyperion*. To a great extent the boat had been reduced to information. The information had its own logic. The sensors measured everything that Clark could think to measure, including the pressure on the engine. They passed these measurements up to the programmable logic controllers. The PLCs in turn passed the data down wires to the high-speed Silicon Graphics computers. The computers organized and presented the data to the captain and crew. Somewhere along that chain was a kink. The question was: Where? It could be inside the sensor itself, or in the PLCs, or in the fancy Silicon Graphics computers. After prodding the sensor a bit, Robert said, "I don't think it is the sensor."

Robert's mind was working its way upstream. If it wasn't the engine and it wasn't the sensor, then the problem lay somewhere between the sensor and the computers. The closer Robert came to the computers, the less sure of himself he became. "I've got to work out how the system is getting its information—how the PLCs sends it to SCADA," said Robert. SCADA was an acronym for the hopeful title they'd given to their software: Superior Control and Data Acquisition. SCADA was what Steve and Lance and Tim and Clark had spent most of their time writing. It picked up the digitized information from all over the boat and manipulated it in any way it needed to be manipulated. Steve and Robert left the engine room and made for the neighboring computer room, to find out what SCADA had to say.

The twenty-five slender black machines were arranged lengthwise along a wall, which resembled a sales rack in a discount outlet for VCRs. Robert had little patience for what went on inside them. ("They just make my job more complicated.") He had spent a great deal of the last year trying to explain the engine room to Tim and Lance and Steve to avoid problems just like this one. Of the computer people the only one who had impressed Robert *as an engineer* was Clark himself. "Take Lance," Robert said, when Steve popped upstairs. I'd missed Lance on this trip, and his attempt to infuse computer programming with the romantic spirit. "Lance is an unusually intelligent man," said Robert. "Yet the guy can't remember where he left his shoes. And when he goes to Amsterdam for a visit, he gets ripped off. What you need to be a good engineer is a set of skills, in addition to a logical process. Some people have an aptitude for it; some people never will."

The programmers came at the boat from the top down. Robert came at it from the bottom up. Robert believed his approach led to a deeper understanding of the machine. While Steve was gone, he said, "One of the problems here is that the computer program is designed to control things that the programmers themselves do not understand." Robert's resistance to the computer was a resistance to abstraction. The computer engineer has a postmodern flavor to him—which is perhaps why it is so difficult for him to explain even to other computer engineers what he does for a living. The honest answer is that he gazes into a screen and thinks. He is a creator of concepts. Robert, by contrast, was a practical man. He wanted to *see* what he was fixing.

At length Steve returned. Together, he and Robert hunted for the lines of code that concerned the engine. Steve pulled up one page of obscure-looking numbers, and Robert snorted, "That's the first time I've even *seen* that bloody page."

To anyone who has not seen it before, computer code is meaningless. Robert had taught himself to program a bit, but he was nevertheless disturbed by the way it removed real-world problems from the real world. As Steve looked on, Robert complained. "The only way I can read the life functions of the engine is via the computer system," he said. "The only way I can know what stopped the engine is this page here." He hit a few buttons, and up popped a screen filled with numbers. "The old way I'd have gauges on everything that would let me interact directly with the engine. On this boat you have to go to a computer screen and go looking for it." He paused. "On this boat if I want to turn on the light, I have to go to a computer screen."

"It's the modern world," said Steve.

"There are a million lines of code in there," said Robert, motioning to the twenty-five computers, "and nowhere in them will you find the word 'boat.'"

After an hour of digging around in the code, both Robert and Steve decided that the problem was beyond their grasp and would probably take a long time to repair. Given that they couldn't find the break in the chain of information running from the engine to the computers, the only thing to do was to remove the chain. "My next move," said Robert, "is to bypass the sensor. I can always fool the engine into thinking the sensor is not there."

And that is what he did, though he dreaded doing it. "It's the very worst thing an engineer can do," he explained, "to pull a plug and leave something unprotected." He went into the engine and yanked out the sensors. By yanking out the sensor he yanked out the link between the engine and Clark's computers, and thus prevented the computers from shutting the engine down arbitrarily. Unfortunately, it also prevented the computer from shutting down the engine when it needed to be shut down. Effectively, he removed the engine entirely from the computer's monitoring system. This small rebellion against the new technology, staged at four in the morning, earned Robert the right to return to bed. But he did so uneasily. With the sensor gone the engine could overheat without anyone's noticing. It could catch fire, even blow up, without warning. The boat was suddenly a lot more dangerous.

For two full days we motor sailed along without incident. The tedium exceeded even Clark's expectations. Every hour or so I'd check the computer screen to see how far we'd gone; every hour we'd traveled a mere eleven miles more.

The seventh night out there brought a new kind of trouble. Why the crises on Clark's boat could not occur at one in the afternoon rather than one in the morning, I do not know. But they never did. At one in the morning an hour into his watch, Steve wandered out onto the aft deck, looked up at the sail, and saw what looked like a pillow coming off the side. The pillow was growing. Finally, the night sky was filled with a chaotic whiteness. The sail was collapsing onto the deck. Its billowy heaps collected at the base of the mast, a kite the size of a mansion struggling to take flight.

The strange thing about the event was the silence that accompanied it. The main halyard had broken. The halyard was the rope that kept the sail hoisted. Clearly it was a bad moment. The world's largest sail, containing more wind than any sail in history, was on the loose. Fifty-five hundred square feet of sail flapped violently in the wind, with only a rope at the bottom of the mast to hold it in place. Flap one way, and it would have sailed off the side of the boat; flap the other way, and it would have knocked Steve off the side of the boat. And the computer had nothing to say about any of it. No alarm. No sound of any kind. Steve sounded the alarm, inadvertently. He hollered.

Up from the bowels of the ship came running the entire crew, Clark, and Louie. Barely awake, they threw their bodies recklessly on top of the sail in an attempt to take the wind out of it and to prevent it from flying overboard.

It took the crew about fifteen minutes of pouncing on air pockets to remove the last trace of wind from the sail. Once they'd subdued it, they found another rope, replaced the broken halyard, and hoisted the sail. As they worked, Clark looked on with a curiously detached expression. It was not, as you might think, the look of a man distressed that his boat is falling apart in the middle of the Atlantic Ocean. With all hell breaking loose on the foredeck, Clark was the calmest thing on board. Indeed, he wore an expression I hadn't ever really seen on him: one of contentment. Clark often struggled mightily to fake a contentment he did not feel. When *Fortune* magazine turned up to take his picture for the cover, for instance, he'd leaned back with a big cigar in his mouth and offered them the picture they wanted, of a successful California entrepreneur. (He really did feel some strong impulse to meet other people's initial expectations of him.) He did this without ever actually feeling contented. He was living disproof of the idea that California is home to people with a gift for relaxing. California was, at best, the place for people who wish to appear relaxed.

At any rate, now that his boat was falling apart, Clark actually appeared to be happy. A few months earlier, at the boatyard, he had explained to me what was so unusual about *Hyperion*. "Everything on board is measured," he had said, "*everything*." Everything had to be measured, or quantified, for the computer to get its mind around it. Clearly that statement was not true: the rope that held the sail up was not measured. It had broken without the slightest reaction from the computer. Seeing this, Clark said, "You could probably figure out a way to put sensors on the ropes so that you can tell when they frayed." That thought— he might have something more to tinker with—gave Clark a sense of purpose. He was perhaps the first owner of a mega-yacht who enjoyed his boat better when it was broken.

Once they'd tamed the sail, the crew members, led by Jaime, threaded a new rope through the sail and hoisted it up the mast. Clark watched them work with a mixture of admiration (toward Jaime) and intrigue (that there were parts of the boat that his computers did not yet control). Finally, as the sail rose again, he turned to me and asked, "Do you ever get scared?"

The moment he asked the question, I realized that I didn't. Not really. I was the ideal recipient of his new technology. Technically inept, thoroughly lazy, I was quick to place my trust in people who professed to understand how the various machines on which my life depended worked. Of course, every now and then, say, when an airplane went bump in a storm, my stomach clenched and all assumptions momentarily were called into doubt. But those moments always passed.

"No," I said.

"I do," he said, seriously. He must have noticed the new uncertainty on my face. "On some fundamental level I'm astonished that any of it works." Then he laughed and returned to his cabin. That was the burden of the technical man. He knew the many ways technology could fail. And he realized that he alone was responsible for its success.


The next evening it was Jaime who first sensed something new was wrong: he heard a sound as he walked past the mast. The sound, whatever it was, was not something the computers picked up on; there was no obvious sign of anything wrong. But the mast did make a faint clicking sound that Jaime had never heard it make, and he made a point of knowing all the sounds on the boat. This one, so faint that it barely registered, was entirely new. Click . . . click . . . click. It bothered Jaime enough that he decided to climb the mast to see what might be causing it.

This in itself seemed an act of madness. It crossed my mind that the computers had taken over so much of the business on the boat that the human beings strained their imaginations to remain relevant. The whole point of the computers was to reduce the sailing to a science, and to eliminate the dependency on human nerve and instinct or, at any rate, limit it to the nerve and instinct of computer programmers. Jaime was reasserting the need for nerve and instinct. The seas were rougher than they had been in days. The boat pitched and rolled with sufficient violence that you had to concentrate to remain upright on deck. The top of the mast was two hundred feet off the ocean, or about seventeen stories. The slightest sway on the deck was experienced at the top of the mast as a violent rock. Even in calm seas it was hurled back and forth like a particularly treacherous ride at an amusement park. Now, with each roll of the boat below, it swung hundreds of feet across the sky, with an ugly corkscrewing motion.

Jaime was, in a sense, the most articulate expression of Allan Prior's sailing skill. He'd been hired by the captain to be *Hyperion's* first mate. He had sailed with Allan in around-the-world races and was generally acknowledged by the crew to have a special knack. Whatever it was that made a sailor a sailor, Jaime, like Allan, had it. He was one of those people who seem to have been born to their assigned role. Only he wasn't. Jaime had come to sailing by circumstance and not choice. He'd started his career farming the Australian outback. In the early 1980s a drought drove him from the land and sent him seaward, looking for some other way to make a living. A friend told him about a job on a sailboat that was making an Atlantic crossing. Jaime knew so little about boats that when he was awakened at three in the morning for his first watch his first instinct was to punch the guy who had woken him up.

That all happened fifteen years before, when Jaime was in his midtwenties. Now, on our seventh evening at sea, he'd heard a sound that no one else had heard. In response to that sound he donned a thin harness shaped like a jockstrap and asked Celcelia, who was making her first long sailboat trip, to belay him up in it. The comely Celcelia spent a large part of each day with her nose buried in books with titles like *Sailing across the Atlantic Made Easy.* Now Jaime's life was in her hands. Up, up, up the mast he went, using his feet to keep him attached until he was a pale white dot in the dusky sky. By the time he signaled Celcelia to stop cranking, he was near the top of the seventeen-story building, clinging to its sides with his legs. One slip and he'd be finished. He would have been hurled out into space like a shot from a sling and then back into the mast. He'd have been crushed, and crushed again.

At first Jaime had thought the sound in the mast might be the satellite dish. But he rose past the satellite dish on the second spreader, and the noise only grew louder. It grew louder, in fact, all the way to the top. Only when he arrived at the top of the mast did Jaime find its origin. The rope that had been strung up in place of the main halyard— that is, the rope that held up the massive sail—had ripped the sail. A fresh tear nearly a yard long ran down from the top. That is, what Jaime had detected when he walked by the mast was the very slight difference in the sound made by a 5,500-square-foot sail that is fully intact and a 5,500-square-foot sail that has a slight tear in it, two hundred feet off the ground. As his body hurtled through the night sky, Jaime explained all this into a walkie-talkie. The entire sail was like a giant stocking on the verge of a run, he said. A strong gust of wind would rip it in two. One half would probably blow clear off the side; the other would flap crazily from its moorings at the base of the mast. The force of this event, on a sail of this size, might easily cause the mast to snap.

The tear in the sail put an end to our sailing trip. The computers would learn no more about sailing on this trip. The only solution was to reel the sail back into the boom and to put ourselves at the mercy of the quixotic engine. After an hour of flying through the dark at the top of the world's tallest mast, Jaime shimmied back to the deck. The rest of the crew members sensed they had just witnessed an extraordinary piece of seamanship, though no one said much about it. But the next morning I did hear one person say, "I've been on boats where the mast has broken but nothing like this. This is a whole 'nother beast. Thank God he went up there."

This being Jim Clark's trip, it could not follow its expected course and arrive at its intended destination. When we set sail from the Canaries, we were headed to St. Bart's. Five days into the ten-day crossing, Clark decided that St. Martin's made for a better landing. On the ninth day he changed his mind again and told Allan to take the boat to Antigua. Antigua was closer. Antigua was also new. New was good. Clark was far happier doing something that he had just decided to do than something he had decided long ago. No decision was worth sticking to unless it had replaced several other decisions.

We groped our way toward Antigua. A couple of hundred miles off-shore a spotted hawk flew overhead. It was a poignant moment; it often is when the first bird appears in the sky. The first bird, like a man ahead of his time, is a tragic figure. Typically, the first bird has flown too far from shore, and is flapping its way to its death. The good news that land is near is quickly followed by the realization that land is not near enough for the bird. The crew gathers on deck and hopes that the bird will roost in the mast, and sail back to shore. It almost never happens.

The bird flapped on toward oblivion. A few hours later Clark's jet plunged down out of the clouds and buzzed the boat. Everyone, Clark included, clambered up top and cheered.

## 17

## The Turning Point

The Gulf Stream rose and banked over the untroubled sea and the bright white sand. As it leveled off, Cliff's voice came over the intercom. Cliff was one of the two pilots employed by Clark to fly his jet.

"Okay, all you billionaires back there," Cliff said. "They opened at one hundred and seventy-four and a half and seventy-four."

There was no need to specify who or what "they" were. Obviously, "they" were the share prices for AOL and Netscape, which six weeks earlier AOL had agreed to purchase. You could hear the smile on Cliff's face. Cliff was a member of ClarkWorld and, therefore, an owner of stock options in both Netscape and Healtheon. Clark reached a bit too casually behind his seat and found a pocket calculator. Cliff's news was the cherry on top of the ice cream sundae of his relief that the crossing was finally over. AOL had agreed to swap .45 of its own shares for each outstanding share of Netscape. Clark owned 14.2 million shares of Netscape. He punched .45 times 14.2 million into the calculator. Six point three million—the number of AOL shares he effectively owned, making his the biggest single chunk of AOL stock, larger even than that of Steve

Case, who created and ran the company. He multiplied 6.3 million by 174.5. One point one billion dollars. In our ten days at sea the value of his Netscape holdings had nearly tripled, from $25 a share to $74.

It was late January 1999 and the stock market was rising even faster than it had fallen in the fall of 1998: Healtheon was soon to make its second bid to go public. And once Healtheon went public, Clark would be even richer. More to the point, he'd be free to move again. That was the unofficial sequence: start it, sell it to the public, then announce the new new thing. The stock market collapse had forced him to put off the public side of his quest for the new new thing, though, of course, he had continued feverishly with his private search. Now the two were about to converge.

"This is fantasy land," he said, putting his calculator away.

All the way back to the United States he marveled at the miracle of the stock market. Before we landed he said, "When Healtheon goes public, I'm going to get a lot of attention very quickly. I have to figure out what to do with it."

In mid-February, Healtheon finally went public. There was no transition between the failed IPO five months earlier and this one. No one asked how a company that the stock market deemed unworthy was now, suddenly, desirable. It just happened. The company now employed nearly six hundred people. Three hundred of them were housed in the main office in an industrial park just north of San Jose. By five in the morning on the day of the public share offering, they were all at work.

There was almost nothing good to say about Healtheon's offices, except that they were no worse than most offices in Silicon Valley. Outside, it was a low white stucco warehouse plopped down in a sea of asphalt and dressed up with a corporate logo to pass for an office building. Inside, you could count on one hand the attempts to enrich the employee's state of mind: the cheap fountain across from the reception desk, the etiolated plants, the Universal weight-lifting machine tucked away in the corner of the otherwise vacant rec room, the cappuccino maker Clark had bought and installed the day he founded the company. Otherwise, it was a sea of gray fuzz cubes. Some of the cubes were slightly larger than others. Some had a view of the parking lot. Other than that, the place was as drably uniform as a commune. No number of balloons in the lobby or streamers in the rec room would turn it into a space anyone would regret leaving behind. The companies were built to change. No one was encouraged to grow attached to his personal space.

By five-thirty the employees had assembled in the big rec room, in front of the television set. Pavan, Kittu, Stuart, the Band of Indians—they were all crammed into this one room. It smelled, faintly, of curry. The only sounds came from the television, tuned to CNBC. The ticker tape ran across the bottom of the screen. The Nasdaq opened up 64 points, or better than 2 percent. Yahoo and @Home were both up almost 10 points. No one could say what Healtheon had done, since trading in the stock was suspended before it began, because of an imbalance of orders. Healtheon had offered five million shares in itself, or about 8 percent of the company. The initial demand, mainly from the big institutions, was more than five million shares. How much more no one could be sure. Morgan Stanley and Goldman Sachs had ginned up a lot of interest. The deal was hot, or appeared to be, which amounted to the same thing. Healtheon's shares had been offered at seven dollars apiece, but that was just what people paid who were lucky enough to receive what they signed up for. The important question was: At what price would the first trade occur? How much would people pay for shares in Healtheon who didn't get as many as they wanted? At what price would the investors who paid seven dollars willingly part with their shares? Healtheon's CFO, Jay Westerman, stood beside the trader at Morgan Stanley in midtown Manhattan who was making the book in Healtheon's shares. He'd tell Pavan the price. Pavan would announce it to the room.

Once the employees were informed trading had been suspended, attention shifted back and forth between the television and Pavan. Pavan would get the news about the stock price before CNBC. CNBC would get Jim Clark. The cable reporter was scheduled to interview Clark, though it was unclear exactly where Clark was at that moment. Mike Long sat on the Morgan Stanley trading desk in New York City; Clark was nowhere to be found. For the next thirty minutes Pavan stood stoically in the front of the room with a cell phone to his ear, while the employees around him tittered. Among them they controlled about 15 million shares out of the 69 million shares outstanding. Pavan alone owned a million. Kittu, who stood beside Pavan, had 350,000. Stuart, who stood a bit off to one side, owned perhaps 100,000—though Stuart was coy about this. All together the employees owned only a bit more than Clark, who, at the time of the offering, controlled 11.5 million shares. It was a tribute to their belief in Silicon Valley's class system that they felt they had been treated generously.

There had been no road show this time around. Instead, Mike Long had sat down with a handful of large institutional investors that the Morgan Stanley bankers felt would lead public opinion about the company. Long had decided in his mind that he deserved some of the blame for the failure of the IPO the first time around. "The story in the fall was too complex," he said. He had learned that, in a business climate that changed as rapidly as this one did, no one on the outside had time to "study the details" of the business. That was a polite way of saying that a lot of potential investors had no idea what Healtheon actually did. Healtheon, like a lot of Internet companies, was an ever-shifting abstraction. When asked what advice he might give to other Serious American Executives who were talked into running one of these Silicon Valley businesses, he'd say, "It's not about business plans. You can't plan chaos."

This time Long made his presentation to investors even simpler than before. Gone was any mention of the software, which no one understood anyway. All that mattered was that Long could say, truthfully, that the software had been installed successfully in doctors' computers, just a few days after the nasty article in the *Wall Street Journal* implied that the software might never see the light of day. Gone, too, was the Chart of Many Bubbles. Just as the Magic Diamond had given way to the Chart of Many Bubbles, the Chart of Many Bubbles now gave way to the Golden Triangle. The Golden Triangle distilled the high concept behind Healtheon to its essential components:

Doctors
*

Patients *                    *Health Care Institutions

Leaving just enough room for one asshole in the middle. The notion of one asshole in the middle was easier to put across when you sum-

marized the entire Byzantine health care bureaucracy, most of which
you intended to gut, with the phrase "health care institutions." The math
that Long asked investors to do was also even simpler than before.
Healtheon now had 200,000 physicians under contract; soon enough
they'd all be wired into Healtheon's system. Each time a physician hit
a button on his computer to order a lab test, or a prescription, or a
patient's medical record, Healtheon would be paid between 9 and 35
cents. Long told investors that the company had handled 5 million
transactions in 1998, and expected to handle 500 million in 1999, 1.5
billion in 2000, and so on for some time until, presumably, every single health care transaction in America ran through its computers. *You
do the math.*

On top of that, Long said, Healtheon could be the leading health
care Internet portal. People would come to the Healtheon Web site for
information; once there, they could be sold all sorts of things.

Healtheon's story had improved in the retelling. The story may not
have been quite as important as the willingness of the stock market to
hear it, but the story still mattered a lot. No one could honestly claim
to know what Healtheon was worth. The company in its brief history
had made nothing but losses. It would run through another several hundred million dollars before it ever earned a dime. It could offer only a
rough estimate of its revenues for the next few years, which no knowledgeable person, or even intelligent ignoramus, could take seriously.
Healtheon was worth whatever investors felt like paying for it, and that
depended largely on public opinion. Healtheon was running for president. The IPO was election day. The polls were moving in the right
direction. Just a year earlier the venture capitalists who had backed it
thought its stock was worth zero; just six months ago the investment
bankers who were taking it to market said they might be able to unload
the stock at a price that implied a total value of a bit more than $500
million. Now there was talk in the rec room that the company might
be worth a billion dollars.

And why not? The stock market was once again cooking up miracles. It was now possible that the big Internet investors—Fidelity,
Vanguard, Bowman Capital, Nicholas-Applegate, Amerindo—would
be intoxicated by Mike Long's story. If so, their excitement might well
percolate all the way down to small investors like Captain Allan Prior,

poised in front of the one computer screen on *Hyperion* he felt happy about, ready to buy something new.

The employees waited nearly two hours. At nine-fifteen Pavan shushed the room. A big smile flitted across his face, which he quickly swallowed in the interest of preserving his air of authority. "They have demand for forty million shares!" he shouted. A cheer went up.

They waited another fifteen minutes. At nine-thirty Pavan quieted the room again. His expression suddenly became more serious. Beyond serious. Pained. He looked like a man with a stomachache. The excitement of what he was about to say was nearly too much for him. "Twenty-one and a half!" he shouted. The four hundred people in the room went wild. The ragtag collection of engineers and engineers' helpers suddenly were worth three hundred million dollars. Pavan waved his hand for silence. The room went quiet.

"Twenty-four!" Pavan shouted.

More cheers.

Again, Pavan raised his hand; again, silence. "Twenty-eight!" Pavan shouted.

More cheers.

Now Pavan's hand was raised high and straight, like a Roman orator's. The room went completely silent. It was filled with people whose fortunes were rocketing; at the rate they were going, they'd all be billionaires by nightfall. Rather gravely Pavan announced, "One million shares just traded at thirty-three and a quarter!"

This time a new sound greeted the news. Not cheering. Laughing! Healtheon's employees were turning and clapping each other on the back and laughing. Thirty-three and a quarter! At that price they ceased to be the justly rewarded victors of the race that went to the swift. They became the lucky holders of a winning lottery ticket. One of the Indian engineers threw up his hands and jogged back to his cubicle and wrote a program that installed the Wall Street ticker tape on the top of his computer screen. Thirty-three and a quarter! At thirty-three the company was worth $2.2 billion. Pavan Nigam was worth $33 million. Kittu Kolluri was worth $10 million. Stuart was worth $3.5 million. Jim Clark was worth another $375 million. When you added in his stake in AOL, he was now worth $1.5 billion.

All attention now shifted to the television set. One cheer went up when Healtheon's stock price raced across the bottom, another when the talking head announced that Healtheon's was one of the most successful IPOs of all time. They were, collectively, a success. What the four hundred people in the room wanted to see now was Jim Clark. A long time ago Clark had told several of them personally what was going to happen. "At the end of the first trading day Healtheon will be worth two billion plus," he'd said. "And I don't see any reason why it shouldn't go to five billion fairly quickly. It depends on what kind of publicity we get." To the engineers this was a mythical Clark moment; and I knew it to be a true myth because he had said that very thing to me, a year and a half earlier. How often did a man say to you, "Come with me, I'll make you rich," and then tell you exactly how rich he was going to make you, and then do it. It was a bit like watching Babe Ruth stride to the plate and point to the fence with his bat.

It went without saying that Clark was making it up as he went along: no one could know even the day before what financial public opinion would make of Healtheon if and when it finally went public. But crack engineers like Pavan and Kittu and Stuart had believed him, and their faith trickled down. Not a single engineer had quit the company after the failed IPO. Each of them could have worked for any Silicon Valley start-up he wanted to work for. The decision of where to work was, at that moment, monumentally important. Work for a flop, and you miss this golden moment—perhaps the one chance you'll have in your whole life to get rich. And all had stuck with Healtheon. And now their faith had been rewarded. That is why they sat and waited half the day for Jim Clark to appear on the screen.

They waited for an hour and . . . nothing. Something was holding up Clark's appearance. Pavan tried to discover what. The people at Morgan Stanley in New York had no idea. Finally, Pavan announced that Clark was off on his boat. Of course, Clark had designed the search for the new new thing so that it could occur wherever he happened to be. At that moment he happened to be on his boat, docked in some Caribbean harbor. A camera crew from CNBC waited on the dock, hoping to record Clark's reaction to being the first man to create three different multibillion-dollar technology companies. They couldn't possibly know that his mind was now fully occupied by the fourth. At any rate, Clark decided he didn't want to go on the television. The

CNBC reporter had hinted he might show a map of the Caribbean with the boat on it. Clark didn't like the idea.

When Pavan relayed that news, the energy went out of the event. Healtheon's engineers trickled reluctantly from the conference room. Pavan and Kittu left together. Kittu was jolly, Pavan sober. As he walked back to his cube, his legs trembled. Kittu put his arm around him, and they shared a laugh.

Pavan's cube was no kind of place for a man worth thirty-three million dollars. It had a computer, a desk, and a giant white board. Pavan went to his white board, stood there for a minute, and quit. There was nothing to draw. The lines, graphs, and charts that he was forever scribbling on the board no longer expressed his meaning. He resembled a man who has swallowed an earthquake whole and was now trying to contain the aftershocks within his frame. He shook involuntarily. He had imagined this moment for nearly five years, since he first read in *USA Today*, while sitting in a Delhi hotel, about the Netscape IPO. He had met his destiny, and he did not know exactly what to make of it. Pavan Nigam was a rich man.

That night I came home and found an e-mail from Stuart Liroff. Stuart had been more reticent about his good fortune than either Pavan or Kittu. When I asked him whether on balance the sacrifice had been worth it to his wife, he made a face that suggested he wasn't sure. "History will document this as the largest financial bubble in the history of the world economy," he said, at one point. I think deep down Stuart did not really expect to make millions of dollars: he was so happy without them. After the IPO I had asked him if he ever thought about retiring. He said that the thought never crossed his mind, nor should it. Now he wrote,

My grandfather was a Kosher butcher and my father was in the "rag trade." I think my reaction to the word "retire" was almost visceral. . . .
But you wouldn't believe what happened to me this evening.
As I mentioned, I went with my wife to a local charitable event. . . . There were no less than 500 people there. . . . It was mind boggling. It seemed like almost everyone came up to me and gushed about how rich I was, and about how I could retire, and wanted to know what I was "going to do now"!? I felt like I had been Bar

Mitzvah'd or just had a baby! You have to understand: I never talk to anyone about my personal finances; in my family, it was always considered "bad taste" to talk about your finances publicly. And, here I was, in the middle of a public event, and it seemed like 250 people knew that I was "rich." I felt somehow exposed in public, and you know what, it felt great!

A few days after the Healtheon IPO, Mike Long was invited onto CNBC to talk about his hot new company, which, at $44 a share, was now worth $3 billion. There wasn't any question about accepting. CNBC was the cable channel of choice for the speculators who bid up Healtheon's stock price. There was a room wired on the Stanford campus—it was used by all the TV shows back East. The room was where Silicon Valley executives went when they wanted to talk to their investors. Long drove over to it at four in the morning. He clipped the microphone to his tie and the earphone to his ear. He looked high up on the wall at the black eye of a single camera. Look straight into the black eye when you speak, he'd been told. A woman's voice—he'd never actually laid eyes on her—was piped through his earpiece. The lady welcomed Mike Long to CNBC, told him he was on the air, and then asked him a list of questions. A few questions into the list Long was able to mention "our new relationship with IBM."

"Let's pick up on that," said the woman at CNBC. "You picking up this company and going forward. How has this acquisition helped you?"

Long had to think about that one. IBM was worth about $240 billion. It had 290,000 employees, $82 billion a year in revenues, and a long, glorious history dating back to 1911. IBM wasn't a company; it was a country. Healtheon . . . well, until a few days before, no one had even heard of Healtheon. Now the company was being accused on the official cable channel of the speculating classes of having acquired IBM.

Back when Mike Long had been a Serious American Executive he had no truck with the wider public. Maybe once or twice his name turned up in the local newspapers when he and his wife attended a United Way dinner. Now he was expected to play a role that was one part commercial celebrity and one part carnival barker. His new role required him to stifle a great deal of bewilderment. He had to find a way to be adaptable enough to keep a straight face when some journalist asked him why he'd bought IBM, but not so adaptable that he lost his self-respect. His central nervous system was busy making the necessary adjustments.

One of the many things Mike Long had learned in the transition from Serious American Executive to keeper of the new new thing was to keep the story moving along. Or, as he put it, "You have to stay ahead of the public road map." The minute investors understood what you were doing, they held you in lower estimation. Solid performance was no longer interesting; familiarity bred contempt. The dollars invested in Healtheon were always threatening to move on to the latest IPO. To woo investors enamored of the new—and thus keep your stock price rising—you had to remain in a state of pure possibility.

In this question about his acquisition of IBM, Long sensed an opportunity. Healtheon buys IBM—that's new! On the television screen Long's face contorted slightly, in the way it might if a lunatic on the street approached him to say that he had a little green man perched on his shoulder. But before it reached that point, it froze. He smiled. He said that while Healtheon had not purchased IBM, it had agreed to provide IBM with technology, thus leaving CNBC viewers with the vague impression that the question was not implausible. Healtheon might well have bought IBM but found it more useful to partner with them.


In the month after the IPO Healtheon's stock price behaved like a manic-depressive off his medication. First it fell, from $44 to $29 a share. Then, on March 8, the investment bankers Morgan Stanley and Goldman Sachs issued buy recommendations. The next day the stock shot up 19 points, to $48 a share. The enthusiasm, however, was temporary. In early April it drifted down and then back up some more, to $59 a share. From there it tailed off badly. From the beginning of April to early May it fell 20 points, to $39 a share. Something was holding it back.

What that something was soon became clear. Around this time Clark heard from a friend—he won't say which one—that Microsoft was taking a new interest in the health care industry. The rumor was that Microsoft intended to invest $700 million in a new Atlanta company called Web MD. Web MD wasn't much more than a shell for a brilliant marketing campaign. Its twenty-nine-year-old CEO, Jeff Arnold, had persuaded a lot of health care organizations that he could make the Internet work for them, and persuaded them to sign contracts, but he didn't actually have a product. For that reason Clark hadn't paid Web MD all that much attention. Microsoft's backing changed his attitude. With Microsoft behind it there was every chance that Web MD would go public at a higher valuation than Healtheon and then establish itself as the leading brand in Internet medicine. "I couldn't let that happen," said Clark.

In mid-May, Clark and Long flew to Atlanta to meet with Jeff Arnold. When they left the meeting, they had agreed to purchase Web MD— exchanging 1.85 Healtheon shares for each Web MD share. Microsoft would own a 17 percent stake in the combination. It was Clark's original coming to terms with Microsoft. Netscape had taught him the hard way that it was not worth the trouble to resist what he regarded as the evil empire. The Microsoft antitrust trial looked as if it might drag on for several more years; there wasn't even a faint hope that the company would be constrained by the government, at least in time to make a difference to Clark. On balance, Clark decided, it was better to pay protection money. Microsoft's response to Healtheon hadn't been as crude as its response to Netscape: give us a piece of your company, or we'll put you out of business. All the same, its investment in Web MD amounted to a shakedown: give us a piece of the action, or we'll sponsor some other company to compete with you. "It's grotesquely unfair," Clark said. "And I hate it. But there's nothing I can do about it."

On May 20 the companies announced their merger. The market interpreted the deal as a sign that a new monopoly was being created, and perhaps the market was right. Certainly, the effect of combining ClarkWorld with Microsoft would be to frighten a lot of potential competitors out of the market. Anyone insufficiently frightened could be acquired. Healtheon's stock ran up nearly 70 points in two days, to 105. The company was now valued at $16 billion. Out of thin air, it seemed, $16 billion had been plucked. Clark's stake in the enterprise had been whittled down to 6 percent, worth about $1.3 billion. "It's enough to keep my interest level," he said, a disenchantment I was now familiar with creeping into his voice, "but it isn't what I'd like to have." He also said, "When I formed Netscape, I thought about sleeping with the enemy. Now I know I should have done it. I've gone over to the dark side."

The truth was it was time for him to move again. On the eve of the new new thing, the Netdex, as the brokerage analyst Keith Benjamin described his index of all Internet companies, was worth $405 billion. That was up 654 percent in the past year. To put that number in perspective, the top twenty media companies—Time Warner, Disney CBS, etc.—had a combined value of $527 billion. Just how much of the Netdex belonged to people associated with Clark's various ventures was hard to say; but in the spring of 1999 I made some quick back-of-the-envelope calculations. They amounted to a rich list of the people in ClarkWorld I'd come to know a bit. The back of the envelope read like this:

The CEOs:
   Mike Long (Healtheon): $400,000,000
   Jim Barksdale (Netscape): $1,000,000,000
   Tom Jermoluk (@Home): $550,000,000

The VCs:
   Kleiner Perkins (John Doerr): $1,800,000,000
   New Enterprise Associates (Dick Kramlich): $700,000,000
   Mayfield Fund (Glenn Mueller): $400,000,000

The cofounding engineers:
   Pavan Nigam (Healtheon): $85,000,000
   Kittu Kolluri (Healtheon): $30,000,000
   Stuart Liroff (Healtheon): $8,500,000
   Marc Andreessen (Netscape): $80,000,000
   Tom Davis (Silicon Graphics): $10,000,000
   Rocky Rhodes (Silicon Graphics): $5,000,000
   Kurt Akeley: (Silicon Graphics): $5,000,000

The captain and programmers of *Hyperion*:
   Allan Prior: $1,062,500
   Steve Hague: $1,000,000
   Lance Welsh: $1,000,000
   Tim Powell: $1,000,000

Jim Clark's piece of the Netdex came to $3,200,000,000. He was a real after-tax billionaire. He had, as they say, achieved his financial goals.

**The New New Thing**

Different people have used different phrases to describe the path Clark's mind took as he wandered along the top of the cliff overlooking the U.S. economy, deciding which rock, if kicked, would wipe out the largest section of the slope below. The venture capitalist John Doerr calls it "amazing over-the-horizon radar." The Healtheon engineer Kittu Kolluri calls it "an animal's sense of smell." Hugh Reinhoff, one of the young men the venture capitalists had assigned to follow Clark wherever he went, calls it "fuzzy logic." His enemies called it "bizarre" or "dysfunctional" or, most often, "lucky." Each time one of Clark's ventures got rolling, some people, even a few people in Silicon Valley, said he was just lucky. Lucky to have popularized the third dimension in computer space at just the right moment, lucky to have met Marc Andreessen and seen his Internet browser, lucky to have triggered the Internet boom, lucky to have sought control of health care, the world's biggest market, just when it was ready to yield itself up.

"Luck" is one of those unfortunate words that are required to do more than their fair share of the work. What happened to Clark in Silicon Valley was far more interesting than luck. It was the interplay of a character who had a deep feel for technology, and a taste for anarchy, with an environment that rewarded both traits. Silicon Valley in the late 1990s was the closest that business has ever come to resembling a child's chemistry experiment. Some tiny invisible hand poured one chemical after another into a test tube in the irresponsible hope of making it go Boom! Clark—and people like him—turned out to be the active ingredient.

At any rate, in the spring of 1999, after Healtheon had established itself as the most successful IPO in a year of fabulously successful IPOs, Clark was a more active ingredient than ever before. There were many reasons for this, but the main one was the Internet. There was no longer much question about what Clark had been saying all along: the Internet was bigger than anyone understood. Pretty much every Serious American Executive now agreed he had no choice but to adapt, or wind up bottled in formaldehyde and displayed on a shelf in the new special exhibit of extinct economic species. In March 1999 Jack Welch, the chairman of General Electric, one of those people who created conventional business wisdom every time he opened his mouth, said that the Internet was "the single most important event in the U.S. economy since the Industrial Revolution." Even the normally understated chairman of the U.S. Federal Reserve, Alan Greenspan, said that "the revolution in information technology has altered the structure of the way the American economy works."

Growth was change, and change was disturbing—and if you doubted it you needed only to ask any Serious American Executive. The business magazines even had a phrase for the pangs of incipient doom that afflicted them: "Internet anxiety." Internet anxiety was simply the sense, now widely shared, that you were about to be put out of business by someone who operated in the spirit of Jim Clark. The Internet created many opportunities for people like Clark—outsiders, troublemakers— to think thoughts that would turn entire industries on their heads. Jeff Bezos, the founder of Amazon.com, had upended the book business; the founders of eBay had upended the auction business; the founders of E*Trade and Ameritrade had upended the Wall Street stock brokerage firms. In 1998 the manager of Merrill Lynch's fifteen thousand stock brokers, John Steffans, had called the Internet trading firms "a serious threat to America's financial lives," and assured his employees that

Merrill Lynch would never do such a thing. The next year Merrill Lynch created an Internet trading department.

Paul Romer, the young economist whose work on New Growth Theory had stressed the importance of technology in economic growth and, by implication, conferred a magnificent importance on the new new thing, hinted at another, deeper reason technological change was so unsettling. In a digression from his otherwise rigorous analysis, in a 1994 issue of the *Journal of Development Economics*, Romer wrote, "Once we admit that there is room for newness—that there are vastly more conceivable possibilities than realized outcomes—we must confront the fact that there is no special logic behind the world we inhabit, no particular justification for why things are the way they are. Any number of arbitrarily small perturbations along the way could have made the world as we know it turn out very differently. . . .We are forced to admit that the world as we know it is the result of a long string of chance outcomes."

Clark, the inventor of chance outcomes, was himself a kind of chance outcome. Not long after I'd first met him, back when Netscape's stock was speeding to zero, and Healtheon's stock was considered worthless, he announced his plan to retire once he became a real after-tax billionaire. He intended to float around the world on his new boat, as soon as it was finished. Even then you could see he couldn't possibly believe what he was saying. His life was an adventure story: without suspense it lost its purpose. Besides, he was still curious to find out what happened next. How would he know unless he set out to make it happen? The near certainty that something important was about to bubble up out of him, the sense that he had some peculiar gift for letting the right thing bubble up, had him and a lot of other people in Silicon Valley on the edge of their seats. By April of 1999, people outside of the Valley wanted to talk to Clark about Healtheon, which now seemed poised to turn the U.S. health care industry on its head. Clark's interest in Healtheon was draining out of him. He wasn't even sure he wanted to keep his investment in Healtheon. Healtheon was the past. The time had come for the new new thing.


In the spring of 1999 Clark started thinking seriously about his money. Actually, he was always thinking seriously about his money, and so I should have seen what was coming next, but I'd been distracted by all the talk about turning *Hyperion*'s software into the Home of the Future. He'd even gone and paid twelve million dollars for a 35-bedroom, 32,000-square-foot mansion in Palm Beach, mainly, it seemed, so that he'd have a place to test his software. Il Palmetto, the mansion was called. It had been built by Joseph Widener back in the 1930s, when rich people were meant to be idle. If he could reduce a 32,000-square-foot home to the sum of its digital data and administer that data over the Internet, Clark figured, he could do the same thing with any home. Clark had bought Il Palmetto after Steve Hague, the boat's programmer, had explained to him, in an e-mail, "how the software that controls the boat can become a dot com company." The new company was to be called Landscape. Landscape, and Il Palmetto, turned out to be just another false lead.

At some point, probably as we crossed the ocean, Clark had lost interest in the Home of the Future. The Home of the Future would have to wait. He decided, first, to change as much as he could of what he disliked about being really rich.

He'd accumulated a long list of grievances from his brief experience with real wealth. He disliked paying California's capital gains tax—so much that he had moved his official residence to Palm Beach, Florida. He disliked the hassle of paying bills—so much that he'd hired a fellow named Harvey to take care of it. He disliked stock brokers—so much that he ignored their advice to diversify and kept all his wealth in Netscape and Healtheon. He disliked venture capitalists and investment bankers and, in general, the phalanx of financial intermediaries who sat between the creators of wealth and their just desserts.

At first he decided that what he really wanted was what rich people have always had: a family office. The rich man's family office is normally a staff of people who do nothing but take care of the rich man's money. Money butlers. Pretty quickly, however, he realized he wanted more than a money butler. He wanted to be able to watch what his money butlers did. He wanted to be able to take in every aspect of his money at a glace, no matter where on earth he happened to be, and at what time. The Internet was perfectly suited to what he had in mind.

The more Clark thought about it, the more he thought that the best money butler would use the Internet. The Internet would spare him endless headaches: no more phone calls to banks or accountants, no more looking around for a pocket calculator to figure out how much he was worth, no more digging for receipts to find out how much he'd paid for the Picasso. Before he knew it, he had an idea for a business. He called his new company myCFO.

His thinking ran something like this. There were a lot of people just like him who'd made millions of dollars and were now coping with the hassle of handling it. Clark had read somewhere that there were now 180,000 American decamillionaires—people with at least ten million dollars in assets. Together they controlled something like fifteen trillion dollars in assets. "The wealthy masses," Clark called them. He figured that the wealthy masses were just waiting to be organized into a fighting unit. (They had nothing to lose but their gold chains.) Certainly, they shared some basic financial objectives: they wanted to minimize taxes and hassles; they wanted to maximize wealth. myCFO would help rich people achieve their objectives. It would be, in the first place, a home for money. "The idea is that everything to do with their finances goes through this one place," Clark said. Once he'd persuaded the wealthy masses to collect their wealth in this one place, he could negotiate on behalf of that wealth, almost as if it belonged to one person. "Say you had two trillion dollars under one roof," Clark explained, "or even a trillion. The power of that money is huge. You could go and cut deals with banks or brokerage firms or insurance companies or anyone else who wanted to do business with the money." The rich people who held in myCFO would wind up with a long list of special deals.

What he was groping toward wasn't just a new company. It was a new kind of financial institution, and, as murky as it was in its conception, it posed a fantastic threat to old, established financial institutions. The Internet had made it possible for people to organize themselves in new ways. It made it possible for *rich* people to organize themselves. No one said that the new organization of rich people had to behave like other financial organizations. The people who joined forces in myCFO would have great bargaining power with traditional financial institutions. They wouldn't be constrained in the way that say, the people who had deposited $1.5 trillion in Merrill Lynch accounts were constrained. When a Merrill Lynch customer wanted to buy stocks, he had to call a Merrill Lynch broker. Jim Clark's pile of money—which he figured could easily be the world's biggest pile of money—would operate independently. Anarchically. Its customers, as a group, could play Silicon Valley venture capitalists and Wall Street investment bankers and Main Street stock brokers and Swiss private bankers off each other, much the way Clark already did in his own private business life. If myCFO did not seize control of the levers of capitalism, it could at least remove the lever from the capitalists' hands. And the bigger the pile of money inside myCFO, the more market clout this cartel of the very rich would have. Once the number of dollars became sufficiently huge, they could sit on top of the financial world like an operating system sat on top of a personal computer.

As usual, Clark felt he had to move quickly. This time he didn't even have a drawing on a piece of paper, just a vague idea in his head. He wanted myCFO to be a multibillion-dollar public company within a year, so that it might be better positioned to gobble up the inevitable competition. He thought its market value should exceed Healtheon's, which now exceeded fifteen billion dollars. In late April he visited a few Silicon Valley opinion leaders, whose commercial success gave them a great deal of influence with the wealthy masses. John Chambers, the CEO of Cisco, the maker of hardware for the Internet, was himself a billionaire. He was also an engineer. He also had long admired Clark's ability to change with the times. The Valley was filled with people who had created a couple of successful companies of the same type. Clark alone moved from one ruling concept to the next. After hearing Clark out, Chambers had said, "You control 80 percent of the wealth, and everything else follows. This thing has the potential to change financial services, forever. " Saying that "this could be a breakaway situation," he asked to buy a 5 percent stake in myCFO, and said he intended to be the company's first customer. Tom Jermoluk, the CEO of @Home, had the same reaction. "Jim's changed the deals people get from venture capitalists," T. J. said, "There's no reason he can't take it a step further." T. J. also bought 5 percent of myCFO.

In the Valley equivalent of noblesse oblige, Clark offered smaller stakes in myCFO to the captains who had served him well, Jim Barksdale and Mike Long. Long bought 2.5 percent of the company; Barksdale called and asked to see "the business plan." "I don't have a business plan," Clark said. Barskdale, too, said he wanted a stake.

In early June, Clark drove up Sand Hill Road to Benchmark Capital, the venture capitalists who'd just made a name for themselves by backing eBay. A few more glamorous deals like that, and Benchmark could offer the same sort of imprimatur as Kleiner Perkins—which was perhaps the biggest reason that people like Clark sought Kleiner Perkins' money. The Kleiner halo, as it was called. The trouble with the Kleiner halo is that it was as up for grabs as everything else in the Valley. Out of fear of losing yet another very public success to Benchmark, Kleiner Perkins had just paid $25 million for a 33 percent stake in a new company called Google.com. Google.com consisted of a pair of Stanford graduate students who had a piece of software that might or might not make it easier to search the Internet.

In short, Kleiner Perkins was already feeling a bit of the pressure on capitalists that Clark, with myCFO, wanted to create a lot more of. He did not seriously think he'd allow Benchmark to invest in his new company. He hoped only that word of his trip to Benchmark would reach John Doerr at Kleiner Perkins.

A week or so after he visited Benchmark Capital, Clark drove back up Sand Hill Road to Kleiner Perkins. John Doerr had gathered his partners in the conference room. Outside of Jim Clark's soul, the Kleiner conference room was the closest thing to ground zero of the Internet boom. Sitting in their conference room, Kleiner partners had backed half a dozen of the most sensational new enterprises: Netscape, Amazon.com, Excite, @Home, Healtheon. The firm claimed, plausibly, to have funded companies worth more than half a trillion dollars. The conference room seemed an unlikely place to create such a pile. The walls were made of glass, the wood was a light bird's eye maple, and the sunlight streamed in from every direction. You could scour the room for weeks and, unless you could enter the minds of the men inside the place, would never find a shadow. The space in which the most important financial decisions of the 1990s had been made was as light and airy as a ski lodge. The iconology of financial power had changed.

Clark took his seat in the sun and explained all about the wealthy masses, and his plans to organize them into a fighting unit. One of the Kleiner partners asked about his business model. "Business model" is one of those terms of art that were central to the Internet boom: it glorified all manner of half-baked plans. All it really meant was how you planned to make money. The "business model" for Microsoft, for instance, was to sell software for 120 bucks a pop that cost fifty cents to manufacture. The "business model" for Healtheon was to add a few pennies to every bill or order or request that emanated from a doctor's office. The "business model" for Netscape was a work in progress; no one ever did really figure out how to make money from Netscape; in its brief life Netscape had lost money. The "business model" of most Internet companies was to attract huge crowds of people to a Web site, and then sell others the chance to advertise products to the crowds. It was still not clear that the model made sense.

The "business model" for myCFO, such as it was, was curiously old-fashioned. Indeed, it marked a departure from the now common approach to creating a business on the Internet. Rather than maximizing the number of people who viewed his Web site, Clark would set out to maximize the number of dollars. myCFO would charge the wealthy masses, on the average, fifty thousand dollars a year each to use the service. They'd pay it because the service would save them at least as much again. Clark figured he might ultimately attract 100,000 wealthy customers; right there you had five billion a year in revenues. He put it another way: an accountant with an established practice who demanded a salary of about two hundred thousand dollars a year brought in nearly two million a year in revenues. Within a year, Clark figured, he'd have hired 400 accountants, mainly from the big accounting firms, who already advised rich people. In exchange for leaving their stable jobs with their big companies, the accountants would receive stock options. They'd come because, like everyone else in America, they were frantically eager to participate in the Internet boom. "How often do accountants have the chance to get rich?" Clark asked the Kleiner partners, rhetorically.

It was a business model even a Graham and Dodd investor could love—which meant it was relatively immune to stock market reversals. It would have profits, lots of them. With companies called Google going for $75 million, Clark did not see much point in selling air: everyone else was already doing that. The revolution had consumed the revolutionary. The revolutionary responded by setting out to consume the revolution. "Old Internet thinking" is how he dismissed the hundreds of companies modeled on Netscape. He then went on to explain what did not need explaining to partners at Kleiner Perkins: the power of a trillion or so dollars pooled into a kind of cartel. There was no end to what might be done with it, once it was collected. He concluded by saying what the Kleiner partners had already figured out: that he had "a much, much better idea how I'm going to make money than I did when I sat here five years ago and told you about Netscape." He called it "one of the biggest opportunities I've ever seen."

When Clark finished, John Doerr took over the meeting. Doerr was wonderful, in the literal sense of the word: he was full of wonder. In Silicon Valley, as in every highly strung status culture, there was a tendency for people to know it all. Doerr retained an almost childlike capacity for curiosity and awe. His feelings for Clark were a case in point. Even in the dark periods of their relationship, he spoke of Clark, behind his back, as "a national treasure." That's what he told his fellow Kleiner partners, who sometimes wondered why Doerr took so much trouble to keep Clark sweet—Jim Clark was a national treasure. He understood exactly how deep and mysterious was this force seated on the other side of the Kleiner Perkins conference room table.

Normally, Kleiner partners deliberated for a few days before deciding whether to invest in a new company. They didn't do that with Netscape, Doerr now reminded Clark. He'd called Clark an hour and a half after he had explained that particular new new thing and agreed to the most onerous terms ever demanded from venture capitalists. The terms were even more onerous this time, but Doerr wanted to move even faster. He turned to Clark and said, "Would you like us to have a show of hands right now?" Clark said that wasn't necessary; in any case, the decision was a formality. An hour and a half later Doerr called him and said that Kleiner wanted to buy as much of myCFO as Clark was willing to sell and that he would like to sit on its board of directors.

For the next few weeks Clark went back and forth on how much Kleiner should be permitted to invest, or whether they should be permitted to invest at all. "I don't need them," he said one day; the next day he said, "If I don't let them invest, they'll start a competitor." Finally, he decided to let Doerr buy a 12 percent stake in myCFO. At the same time he leaked word of the new venture to the press. He'd once told me that he didn't understand why business journalists thought that businessmen would tell them the truth about their affairs. A good businessman was obliged to manipulate public opinion, especially now that public opinion was so important to the future of the business. In the summer of 1999 he demonstrated the point. He presented to reporters a distorted, slimmed-down version of his ambition. The idea was to get the word out to the accountants he wanted to hire and to create a buzz about the company, without alerting the competition. Once again, he was fairly clear in his mind who the competition was. "I want to avoid waving a red flag to Microsoft," he explained to me, "so instead of 'the wealthy masses' I've been saying 'high net worth individuals,' and instead of laying out the whole idea I just say we'll be doing tax planning."

Sure enough, not long after Clark leaked his new story to the press, the accountants began to call. In just a few weeks several hundred people Clark had never heard of came looking to be a part of the new enterprise. The sheer volume of the calls suggested that the accountants at the big accounting firms were spreading the word among themselves. Like everyone else, they'd become attuned to the frequency of the new new thing. A financial adviser at the accounting firm of Price/Waterhouse/Coopers, for instance, called Harvey, whom Clark had installed temporarily as CEO of myCFO, and asked if what he'd read in some business publication was accurate. Harvey said it was. "You guys will control all the financial data," said the accountant, "and if you control the data, you can control everything else. Can I come work for you?" The accountant was making half a million dollars a year, and he was calling to inquire about a job with a start-up. In his voice Clark was able to detect the creaking sound of the American professional class capitulating to a new order.

One evening as we sat in his kitchen I reminded Clark that he had said that once he became a real after-tax billionaire he'd retire. He said, without missing a beat, "I just want to make more money than Larry Ellison. Then I'll stop."

This was news. I pointed out that he'd never before mentioned this ambition. "I just want to have more money than Larry Ellison," he said again. "I don't know why. But once I have more money than Larry Ellison, I'll be satisfied." Larry Ellison, the CEO of Oracle, the biggest software company in the Valley, was worth about nine billion dollars; Clark was worth a bit more than three billion. On the other hand, Ellison's wealth was completely tied up in Oracle stock, which had mostly missed out on the boom. At the rate Clark's wealth was growing, he'd pass Ellison within six months. I pointed this out and asked the obvious question: "What happens after you have more than Larry Ellison? Would you want to have more money than, say, Bill Gates? "Oh, no," Clark said, waving my question to the side of the room where the ridiculous ideas gather to commiserate with each other. "That'll never happen." A few minutes later, after the conversation had turned to other matters, he came clean. "You know," he said, "just for one moment, I would kind of like to have the most. Just for one tiny moment."

It was one of those tiny moments when it was good to have a record of our conversations. Just a few months before, when he was worth a mere $600 million, Clark had said, "I just want to have a billion dollars, after taxes. Then I'll be satisfied." Back further, before he started Netscape, he'd told Mark Grossman, one of the young engineers who had helped him create Silicon Graphics, something similar. Grossman recalled, "Jim came into my office just before he left to start Netscape and said SGI is okay but I'd really like to have $100 million." Back even further, before he'd started Silicon Graphics, he'd told Tom Davis "that what he really wanted was to have ten million dollars." The numbers! They kept moving! And, yet, he was earnest about them. What Clark meant when he said, "I'd really like to have," was "I will do what I need to do to get." It was not exactly wishful thinking. A world in which Larry Ellison had more money than he did was suddenly unacceptable.

Why do people perpetually create for themselves the condition for their own dissatisfaction? Listening to Clark talk about how much money he needed to make was like watching the racing dog who had the wit to grab hold of the remote device that controls the mechanical rabbit. Rather than slow it down, however, he speeds it up. Clark played these little tricks on himself so that he would have an excuse, however flimsy, to keep running as fast as he could. It was the same way with his resentments. He treated those who had done him wrong in much the same way he treated those he did not like who had more money than he did. They were all motives. Plainview, the Navy, Glenn Mueller, Ed

McCracken, various venture capitalists: he needed people or places to doubt him so that he could prove them wrong.

Obviously, Clark couldn't stop using technology to change the world, and so he needed an excuse not to stop. The reasons he couldn't stop were ultimately unknowable; but I assumed that the best and most lasting motive for wanting to change the way things are is to be unhappy with the way things are. People who are unhappy with the way things are tend to remain unhappy even after they have changed them. The nature of their unhappiness is such that change does not slake it. The difference with Clark is that he continued to believe in the endless possibilities of change, even after he'd experienced its limitations. He was the least happy optimist there ever was. No matter how well Jim Clark did for himself, it was always two in the morning in his heart, and he was lying awake.

Above all, one thing was clear: his pursuit of the new new thing depended on his curious amnesia. His ability to forget what he said he would do next, or what he'd thought would make him happy, was the mortar on which he laid his endless tiers of self-renewal. He'd made a kind of religion of keeping only those parts of his past he needed for fuel, on his journey into the future.

His escape from the past was necessarily incomplete. The drug hasn't been invented that permits people to forget as perfectly as they would sometimes like to forget. He still had his tuba, for instance. The tarnished old instrument sat mysteriously in the corner of the guest room upstairs—the one that stored the cardboard boxes filled with the scraps of paper his former secretary had rescued from Clark's past. It was such an odd thing to stumble across in a house that otherwise said so little about who its inhabitant was, or where he was from, that I had asked him about it. He'd played the tuba as a child, he'd said. Twenty years before, just after he'd founded Silicon Graphics, and made his first millions, he'd been seized by the desire to play again. And so he bought this tuba. He soon found he'd lost interest in it. Only the idea of playing his tuba pleased him now. So he propped it in the corner of the guest bedroom, and left it there, as a lone reminder of something he couldn't quite explain.

## The Past outside the Box

A large aquifer beneath the flatlands between Amarillo and Lubbock supplies Plainview with more water than any other town in West Texas. The water was discovered not long after the Civil War. By the end of the nineteenth century Plainview tilled the most fertile cotton farming land in the United States. The local economy was premised on the family farm—a premise called into doubt in Clark's boyhood, when the modern high-tech farm moved in. Since then all news for Plainview has been bad news. Such is the economic history of Plainview, Texas.

I drove into the town one bright winter morning. Poor places are slower to change than rich places; perhaps poor people are slower to change than rich people, too. The neat brick school, the tiny house, the church, the people who, as Clark had once said, "watched the outside world as if it was a television program" were pretty much as he must have left them back in the early 1960s. The sound at the center of town was the sound of the inside of a conch shell. The wind howled. The irredeemably beige buildings perched low across the flat yellow grass as if designed to diminish the human imagination. The skyline was unmarked either by windbreaks or by ambition; the lone exception was the water tower on the edge of town. Plainview was built on water, and the tower that held that water was painted proudly. Only it didn't say Plainview; it said Rust Water. In 1992 Paramount Pictures used Plainview as a movie set for a comedy called *Leap of Faith*, about a prairie evangelist, played by Steve Martin. The Hollywood people came for a few weeks, got everyone worked up, and left behind more money than the town had seen in a long time. In the bargain they repainted the Plainview water tower with the name of the fictional town in the movie. Plainview never bothered to repaint it.

Other than that, Plainview seemed to have settled on an old idea of itself. It was staying pat, declining the dealer's offer of another card. It had become one of those places defined by what they do not have rather than what they have, and by who has left, rather than who has stayed. The man whose departure defined the town with the most dreadful clarity was Jim Clark.

On that bright winter day I followed the directions Clark's mother, Hazel McClure, had given me to her brick house, slightly bigger than the houses on either side of it. Waiting inside were Clark's younger sister, Sue, and her husband, Roger. I had come to ask them some questions, but it turned out that Hazel had a question for me. "Do you know when Jim will come and visit next?" she asked, after we'd settled into our chairs.

On the rare occasions Clark visits Plainview, Texas, he lands at the airfield on the outskirts of town, has lunch with his mother, and then flies off to someplace else as quickly as he can. He seldom drives into the town and never visits home. He's never seen the house his mother bought with the stock options he gave her in Silicon Graphics. The few stops he's made have all been unscheduled. The flight path from Palm Beach to San Jose just happens to pass directly over Plainview, Texas, and every so often Clark drops out of the sky. Almost always he takes his mother by surprise. For instance, Hazel learned of Clark's most recent visit, a year earlier, from her answering machine. She found a message on it from Jim saying he was right over her head, in descent, and intended to remain in Plainview just long enough to refuel. If she was around, he said, they could have lunch out at the airfield. "I just turned around and ran out the door to the airport," recalls Hazel. Half the town followed her. The appearance of Clark's jet in the Plainview sky was a public event. All of Plainview's residents knew the plane by sight, and a hundred or so of them rushed out to the airfield, just to watch it land. "They just know that anything the size of Jim's plane just got to be Jim," said Roger, Clark's brother-in-law, "because there is nothing else like that. . . . And, truth is, whenever he comes, Jim kind of buzzes the town."

Hazel now said that most of what she knew about her son's illustrious career she knew from having read it in magazines. She has difficulty squaring the boy she raised with the man she read about. She has no advanced theory why Clark became who he became. All she has is a few memories that might, or might not, offer clues to a person on a search for a character. She remembers him as a four-year-old, when she first suspected he might be smarter than the average little boy. He'd recite back entire nursery rhymes from memory, and boast, "Anything you tell me I can remember as long as I pay attention." A bit later, when he was twelve, she recalls him accidentally shooting a hole through every toe on his left foot with a .22-caliber rifle. He lay in bed with his foot in a cast and built more model airplanes than she'd ever seen anyone build. She also remembers finding, later that year, just before Christmas, a sack of light bulbs tucked away in a closet. Hazel couldn't afford Christmas lights. Yet here were hundreds of bulbs in a sack, waiting to be strung. It turned out that Jim had stolen them off other people's houses.

The telephone rang. Clark's sister, Sue, rose to answer it. In a clipped tone of poorly suppressed irritation she said, "Sorry, we're not investing right now." Pause. Then, more tensely, "I said we're not investing." She hung up. Returning, she explained that the shares in Netscape that Clark had given them had made them rich. "And you have to understand," she said, "that when this happened, we were poor. I was ready to cook the cat." I assumed this was a joke, and laughed. I assumed wrong. She had, in fact, been ready to cook the cat. The Netscape IPO had saved at least one life.

The deprivation Sue recalled occurred only four years ago. Now, all of Plainview thought of her and her family as these walking sacks of cash. People treated them differently. They asked for loans. They asked for stock tips. They asked what kind of company Jim might start next. They asked if they could invest in it. There was now a Clark-sized moat, filled with money, that separated his family from the rest of Plainview.

Hazel resumed the mining of her memory—and she had a lot of material to mine. The most chilling of it concerned Clark's father, who apparently drank all day and beat Hazel up all night. Hazel put up with the routine for years; it became, in a way, normal. She hoped only that Charles—Clark's father—would hit her someplace where people at work couldn't see the bruises. Charles became more and more brutal, however, and Hazel divorced him when Jim was fourteen. Charles moved out onto the streets of Plainview. From there he terrorized his family with an ingenuity he showed in no other aspect of his life.

One episode still stood out brightly in Hazel's mind. She glanced out the window of her office one day and spotted Charles standing in front of her car. He'd raised the hood and was tinkering with the engine. She ran down and hollered; Charles ran off. After that she parked in front of a car repair shop and asked the owner to keep an eye on it for her. One evening after work she found a man from the auto shop waiting for her. He told her he'd just seen a man, resembling her ex-husband, working on her transmission. Hazel opened the transmission and discovered steel shavings. The man from the auto shop helped her clean them out. Thinking they'd fixed the problem Hazel set out with her baby daughter (Sue) to visit friends in Amarillo. On the road the car broke down. Whoever had put the steel shavings in the engine had also put sand in the oil. Fixing the engine cost Hazel two months' pay.

That night she told her son what had happened. Clark had just turned sixteen. "Jim got up and left the house," said Hazel, "and went to find his father. When he came back he was crying."

"I never found out what happened," said Sue, who was clearly feeling left out.

"I never knew what happened," said Hazel.

"But I tell you what," said Sue. "After that my father never bothered my mother again."

It turned out that Hazel also remembered the tuba—how could she forget it? The tarnished brass instrument propped in the corner of Clark's guest bedroom had struck me as doubly odd, and I now said as much. It was the only artifact of his past that he thought worthy of display; it was also, for someone as willful and individualistic as Clark, a poor choice of instrument. The job of the tuba player is to blend with the orchestra. No one who wanted to stand out from the crowd would choose it for himself.

The tuba had come as a surprise to Hazel. "One day Jim came home from school with it," she said, "And he could play a little. He used to go into the bathroom where he could hear himself better and sit on the commode—with the seat down, you know—and practice. I never knew where he got the tuba from. I guess the school gave it to him. I could never have afforded to buy any instrument." Hazel supported a family of four on the $225 a month she took home from the hospital, where she worked as a doctor's assistant. After she had paid the bills, she had $5 a month to spend on groceries. Clark was obviously well aware of their situation from a very young age. He had chosen to play the tuba because the tuba was the one instrument supplied to the pupil by the school, free of charge. Hazel never knew that, but it was true. Clark's old band director, O. T. Ryan, said as much. At the Plainview middle school the students who wished to play flutes, clarinets, trumpets, and trombones were required to buy their own instruments. The tuba players alone received a loaner from the school.

Not long after he'd come home in tears, from what turned out to be his final meeting with his father, Clark quit playing his tuba. Soon after that he was expelled from school, and left town. Once he'd left, he became a stranger to his family. He'd turn up every now and again, and the family now recalled something about each visit. One time not long after he'd left, for instance, he came home talking about nothing but computers. "No one in Plainview had seen a computer, except in the movies," said Hazel. Another time he came home with financial ambition. "When Jim came home from the Navy," Hazel recalled, "he told his uncle that someday he was going to make fifty thousand dollars a year."

Sue hooted and clapped, "He done a bit better than that!"

Hazel continued, "I remember him telling me when he came back from the Navy, 'Mama, I'm going to *show* Plainview.'"

T he sun shone brightly on the clear untroubled sea. When Allan Prior maneuvered *Hyperion* into the narrow channel leading to the shallow harbor on the south coast of Antigua, he probably knew that he would be fired. Not long after the boat reached the dock, Clark dismissed Allan as his captain. Clark had no one reason for replacing him. Allan just wasn't well suited to managing the crew of a computerized sailboat. By the time, six months later, that *Hyperion* sailed beneath the Golden Gate Bridge and into the San Francisco Bay, Jaime, too, would be gone. *Hyperion*'s captain and half of its crew would be new.

But for that one, final moment Allan Prior was still Jim Clark's captain. He guided *Hyperion* skillfully toward the shore, without so much as a glance at the computer screen beneath the wheel. The computer offered up all sorts of useful information: the depth of the sea, the speed of the ship, the subtle shifts in the wind's strength and direction. Allan snorted and said, "I never look at the computer—I don't trust it," then returned to the business of guiding the boat toward the shore. Slowly, he turned into the harbor; and when he did, Simon, standing on the bow, gave a whoop. Behind a stand of dismasted sailboats was the boat

Simon was working on when Clark stole him away to learn all about computers: *Juliet*. By then the crew knew that *Juliet* was the reason *Hyperion* existed—that after he had boarded *Juliet* in the San Francisco Bay, Clark had decided he wanted one like it, only bigger and smarter. *Juliet* had led to *Hyperion* and *Hyperion* had led to Netscape's IPO and Netscape's IPO had triggered the Internet boom. Of course, the boom probably would have happened without *Juliet*, or for that matter, without Netscape. But I doubt it would have happened quite the same way. Clark's first sighting of *Juliet* was one of those small perturbations that radically altered the world we inhabit.

Now *Juliet* felt small and insignificant. The crew of *Hyperion* waved to her crew in the same spirit that the winner of a beauty pageant hugs the runner-up. Clark waved, too. Once he had the biggest mast and the finest boat, he didn't care to rub it in. He was a good winner; poor losers often are. The joy of winning was only slightly diminished by the sighting of Larry Ellison's much bigger power boat (this was a curiously small world). We docked right beside it, and then left quickly for Clark's plane.

But before we did I went down to Clark's cabin. I wanted to hear whatever he'd concluded about the crossing—and whether he thought there was a business in the boat's software. I found him hovering over an architectural drawing. It was neatly spread out on his desk, beside his computer. It looked very much like a drawing of a boat, I said, coming up behind him. It is a boat, he said. He'd asked the man who had designed *Hyperion* to draw the lines for a sailboat half again as big as *Hyperion*, or a bit longer than 250 feet. He'd already spoken to Wolter Huisman about it, and Wolter was willing to build it, even if it meant building a new building that could hold it. The drawing was what Clark thought of as his "new boat."

I suppose he must have seen me flinch, because pretty quickly he was explaining why he needed to be thinking about building another boat. He'd spent the last five years, and upended the U.S. economy, to get his hands on the one we'd just sailed across the Atlantic Ocean. "*Hyperion* is a beautiful boat," he said, and I knew when he said it what the next word would be. "But . . ." His finger traced the lines of his new boat, which was still no more than a figment of his imagination. Pure possibility. A smile lengthened across his face. *Hyperion* was nice, but this . . . this was the perfect boat.

## Acknowledgments

Andy Kessler and Fred Kittler introduced me to the Valley, and helped make this book what it is. Jim and Nancy Rutter Clark put up with a writer in ways that no one should have to. Clark has made a career of taking risks others avoid. He took another when he let me talk my way into his life, and I'll always be grateful for that. I'd also like to thank Pham Nguyen for checking my facts and Chris Wiman for checking my sentiment. Eric Ver Ploeg read the manuscript for technical illiteracy; Paul Romer read it for economic illiteracy; Patricia Chui read it for just plain old-fashioned illiteracy. Any mistakes they failed to detect are obviously their fault; indeed they can be blamed handily for anything the reader might disapprove of. A special thanks to my editor Starling Lawrence, who navigates rough drafts, as he navigates life, with great grace. It's good to be back on board.